DESIGNING AND BUILDING SCHOOLS

A Manual for Phase 0

Montag Stiftung Jugend und Gesellschaft (Ed.)
Ernst Hubeli, Meike Kricke, Barbara Pampe, Ulrich Paßlick, Kersten Reich, Jochem Schneider, Otto Seydel

jovis

Montag Stiftung
Jugend und Gesellschaft

TABLE OF CONTENTS

4

5

6

7

FOREWORD

Since the first publication of this book, the importance of school construction has increasingly moved to the center of social and political debate. The issue is no longer merely about addressing serious structural deficiencies in schools—it is about nothing less than the structural renewal of our school and educational landscape. And one thing has become increasingly clear: good schools need good spaces. The educational challenges of our time—all-day schooling, inclusion, digitalization, education for sustainable development, and the fostering of 21st-century skills—require learning environments that are flexible, open, and geared towards participation.

We must succeed in channeling all investments away from the refurbishment of school with an outdated corridor-classroom layout and instead towards future-ready typologies for learning spaces and efficient school buildings. These must be capable of reflecting the requirements of forward-looking education in the necessary concepts within the built environment. Not only new construction, extensions, and annexes, but also refurbishment and conversion projects provide opportunities to enhance school buildings and gradually adapt them to forms of learning that already differ significantly from those prevalent at the time when most of our schools were built.

For nearly 20 years, the Montag Stiftung Jugend und Gesellschaft has been advocating for a new mindset and new practices in school construction. Working together with experts from education, architecture, planning, and administration, we are developing foundations, guidelines, and concepts—and are striving to implement them in practice.

With this new edition, we hope to further support this transformation actively, sustainably and on a broad scale—through knowledge, experience, and a strong commitment to school construction that fosters educational quality and enables social participation.

We would like to express our special thanks to all those who have contributed—and continue to contribute—to this endeavor with their expertise, dedication, and spirit of cooperation.

Bonn, July 2025

Dr. Meike Kricke, Barbara Pampe
Executive Directors, Montag Stiftung Jugend und Gesellschaft

INTRODUCTION

INITIAL SITUATION

Those responsible for school construction in Germany are facing major challenges: There is a massive backlog of school buildings to be renovated. This is due to significant population growth in urban areas, additional demand for school space, new requirements resulting from the increasing introduction of all-day schools, the implementation of inclusion, the demands of digitalization, and, last but not least, the far-reaching change in the pedagogical understanding of schools and teaching. School construction is burdened by the high investment backlog and the need for renovation and expansion, which is a recurring theme in the media.[1]

1
The perceived investment backlog of municipalities in school construction amounts to 67.8 billion euros in 2025 (KfW Bankengruppe (Eds.) (2025)). This corresponds to 31 percent of the total investment backlog. Once again, the largest investment backlog is in school buildings. Although extensive efforts have been made to improve the structural situation in schools for over 15 years, the need for investment has risen continuously since then.

The need for structural renewal is also accompanied by a need for innovation regarding content. Much has happened in the last 10 years, and contemporary spatial concepts for future-oriented pedagogy are increasingly being implemented. However, the common practice of calculating space requirements by counting the number of classrooms required—thus reproducing the rigid concept of the classroom-corridor school—remains widespread. In addition, past investment boosts[2] have tended to support only fragmented, sectoral structural implementations (equipment for all-day schooling, energy-oriented refurbishment). Despite many encouraging projects and programs, it is not yet possible to speak of a fundamental change. Due to time and financial pressures, as well as a lack of human resources in municipal administrations, projects continue to be implemented that do not meet current needs.

2
For example, through the federal programs »Future of Education and Care« (2003–2009, 4 billion euros) and »Economic Stimulus Package II« (2009). Currently, the All-Day Promotion Act with the recommendations of the KMK (Conference of the Ministers of Education and Cultural Affairs) and the federal »Startchancen« program offer opportunities to implement innovations in school construction; see below.

☞ Chapter 1, *Funding programs*, p. 19

If this unsatisfactory situation is to be remedied, then, in the interests of quality assurance, the requirements for use and space must be defined collaboratively in a dialog between users on the one side and administrations, architects, and municipal political bodies on the other. This concerns an investment area that often accounts for a quarter of project-related municipal expenditures.

AIM OF THE MANUAL

This book provides a guide for practitioners from schools, architecture firms, and local authorities on the reconstruction of existing and design of new school buildings. The aim is to bring together and interweave pedagogical and planning perspectives to help those responsible find a common basis at the beginning of the project. In this »Phase 0«, i.e. before the actual design planning begins, the decisive course is set with the definition of the usage requirements, the space allocation program, and the spatial organizational structure.

Chapter 4.3, *Phase 0,* p. 106 ff.

Today more than ever, the obligation of school authorities to use scarce financial resources economically and the need for sustainable planning and construction require a reliable basis at the start of the planning process. A basic rule of project development also speaks in favor of solid groundwork, concept development, and reliable coordination: The later changes are made in the planning process, the more expensive they are. To avoid the dilemma of costly design changes, the manual »Designing and Building Schools« is both a guide and a source of inspiration for Phase 0.

This is a challenging task. If the school is to define its spatial requirements for planning purposes, the pedagogical concept must be specified and described, considering foreseeable future development goals, in order to be resilient. Adaptability to future pedagogical-conceptual developments in spatial organization must be taken into account. At the same time, a building per se represents longevity and durability and can only allow for structural flexibility within clear limits. Accordingly, basic pedagogical considerations must be translated into a robust building structure. Challenges must be precisely formulated and can only be solved where they arise: at the interface of all disciplines involved on site—in Phase 0.

MOTIVATION FOR AND CHANGES TO THE NEW EDITION COMPARED TO THE FIRST EDITION

This edition presents updated content in a refreshed format. Since the first edition was published in 2012 and the revised version in 2017, much has changed in the field of school construction in Germany. The approach of designing and planning school buildings specifically and based on local needs has become more widespread. More and more municipalities, cities, and school authorities are recognizing that the significant investment backlog also presents an opportunity to plan and build efficient educational facilities with new concepts. The number of exemplary project and planning process is growing.

Phase 0 is now an established, recognized, and efficient component of successful planning processes in school construction. But what do people in different departments associate with this phase? The following trends have prompted us to once again define the key quality characteristics and objectives of Phase 0 in school construction for a broad readership:

— The success of Phase 0 leads to an inflationary »dissolution of boundaries«: Different, sometimes even contradictory approaches are subsumed under the term. They range from structural surveys to the evaluation of financing models. Furniture manufacturers, as well as architects and project managers, offer shortened »Phase 0 planning processes« during the procurement process—often without addressing pedagogical issues and without involving school communities in the long term.
— Due to the many planning issues that need to be clarified during the project development phase of building or converting a school—such as climate concept, mobility concept, species protection, preservation of historical monuments, etc.—Phase 0 is often overloaded or the specific interfaces between pedagogy and space are neglected. It is therefore all the more important that Phase 0 is not reduced to user participation or technical surveys.

The new edition of the book is intended to make the knowledge and content of a targeted Phase 0 available in an updated form. In addition to the print edition, a digital open access version is available. Both versions are published in English and German.

Example projects are no longer presented as extensively as in the previous editions, as sufficient information on various projects is now available on the Internet. The new edition also includes references to current studies, other sources of information on the topic, and findings from the pilot projects of the Montag Stiftung Jugend und Gesellschaft and its various cooperation partners. The bibliography has been expanded and updated.

Chapter 7, *Examples*, pp. 217 ff.

ADDRESSEES

»Designing and Building Schools« makes knowledge from three fields of action—pedagogy, architecture / construction, and municipal administration—accessible in such a way that a concrete basis for joint action and decision-making can be created. The book is therefore aimed at several target groups simultaneously: different municipal administrative departments, architects, educators, parents and students, as well as political decision-makers within a municipality. It is a book for the different professions and stakeholders, helping them develop a common language in the planning process.

STRUCTURE

The manual has a modular structure. It is divided into the following chapters:

CHAPTER 1 discusses the reasons why school construction needs fresh impetus and why it is a particular priority for all municipal authorities today.

CHAPTER 2 describes the central requirements of school construction today in 10 Theses. For each thesis, there is both an educational and a spatial perspective, showing how the two are linked in a sustainable school building.

CHAPTER 3 entitled »Users and Their Spaces,« provides basic practical knowledge about changing usage patterns and the resulting spatial consequences.

CHAPTER 4 describes the stages and stakeholders in Phase 0, providing basic knowledge about the process of integrated school building design.

CHAPTER 5 offers a selection of modules for implementing Phase 0. They can be used individually or in combination in the different planning phases.

CHAPTER 6 provides background and contextual knowledge: The theses formulated in Chapter II are substantiated in more detail from a professional pedagogical discourse.

The **APPENDIX** completes the handbook with FAQs, a glossary, references and links, a detailed index of terms, and a list of projects with exemplary implementation.

EDITORS AND AUTHORS

The new edition is published by the Montag Stiftung Jugend und Gesellschaft (Montag Foundation Youth and Society). Within the Montag Foundations, this foundation is responsible for the field of »Educational Architecture.« The Montag Stiftung Urbane Räume was one of the co-initiators of the first edition. The authors Dr. Meike Kricke, Barbara Pampe, Prof. Dr. Kersten Reich, Jochem Schneider, and Dr. Otto Seydel were responsible for this update. The interdisciplinary team of authors and editors since the first edition includes:

Prof. Ernst Hubeli, Dipl.-Architekt ETH, co-owner of the office Herczog Hubeli, Zurich; from 1982 to 2000 editor-in-chief of the Swiss architecture magazine *werk, bauen and wohnen;* from 2000 to 2007 head of the Institute for Urban Design at the Graz University of Technology; since 2008 research on urban future scenarios.

Dr. Karl-Heinz Imhäuser, teacher and educationalist, member of the board of the Carl Richard Montag Förderstiftung and the Montag Stiftung Denkwerkstatt; research activities at universities and state institutes, teaching assignments on inclusive didactics; consultant for school construction projects; member of the Education Committee of the German UNESCO Commission, long-standing member of the board of trustees of the IBA Heidelberg.

Dr. Meike Kricke, elementary school teacher and educational scientist, since 2019 board member of the Montag Stiftung Jugend und Gesellschaft, research assistant at the University of Cologne in projects on inclusive education; lecturer at international universities and in vocational education; author and co-editor of publications at the intersection of future-oriented education and school construction.

Barbara Pampe, Dipl.-Ing. Architektin M. Eng., since 2019 board member of the Montag Stiftung Jugend und Gesellschaft, collaboration in various architectural offices, co-founder of baladilab, research and teaching assignments at various universities in Germany and abroad; professor at the German University in Cairo; author and co-editor of numerous publications on school construction.

Ulrich Paßlick, graduate engineer in spatial planning, DASL, construction assessor specializing in urban planning, freelance planner; 1992 to 2016 City Planning Councilor of the City of Bocholt, Administrative Director for Planning, Building, the Environment and Real Estate Management; long-standing chairman of the NRW City Center Network and the Construction and Transport Committee of the Association of Cities of North Rhine-Westphalia. Member of the Construction and Transport Committee of the German Association of Cities until 2016.

Prof. Dr. Kersten Reich, professor emeritus for international teaching and learning research and director of the Dewey Center at the University of Cologne; author of numerous books on constructivism, educational equity, inclusion, and sustainability; most recently *Faire Bildung für alle* and, with Charlotte Reich, *Digitale Didaktik;* scientific support in the development of the Inclusive University School Cologne; many years of experience in supporting school development processes.

Jochem Schneider, Dipl.-Ing. SRL DASL, freelance planner and partner at bueroschneidermeyer; many years of experience in advising municipal school authorities on the development of over 50 school construction projects and educational facilities in Germany; author of various planning frameworks for school construction; advisor to the state government of Baden-Württemberg on school construction funding guidelines; numerous publications on the subject of school construction.

Dr. Otto Seydel, from 1976 to 2001 teacher and member of the school administration at Schule Schloss Salem; since 2001 director of the Institute for School Development; member of the jury for the German School Award; coordinator of the school network »Blick über den Zaun«; head of the Bremen school inspectorate; since 2010 support for school development projects and school construction planning in Phase 0.

Frauke Burgdorff, Dipl.-Ing. Raumplanung DASL, freelance planner and urban developer; since 2019 Councilor for Planning, Building, and Mobility of the City of Aachen; was also involved in the conception of the first edition of this book as a former board member of the Montag Stiftung Urbane Räume.

Schulbau Open Source

Schulen Planen und Bauen

Phase Zehn—Playbook

Akustik im Schulbau

Ganztag und Raum

Leitlinien für leistungsfähige Schulbauten in Deutschland

Brandschutz im Schulbau

Bildungsband Osdorfer Born

Phase Null—Der Film

Fünfmal Phase Null

SET OF TOOLS

The manual is part of a program of the Montag Stiftung Jugend und Gesellschaft to provide support and assistance for forward-looking school construction projects—both for new buildings and reconstructions. In the meantime, the foundation has published numerous works on the subject, providing an integrated set of tools to support the planning and implementation of educational architecture (all publications in German language):

»Schulbau Open Source—Planungswissen für Innovationen im Schulbau,« online platform of the Montag Stiftung Jugend und Gesellschaft. Bonn 2025.

»Schulen planen and bauen,« blog of the Montag Stiftung Jugend und Gesellschaft on educational architecture. Bonn 2025.

»Phase Zehn—Playbook,« a playful guide to discovering and designing new spaces together (»Phase 10«). Bonn 2025.

»Akustik im Schulbau. Neue Konzepte und Empfehlungen,« published by Montag Stiftung Jugend und Gesellschaft, Bund Deutscher Architektinnen und Architekten (BDA), Verband Bildung und Erziehung (VBE). Bonn, Berlin 2024.

»Ganztag und Raum,« five documentations on the pilot projects of the Montag Stiftung Jugend und Gesellschaft. Bonn 2023–2024.

»Leitlinien für leistungsfähige Schulbauten in Deutschland,« published by the Montag Stiftung Jugend und Gesellschaft, Bund Deutscher Architekten (BDA), and Verband Bildung and Erziehung (VBE). 4th, updated edition. Bonn, Berlin 2022.

»Brandschutz im Schulbau. Neue Konzepte und Empfehlungen,« published by Montag Stiftung Jugend und Gesellschaft, Bund Deutscher Architektinnen und Architekten (BDA), Deutsche Bundesstiftung Umwelt, Technische Universität Kaiserslautern, Unfallkasse NRW, Verband Bildung und Erziehung (VBE). Berlin, Bonn, Düsseldorf, Kaiserslautern, Osnabrück 2017..

»Bildungsband Osdorfer Born. Die Bildungslandschaft Osdorf/Lurup finden and entwerfen,« published by the Montag Stiftung Jugend und Gesellschaft in cooperation with the Free Hanseatic City of Hamburg, the Hamburg-Altona District Office, and the arge studio urbane landschaften – bildung. 72 pages. Bonn 2017.

»Phase Null—Der Film,« a film by Jan Marschner and Flash Filmproduktion Armin Maiwald GmbH on behalf of the Montag Stiftung Jugend und Gesellschaft. Documentation of the Planning Phase 0, edited by bueroschneidermeyer and the Institut für Schulentwicklung at the Geschwister-Scholl-Stadtteilschule in Hamburg. 161 minutes (incl. trailer), with 64-page booklet. Berlin 2015.

»Fünfmal Phase 0. Dokumentation der Pilotprojekte Schulen planen and bauen,« published by the Montag Stiftung Jugend und Gesellschaft. 113 pages. Bonn 2015.

1

REASONS

Why School Construction Needs Fresh Impetus

School construction is only one of the major challenges facing municipalities today. Investment is urgently needed in many areas: housing, digitalization, transport infrastructure, energy supply, and climate protection to reduce CO_2 emissions. Why should schools be given such a high priority? What are the reasons for advocating a new culture of integrated design and construction of educational facilities now? The following are key arguments that underscore the need for a new understanding of school construction. It becomes clear that the framework conditions for educational facilities have changed at all levels: at the macro level, with its overall social, municipal, and institutional conditions, as well as at the micro level, the level of the school itself. Everywhere, a fundamental change can be observed, with significant consequences for the planning, design, and construction of contemporary educational facilities.

EDUCATION IS A HUMAN RIGHT

»Everyone has the right to education« – Article 26 of the Universal Declaration of Human Rights ought to be a given in our country—but it is not. The 2024 Report on Vocational Education and Training highlights an increase in the number of 20- to 34-year-olds without a vocational qualification—nearly 2.9 million young people in 2022. In 2018, 6.2 million people with low literacy skills (reading and writing at a low level of competence), which is 12.1 percent of the working population, were recorded.[3] In key areas such as integration (–39.5 points), school quality (–28.2 points), and educational poverty (–25.7 points), the 2024 Education Monitor identifies »significant deterioration nationwide.«[4]

Exclusion and segregation are well-known problems in the German education system that persist. The practice of segregating students with special needs in special schools has changed little across Germany, despite the obligation to include them.[5] Students with a migrant background are also frequently denied educational opportunities: the three risk factors for educational disadvantage—parents without vocational training or school-leaving qualifications, as well as social or financial vulnerability—are disproportionately common among them.[6]

So far, efforts to reduce social inequalities and the associated disparity of opportunity in the education system have not been successful. The system fails to achieve an education that offers equal opportunities. International comparisons—such as those conducted in the context of the PISA study—make it clear that the explanations commonly offered in this country (»It's their own fault!« or »Nothing can be done about it!«) are inadequate. Educational disadvantage is also the result of inadequate concepts and a lack of commitment that society invests in this sector.[7]

INCLUSION IS AN EDUCATIONAL RIGHT

In 2019, Germany has agreed to the UN Convention on the Rights of Persons with Disabilities, adopted by the UN General Assembly on December 13, 2006, thus initiating a far-reaching systemic change.[8] The UN Convention obliges nations to combat all forms of discrimination and defines a fundamental right to learning together. The implementation of inclusive schooling leads to a significant increase in the heterogeneity of school classes and thus to a student body that requires differentiated care and support.[9] This requires both better staffing ratios and appropriate spatial conditions.

In this understanding, inclusion does not only refer to people with disabilities. The core idea is to provide all children with access to high-quality education together. The reasons for disadvantage and exclusion are manifold. Sociologists such as Aladin El-Mafaalani and others now speak of »super-diversity,« by which they mean an increase in diversity at different levels, with both quantitative and qualitative dimensions.[10] Diversity and heterogeneity are not a special case, but the new normal today.[11]

This claim is confirmed by a second global frame of reference to which the Federal Republic of Germany has committed itself and which defines inclusion and educational equity as the most important global

3 Universität Hamburg (2019)

4 Cf. Anger et al. (2024), p. 205

5 Cf. Klemm (2016c)

6 Autor:innengruppe *Bildungsberichterstattung (2024)*, p. 6

7 The UN Committee on the Rights of Persons with Disabilities is critical of the situation in Germany with regard to the implementation of inclusion. See UN (2023)

8 See Deutsche UNESCO-Kommission (2010)

9 The OECD cites Germany as an example of a system that does particularly little to ensure both vertical and horizontal inclusion (selective schools and segregation in urban planning). See OECD (2024).

10 Cf. El-Mafaalani et al. (2025)

11 See Hattie (2023)

educational goals: the Sustainable Development Goals.[12] Adopted by the United Nations in September 2015, this international frame of reference for the post-millennial decade 2015–2030 defines the following goal for education: »Ensure inclusive and equitable quality education and promote lifelong learning opportunities for all.« The document underlying the adoption of this agenda, »Transforming our world: the 2030 Agenda for Sustainable Development,«[13] which describes the goals—also binding for Germany—and their implementation mechanisms, identifies the following as a key implementation strategy: »Build and modernize educational facilities that are child-, disability-, and gender-sensitive and provide safe, non-violent, inclusive, and effective learning environments for all.«

12 Cf. UN, *Sustainable Development Goals*

13 United Nations (2015b) SDG 4a.

EDUCATION AS A CENTRAL PRODUCTION FACTOR

With the transition from an industrial to a knowledge-based society, the importance of education has not only increased, but has also expanded substantially and structurally. Education is an important production factor for the economy.[14] Investment in education pays off: the cost of non-education is significantly higher than the cost of education.[15] Non-education can also jeopardize the welfare state if the consequential costs can no longer be financed.[16] The figures cited point to alarming scenarios if no major changes are made. The lack of integration of the socially or otherwise disadvantaged into the education system has consequences that are difficult to quantify but are also highly detrimental. In this context, Germany stands out as a negative example in international comparison. Particularly at the elementary level, Germany spends significantly less per pupil than countries such as Austria, Poland, Spain, Belgium, Denmark, Iceland, Norway, Slovenia, Sweden, Switzerland, the United Kingdom, and the United States.[17]

14 Cf., e.g., Wössmann (2007, 2017); Wössmann / Piopiunik (2009)

15 Cf. Schweinhart (2005); Heckman (2008)

16 On the costs, cf., e.g., OECD (2010e)

17 Cf. OECD (2024); Klemm (2016b); DESTATIS (2023).

The economic argument carries even more weight when considering that Germany, due to its lack of natural resources, must rely heavily on education to remain competitive in the global market. In addition, in view of migration and the need for immigration, great efforts are required to maintain an adequate level of education among future skilled workers.

EDUCATION AS A PREREQUISITE FOR A DEMOCRATIC SOCIETY

There is a growing awareness, both within and outside the OECD, that education, in addition to its economic value added, is a prerequisite for social competence, community spirit, responsibility, and the ability to integrate into communal life whether in a state, a village, a municipality, or a city. Indeed, this expanded concept of education must be seen as a fundamental prerequisite for the successful development and continuity of democratic societies. This dual—economic and social—relevance of education also means that it can contribute to making democratic societies more equal in terms of opportunity. In other words: »Education for all«—a commonplace that has been postulated for decades—is becoming a central educational policy mandate that must also be fulfilled by each individual municipality in order to secure its own foundations and not miss out on social developments.

EDUCATION AS A LOCATION FACTOR

The quality of education is an increasingly important location factor for urban and regional development. Even today, the educational facilities of a city or region have a major influence on the choice of where to live and where to locate a business. Kindergartens, schools, and other educational facilities are increasingly coming into focus in the intensifying competition between cities. Good schools are now recognized as an important asset in attracting new residents and businesses. School initiatives launched by the business community underscore the importance of a strong educational infrastructure for recruiting skilled staff. It is precisely from this perspective that municipal expenditure on school construction should be seen not as a cost but as an investment.

THE SCHOOL AS AN URBAN RESOURCE

In the face of tight public budgets, the economic efficiency of school buildings must be significantly increased. As monofunctional, purpose-built structures, they are often underutilized, deserted after school hours, and contradict many economic, environmental, and urban planning imperatives. Multiple and mixed use, as long practiced in cultural buildings and neighborhood centers, can better utilize infrastructure and revitalize the school. Networking complements the school's educational offerings. However, this requires modern management models and effective facility management. Care must be taken to ensure that such openness is compatible with the school's primary mission. For its part, the school will increasingly reach out to the urban public and, in cooperation with partners, use and help shape extracurricular places of learning. Both sides can benefit from the mutual use and networking of school structures and public spaces.

☞ Chapter 2, *Thesis 10*, pp. 49 ff.

DEMOGRAPHIC AND STRUCTURAL CHANGE

From 2023 to 2035, the number of students is projected to increase by 6.8 percent.[18] Although the extent of this increase will depend heavily on future migration policies, there will, in any case, be a tendency to maintain the industrial and residential location and to adapt it to new conditions. In view of the high birth and immigration rates, many new schools will have to be built, especially in metropolitan areas. In many places, the school place situation is precarious.

18 Cf. KMK (2024)

Further school development will trigger a process of consolidation at the municipal and regional levels. There are significant differences in this development: In North Rhine-Westphalia, for example, regional student numbers recorded up to 2020 vary from one municipality to another —ranging from a 10-percent increase to a 28-percent decrease.[19] These large fluctuations do not allow for general conclusions and highlight the need for precise local development analyses.

19 IT.NRW (2010)

In addition, there are differentiations specific to school types. The varying demand for individual school types in a rapidly changing supply landscape leads to imbalances both between and within municipalities and makes reorganization imperative. Structural changes such as the restructuring of school types with the establishment of new comprehensive schools, which are provided in different forms (Gesamtschulen, Gemeinschaftsschulen, Stadtteilschulen), also have an impact on the calculation of space requirements. In addition, the implementation of the legal entitlement to all-day care in elementary schools varies significantly. Federalism in Germany has led to a patchwork of school types, each subject to its own regulations.

However, school construction planning cannot be considered in isolation for each individual location, but must be based on the principles of equality and be carried out from an educational as well as a municipal and regional perspective (integrated school development planning). Funding policy has also reacted to this situation and has launched a number of funding programs at the state and federal levels for the reconstruction of existing municipal educational facilities. These include the »Startchancen-Programm,«[20] the largest and most long-term education initiative in the history of the Federal Republic of Germany to date. It is designed to enable comprehensive investment in the future, improve equality of opportunities, and renew the promise of social advancement through good education, especially for socially disadvantaged students.

20 www.bmbf.de/startchancenprogramm

DELOCALIZATION OF EDUCATION

What is already evident today in the spheres of working, living, and leisure is also becoming more relevant for educational processes: learning is already becoming increasingly location-independent and »nomadic.« This development opens up opportunities but also harbors risks. Access to knowledge is becoming easier and tends to be available to everyone, everywhere. The availability, but especially the polyphony of information, poses new challenges for learners and teachers alike, especially in terms of media literacy. Here, the education system will become significantly more differentiated through self-organizing forms of learning. This process will be greatly accelerated by the further development of the use of artificial intelligence. New categories and spatial »demarcations« of learning locations will emerge—both within and beyond school buildings.

PARADIGM SHIFT IN PEDAGOGY

A pedagogical paradigm shift is currently taking place in German schools—at varying speeds. The key points are: individual support and inclusion, digitalization, rhythmization of instruction, the establishment of all-day schools, activating forms of learning and teaching, collaboration in multi-professional teams, and school as a place to live. Among other things, the change is from teaching to learning schools, from separating to inclusive schools, from closed to open schools, from managed to independent schools. To what extent this change has already been implemented is demonstrated by schools that were awarded the German School Award in recent years or that received the Jacob Muth Prize by Germany's UNESCO Commission.[21] Such a school requires a profound rethinking, not only on the part of teachers and stakeholders at all levels of educational management and administration but also on the part of planners and architects. In addition, the requirements of sustainable development call for a stronger educational mandate that must be firmly anchored in general education schools if sustainability goals are to be achieved.

☞ Chapter 6, *The 10 Theses in the Pedagogical Discourse*, pp. 178 ff.

21 The German School Award is announced and awarded by the Robert Bosch Stiftung and the Heidehof Stiftung in cooperation with Stern magazine and the ARD broadcasting network. The Jakob Muth Prize for Inclusive Schools (2009 to 2019) was integrated into the German School Award in 2020.

SUSTAINABLE CONSTRUCTION, CLIMATE ADAPTATION, AND CIRCULAR PROCESSES

The demands of resource conservation and resilience are leading to fundamental changes in the way we build today. From a resource perspective, criteria such as the preservation of existing buildings, life-cycle costs, sustainable construction methods, as well as requirements for the recyclability of materials used and the ability to demolish buildings using single-origin materials are now as important as energy efficiency, which has long been the focus of attention. For holistic planning and integrated, transdisciplinary conceptual approaches in a post-fossil society, it seems obvious that educational buildings in particular should take on a special role as pacesetters and role models. This raises the question of how the educational facility can make the content of »Education for Sustainable Development« tangible and »graspable« as a matter of course—for example, in a user-friendly spatial design, with recyclable, healthy materials, user-friendly building technology, with climate-adapted outdoor spaces, with a view to integrating the educational facility into its surroundings. This results in a wide range of requirements for school construction, but also opportunities for future-oriented development.

☞ Chapter 2, *Thesis 9*, pp. 46 ff.

GROWING NEED FOR RECONSTRUCTION AND NEW CONSTRUCTION AMID EXISTING REFURBISHMENT REQUIREMENTS

School buildings in Germany are in poor condition. Municipalities—as school authorities—are obliged to maintain their building stock and use financial resources sparingly. Due to the need to reduce CO_2 emissions in the construction sector in order to protect the climate, it is particularly important to renovate and convert existing buildings—conversion takes precedence over new construction. It is also important to consider whether other vacant buildings offer new opportunities for repurposing. For example, office buildings, industrial buildings, and department stores are increasingly being evaluated for potential conversion into future educational facilities. In the case of existing schools with a traditional corridor-classroom layout, it is evident that their rigid basic structure often involves costly reconstruction work to meet future educational requirements. New and innovative ideas therefore arise from the transformation of the existing—extension then primarily means reconstruction or addition.[22] Because of the urgent need to modernize existing buildings and for reasons of sustainability, examples that demonstrate a successful interplay between pedagogical concepts and creative models of spatial organization have a special role model function.[23]

22
Examples of this include the conversion of an organic supermarket into a district school in Hamburg-Ottensen or the conversion of a department store into a school or educational center in Lübeck.

23
Cf. the pilot projects »Ganztag und Raum«

CHANGING SPATIAL CONCEPTS

Many school building layouts date back to the late 19th or early 20th century and no longer meet current requirements. No home, office, or factory is built the same way it was 100 years ago. And the spatial concepts of the buildings that were created in Germany in line with the educational reform 50 years ago also need to be fundamentally revised. With the transformation of schools into places of learning and living, the range of school activities is expanding and requires spatially modified concepts that respond to new pedagogical, structural, and urban planning requirements. A monofunctional view of »one room = one function = one teacher« is no longer up to date and contradicts the diverse forms of learning and teaching required in an inclusive, all-day school with a multi-professional team. Given the potential shifts in use in the future, what is needed is a robust spatial framework for a changing range of uses rather than a specialized, precisely fitting functional room scheme. At the same time, spaces of high design and atmospheric quality must be created. The search for practical answers to these demands will determine the future of school construction—beyond the question of appearance and form, which is often seen as the central architectural challenge.

☞ Chapter 3, *Users and Their Spaces*, pp. 52ff.

OUTDATED CODES AND STANDARDS

For a long time, school construction in Germany was based on standards and codes/guidelines from the post-war period, which largely determined space requirements based on quantitative aspects (= square meters).[24] However, calculating requirements based on spatially precise area indices lead to the perpetuation of traditional functional allocations and spatial stereotypes and prevents profile-oriented prioritization. The result is disproportionate under- and overcapacity. The idea of generalizing codes or guidelines is countered by the demand that all schools should position themselves on the educational market with their own pedagogical profile—integrated into the specific local conditions of a municipal and regional educational landscape. As with almost all other construction tasks, specific usage requirements must be determined for each school construction project and individually tailored spatial and organizational concepts must be developed jointly by all parties involved.[25]

24
In some federal states, these standards and guidelines still apply today. Due to the sovereignty of the federal states in school matters, school construction and funding—and even more so their implementation—currently differ greatly from one state to another, ranging from a high degree of openness to rigid standardization. However, some states have already made adjustments in response to changing pedagogical requirements.

25
Cf. Montag Stiftung Jugend und Gesellschaft, BDA, VBE (Ed.)(2022)

At the same time, a quantitative and qualitative framework is needed to keep costs under control and ensure the sustainability of the building. This framework, however, must be individually interpretable and contain reasonable minimum requirements. Against the background of these requirements, pragmatic solutions have been found in many model building programs, planning frameworks, and funding guidelines in recent years: Instead of specifying individual rooms, space quotas have been defined for all projects based on the number of students in a school, which can then be interpreted with individual priorities depending on the school and educational location.[26] Structural standards (such as lighting, sound insulation, fire protection, etc.) must also be adapted to changes in education.[27]

26 Cf. for example Stadt Frankfurt am Main (Ed.) (2023b)

27 The Montag Stiftung Jugend und Gesellschaft uses pilot projects to show how building standards can be redesigned and adapted to meet future-oriented pedagogy: Montag Stiftung Jugend und Gesellschaft, *Schulbau Open Source*.

FUNDING PROGRAMS

Funding programs can be key enablers and act as important drivers in the transformation and further development of spatial educational structures. In many cases, state and federal programs make it possible for local authorities to initiate comprehensive transformation processes. Funding criteria are therefore an important steering instrument in reshaping Germany's educational landscapes. However, if funding programs are to truly promote future-oriented education and educational buildings, they must not only allow for but also require an integrated approach that combines pedagogy and space. Even current programs such as the »Startchancen-Programm« or the Ganztagsförderungsgesetz (All-Day Support Act), which support not only construction projects but also measures such as school and teaching development as well as the expansion of multi-professional teams, are not sufficiently binding in this regard.[28]

28 www.bmbf.de/startchancenprogramm; KMK (2012)

For all school construction investments planned for the coming years, it must be ensured that furnishings, equipment, and reconstruction are planned in line with educational developments. This, in turn, must be based on verifiable quality criteria and geared to the future needs of learning in a digital world. This applies in particular to the special infrastructure fund approved by the Federal Government in March 2025. Under the title »Qualität im Schulbau – Sondervermögen für Qualitätsoffensive im Schulbau nutzen« (»Quality in school construction—special fund for a quality offensive in school construction«), a list of demands has already been drawn up, with the editors of this book also contributing. It defines key criteria for good school construction to guide the allocation and management of funding.[29] It is the responsibility of the authorities in charge of allocating funding to manage and guarantee the effectiveness of funding through binding quality criteria.

29 Montag Stiftung Jugend und Gesellschaft, BDA, VBE (2025)

2

REQUIREMENTS

10 Theses on Sustainable School Construction

How can old and new educational facilities be made fit for the present and the near future? Which pedagogical concepts are relevant, and how can they be implemented in terms of spatial and urban planning? The following theses deal with ten aspects that set the course for school construction at the interface of pedagogy and architecture.

Based on the changed understanding of school-based learning (Thesis 1), a total of nine further principles—both organizational and content-related—are developed. They all deal with issues of fundamental pedagogical importance and at the same time have direct consequences for the architectural and urban design of schools. Both aspects—pedagogy and architecture / urban development—are described for each thesis.

It is not about universal solutions, new standards, or a new »school theory.« Rather, it is about formulating key questions that—drawing primarily on practical experience—must be answered in each planning process with an individual focus. Background information and evidence for the ten theses can be found at the end of the book: Chapter VI shows how the theses are grounded in educational theory and practice.

THESIS 1
Learning requires many and varied perspectives, approaches, and outcomes.

THESIS 2
Students learn alone, in pairs, in small groups, with the entire year group, across age groups, and also as a class.

THESIS 3
All-day schooling means learning, moving, playing, romping, lingering, talking, eating, and much more—in a healthy rhythm.

THESIS 4
The culture of digitality changes the culture of textbooks and blackboards.

THESIS 5
Support in an inclusive school takes place in heterogeneous groups.

THESIS 6
Cultural and aesthetic education must be conveyed through pedagogy and architecture.

THESIS 7
Learning with a focus on health and movement takes place in stimulating environments.

THESIS 8
Democratic learning requires a democratic school.

THESIS 9
School is a role model in dealing with the environment, materials, and technology.

THESIS 10
The school opens up to the city—the city opens up to the school.

THESIS 1

Learning requires many and varied perspectives, approaches, and outcomes.

Historically, the invention of schooling assumed that it was useful and possible to familiarize students with the entire cosmos of existing knowledge. Activities such as copying, reciting, and coloring dominated: learning by reproduction.

However, the age of encyclopedic scholarship is over. Major drivers of change such as digitalization, artificial intelligence, and climate change have created a new world. Almost everything that can be known today can be accessed at anytime from anywhere in the world. The key concept for the school of the future therefore is—to put it simply—not knowledge but skills. Along with the acquisition of basic knowledge, it is important to acquire the skills to actively use knowledge: to independently acquire, evaluate, and select information, to use information in a targeted and appropriate manner, and to apply it to solve problems, to communicate with others, to critically question and creatively develop one's own work processes and results. This also includes the use of artificial intelligence.

Learning today means actively experiencing the wonder of discovering objects and patterns, facts and occurrences, connections and disconnections, causes and interactions. Learning involves trial and error, experimentation and testing, presentation and change. Learning is an active and interactive, emotional and social process that influences what we memorize as applied knowledge and skills.

It is not just about the rational aspects of cognitive knowledge acquisition. For learning to take place, the inner forces and visions that set learning in motion and drive it must also be taken into account. Learning is particularly effective when intrinsic motivation, recognition by others, self-activity, and self-determination are intertwined. It is therefore important to enable a variety of learning paths and a wide range of learning activities through different active learning approaches.

Learning is not just about reproducing and reflecting on what already exists, but about active co-construction by the learner—in his own mind, in his own body, and together with others.

The variety of learning paths and activities, the interplay of individual and collaborative learning, requires a variety of learning situations. This leads to the need for a dissolution of spatial boundaries: The traditional classroom as a largely static teaching space becomes a dynamic »conversion space« that enables different forms of learning. In combination with adjacent rooms and areas, the range of uses is significantly expanded. This also creates a new challenge: organizing this variability.

Variability primarily means being able to choose between different spatial situations depending on the learning scenario. Accordingly, the rooms are not arranged according to clear hierarchies but can be combined in a variety of ways. Mono-functionality is avoided, multiple uses are made possible, and open-plan layouts gain in importance—which does not mean that the rooms are featureless. The concept of »spatial polyvalence« creates a mixture of fixed and variable, ambiguous and specialized, open and closed spatial sequences that generate different atmospheres.

Spatial adaptations to changing needs should not require extensive alterations but should be as ad hoc as possible. Circulation areas are expanded to create spaces that are as fully usable or communicative as possible, creating »under-determined« in-between spaces for spontaneous and sometimes unpredictable learning situations. Boundaries and transitions are carefully designed—they define the quality of the connections between the individual spaces.

The organizational models that have emerged can generally be assigned to one of the following three categories. In practice, these categories are often not clearly distinguishable—there are many hybrid models:[30]

— Classroom-plus: The traditional classroom is supplemented by additional areas that offer opportunities for differentiation and retreat in close proximity to the classroom. Additional group rooms are added (for example, by transforming three existing classrooms into a tandem model with two classrooms sharing a central group work area), and circulation areas are reimagined as spaces for communication and study. Alternatively, large classrooms are set up to allow for differentiation within the given space.

— Cluster: Classrooms, differentiation areas, and common areas for multiple learning groups are combined into semi-autonomous units with shared spaces. Rooms are grouped to provide a variety of combinations and separations. Open and closed room configurations are possible. By combining teaching and differentiation rooms, all-day areas, teacher team rooms, sanitary facilities, and storage areas into a single unit, a wide range of interpretation and usage options are opened up. At the same time, learners and learning guides are provided with manageable and clearly identifiable spatial (sub)units that ensure good orientation even in very large institutions.

— (Open) Learning Landscape: Farthest removed from the traditional »classroom,« learning situations are created within a large, mostly open spatial structure where students choose their place depending on their activity. Enclosed functional rooms are reduced to a minimum; there are no classrooms in the traditional sense. Teaching spaces alternate with areas for individual work, group activities, and retreat. Circulation spaces are largely avoided. Each student has a variety of choices between learning areas and learning atmospheres. The concept directly reflects the idea of individualization and personal responsibility in learning. It is primarily used in higher grade levels and requires a high degree of independence.

30
Cf. Schneider (2012); Montag Stiftung Jugend und Gesellschaft/BDA/VBE (2022)

THESIS 2

Students learn alone, in pairs, in small groups, with the entire year group, across age groups, and also as a class.

Each child, each young person is different and learns differently—schools need to respond to the individuality of each person. Individualization is a major concept in current educational development: At key stages in the learning process, each student works at his or her own pace, on different topics, in different ways, in different places. It is no longer necessary for everyone to learn the same thing at the same time, in the same place, and in the same way.

At the same time, no child can learn alone. Learning needs role models, recognition, dialog, and interaction with others. The more socially embedded learning is, the more successful it is. It must therefore be possible to gain and reflect on both individual learning experiences and teamwork experiences in small and large groups at school. The school respects the uniqueness of each individual and at the same time uses people's diversity to inspire, complement, and support each other.

This dual requirement necessitates two key external conditions: First, it must be possible to systematically vary the social organization of forms of working to enable individualized learning while fostering social skills.

A rule of thumb for time allocation might be as follows: Work is done

— 30 percent alone—not left alone though, but with clear and binding, monitorable work assignments and a sense of achievement;
— 30 percent in small groups (between two and six learners), who are systematically introduced to cooperative work;
— 10 percent as a class (ideally 15 to 20 learners), where everyone can see each other, so that everyone can really talk to each other and negotiate common issues;
— 30 percent in a frontal format, i.e. the traditional teacher-led instruction, student presentations, or dialogic class discussions.

Second, the implementation of these pedagogical guidelines requires a stimulating learning environment and the provision of a wide range of both differentiating and motivating learning materials that enable students to work alone or in small groups, at their own pace, on different topics, and in very different ways.

Quantitative and qualitative changes are therefore also required at the architectural level. The standard of two square meters per student, which has been used for decades to calculate the size of a classroom, is not sufficient to allow for different teaching and learning formats. It must be possible to vary the forms of learning (circle of chairs, groups of four, frontal instruction, etc.), and areas for differentiation and retreat must be provided. Ultimately, the area required for learning and teaching—optionally with reading corners, experimentation areas, mini-stage, including circulation and storage areas—adds up to four to five square meters of usable space per student.[31] While this figure may initially seem unfeasible given the standards used to date, this assessment is put into perspective by the fact that judicious integration of differentiation and all-day spaces as well as circulation areas can make significant unused spatial capacities available. Space allocation plans based on the above-mentioned pedagogical concepts already apply these figures (e.g., in Cologne, Munich, Hamburg, Berlin, Frankfurt, Darmstadt-Dieburg, Dortmund, etc.).

Beyond pure space requirements, qualitative changes are also essential. The spatial organization depends directly on the permeability and interchangeability of individual spaces. For example, in order to organize parallel work of individuals and small groups, direct spatial interconnectivity is required. It must be possible to share spaces. This kind of integration requires the dissolution of rigid boundaries—whether through large (usually open) doors, transparent wall elements, or sliding/folding partitions. Despite all the permeability and transparency, the need for sufficient acoustic separation must also be guaranteed.

Equipment standards and furnishings must be adapted to the idea of the classroom as both a workshop and stage that is, as a »transformable room«: tables that can be combined in a variety of ways, but also permanently installed »anchor furniture« for specific uses, presentation facilities tailored to the learning information, good technical equipment, storage options, filing and shelving space, moveable boxes that can also be used as room dividers, etc. Corridor areas should be upgraded with lounge and work facilities and become the backbone of the spatial cluster. In any case, a stable media infrastructure (WLAN) must be guaranteed throughout the building.

31
Cf. also Montag Stiftung Jugend und Gesellschaft/BDA/VBE (2022)

THESIS 3

All-day schooling means learning, moving, playing, romping, lingering, talking, eating, and much more— in a healthy rhythm.

Changing societal demands on schools and new teaching and learning concepts require the transformation of half-day schools into all-day schools.[32] Starting in the 2026/27 school year, Germany will gradually introduce a legal entitlement to all-day care for elementary school children. In the medium term, it is expected that the »bound« all-day school (all students attend school for eight hours) will replace the currently still widespread »open« model. This shift will also impact secondary education. Most high schools in Germany already have the characteristics of an all-day school, even in the upper grades, with afternoon classes and study groups on some days, without being labeled, designed, or equipped as such.

All-day schooling makes a decisive contribution to providing a minimum level of educational opportunity for all, without excluding the promotion of special talents. It also ensures that children and adolescents are cared for while their parents or guardians are working.

With the implementation of all-day schooling, the school is becoming a place of learning and living; different times and spaces are required. Work, communication, and recreation must be balanced in an age-appropriate way . School is no longer just about learning, but also about moving, playing, romping, lingering, talking, eating, resting, and much more. Phases of concentration and regeneration alternate. In the past, school was mainly limited to the morning in 45-minute intervals, after which students did their homework and teachers prepared lessons at home. Now, the time structure is changing fundamentally, especially through the collaboration between professionals from the fields of education and youth services working together in all-day schools. In these all-day schools, different rhythms are not only recognizable by the introduction of 60- or 90-minute units, for example. These units usually consist of several variable phases that can be weighted differently from school to school:

- Arrival at school with individual flextime, during which students can practice, deepen their knowledge, and try things out independently (but also »chill out« or simply talk)
- Alternation of frontal instruction and student-centered forms of learning
- Food and drink, movement and regeneration
- Education according to individual interests and aptitudes
- Extracurricular activities
- Collaborative projects or presentations
- Leaving school, possibly again as flextime

Schools vary widely in how they combine, extend, or modify such phases.

32
An all-day school (Ganztagsschule) in Germany often only lasts until 2 p.m.; when we talk about an all-day school, we mean a period that usually lasts from 8 a.m. to 4 p.m.

The spatial expansion to become an all-day school is more than just adding an extension to accommodate a canteen and an all-day recreation area. The widespread practice of spatially separating formal education (lessons) and non-formal education (care) into dedicated, independent spaces, as is the case in many places, exacerbates the lack of space and is not sustainable—especially as this results in significant vacancies when neither teaching nor care are taking place. This problem is even more pressing given that school and »open« all-day care are often still operated as separate entities in terms of organization and staffing, which runs counter to educational goals. In view of the highly differentiated usage cycles that will result from the necessary integration in the future, detailed activity studies are required to better align school design with the needs of future schools: What happens where and when? Even if similar components can be found in every school, they can only be defined on a case-by-case basis in a dialog between users and planners.

The spatial usage requirements must be derived directly from the description of the various phases of concentration and regeneration in everyday school routines. Although this method of spatial notation (»mapping«) has a long tradition in planning, it was long neglected in school construction due to rigid guidelines that often specified room types and sizes. In modern office construction, by contrast, activity-based and communication-oriented organizational models have long been common practice: the traditional office building with only cellular or open-plan layouts has been abandoned in favor of a variety of spaces with different atmospheres. Depending on one's task and emotional state, people organize themselves in the appropriate spaces. These usage studies form the basis for the spatial program and are the starting point for the architectural design.

Given the large number of activities in an inclusive all-day school, continuing a purely additive approach—allocating a separate, monofunctional space for each activity—would result in an unmanageable increase in space requirements. Instead, activity-based and task-oriented spatial concepts are built on the principle of multiple uses and the shared use of all spaces by everyone. The architecture must respond to the changing rhythms of school life: dynamically adaptable spatial models are essential. As work, communication, and recreation become increasingly intertwined, and as informal learning is given high priority alongside intentional learning, the boundaries between instructional and recreational spaces become blurred. Formal and informal, static and dynamic, fixed and flexible, passive and active, individual and collaborative, tired and playful—many activities take place in parallel and next to each other. Therefore, it makes sense not to separate the all-day areas, but to integrate them into the learning spaces.[33]

The cafeteria, forum, and library, as well as the outdoor spaces, become important communication hubs in the all-day school. The quality of these spaces outside the narrow learning zones is critical to a successful everyday school life.

33
How rooms in elementary school can be used by everyone throughout the day and what pedagogical, organizational, and spatial (conversion) measures are needed is demonstrated by the five pilot projects »Ganztag und Raum. Pilotprojekte. Fünf Dokumentationen« by the Montag Stiftung Jugend und Gesellschaft.

THESIS 4

The culture of digitality changes the culture of textbooks and blackboards.

The basic pattern of the still predominant teaching situation in schools emerged in an era before computers, television, Wikipedia, Google, YouTube, or ChatGPT. Teachers were the first and most important gateway to the world beyond the immediate experience of students. This has changed—and will continue to change—especially with the advent of digital media: A far-reaching »culture of digitality« (Felix Stalder) is changing not only our everyday lives and working world but also the school system. This affects not only the way knowledge is accessed and used. AI will also be increasingly able to adapt to the individual learning paths of each learner in ways that would be impossible for a teacher dealing with a class of 30 students. For teachers, this means a fundamental change in their role. The opportunities and risks of all aspects of digitalization must be weighed and become part of the school, just as they are part of society. This makes the personal role model of the learning guide all the more important in the selection and interpretation of these worlds. Despite and because of AI, the Internet, and blended learning, real people will continue to be urgently needed at these new gateways to the world. This is because digital media can offer students only secondary experiences—but not truly formative, primary experiences: personal, active encounters with people and things—especially critical in the context of the skills needed in the 21st century, such as creativity, communication, collaboration, and critical thinking. These skills cannot be adequately addressed through machine learning alone.[34]

The more widespread the use of digital technologies and artificial intelligence becomes, the more important it is to teach basic media skills. This is something students themselves are calling for.[35] At the same time, schools have a compensatory role to play: especially in the humane use of new technologies, schools must occasionally take a step back. Going forward, schools must above all teach responsible use of media and information, awaken children's and young people's intrinsic strengths, and give them time to develop. Findings from learning research emphasize that schools must facilitate a transformation from analog face-to-face experiences to digital formats and vice versa. To improve the learning process, the integration of AI is helpful.[36] Critical and creative use of digital media and AI is best learned through the act of creation itself—when students work with media, do research, create presentations, and revise found or generated content. Before and during the use of digital tools and AI, it is important to develop and strengthen the creative power of one's own senses, hands, and body. In the face of the enormous acceleration made possible by digital technology, it becomes all the more important to systematically slow down: to give one's own sensory impressions time, to allow for a second and third look, and to wait for the inner impulse.

34
Cf. 4C model of learning

35
Shell Youth Study (2024)

36
Cf. Reich / Reich (2025)

Delocalization processes, which are increasingly leading to location-independent workplaces in the world of work, are also likely to fundamentally change students' working habits in the future. It is difficult to predict the extent to which location-independent learning and the possible integration of the school and public spheres will develop. The Corona pandemic showed that German schools were often not sufficiently prepared for digital learning. This is mainly due to a lack of access to digital devices and the Internet for students, a lack of learning management systems, and a lack of qualified teachers who can teach remotely.[37] In any case, digitalization is increasingly blurring the boundaries between formal and informal learning situations, as real and virtual learning worlds merge.

Media development and digitalization in schools have a direct impact on the use of space: »Learning in digital space« must be taken into account in all reconstruction and new construction projects.

The combination of physical and virtual spaces leads to hybrid learning environments where both dimensions are intertwined. Access to information is no longer tied to a specific location. Key educational goals such as individualization and differentiation, self-organization, and personal responsibility can be promoted through the use of digital hardware. Tablets and smartphones already allow a flexible choice of individual learning locations, thus creating the basis for the inclusion of previously unused spatial resources.

Especially if digital media are to be increasingly used to support individualized learning or group work, a high equipment density, reliable technical functionality, and the availability of high-quality software are just as indispensable as critical media education. Only then can media play a key role in the frequently demanded »flexibilization« of spatial structures.

A good technical infrastructure that is available throughout the school is an important prerequisite for the building. A stable network and a reliable Internet connection for students and teachers are a matter of course, as are flexible presentation options. Dedicated computer rooms will sooner or later only be needed as subject-specific rooms. An IT center with servers is available. Multimedia resources are provided for in-house production and networked with the art room, technology and science labs, library, and theater, and the workroom is supplemented by a 3D printer and a robotics workshop in a dust-proof adjoining room. Makerspaces and green screen areas are also added.

Digitalization enables a high degree of adaptability to different work situations. It should be possible to individually determine both acceleration and deceleration. Transitions are smooth, and changeover times can be reduced to a minimum. New, unplanned learning scenarios can arise when space can be used in a variety of ways—for example, when a stair becomes a seat. Informal learning situations are becoming increasingly important, as are room configurations such as reading corners, study cafes, and chill-out lounges. Multimedia studios with the appropriate technology should be made available, although the requirements must be clarified in advance and adapted to the actual learning needs.

Now that knowledge can be accessed anywhere, a wide variety of places and spaces that were previously only suitable for reading and talking can be used for a broad range of educational processes: Parks, cafes, youth centers, homes, and other locations are increasingly becoming temporary and informal places of learning. The ability to freely choose learning environments inside and outside the school building means a significant expansion of learning scenarios.

37
Cf. Anger (2024)

THESIS 5

Support in an inclusive school takes place in heterogeneous groups.

Schools should compensate for young people's disadvantages, whatever they may be: (social) origin, ethnicity, gender, language, or other characteristics. PISA has shown that school systems produce better educational outcomes when students learn together for long periods of time under appropriate staffing and physical conditions. This also applies to special needs—whether physical, mental, or emotional.

The theory that early separation contributes to the development of the individual, which is often used in Germany to justify the multi-track school system, cannot be empirically proven. On the contrary, daily contact with the diversity of people can—with appropriate support—lead to special social, cognitive, and emotional skills that would not be gained without these experiences of shared learning. The results from other countries also show that this applies particularly to high-achieving children and adolescents. Additional factors include the growing shortage of skilled workers and a labor market that values diverse talents. A future-oriented society depends on providing good educational opportunities for all.

»Inclusion« is therefore a key concept in the education policy debate—no one must be excluded. The aim is to provide the best possible opportunities for all students, to foster a sense of belonging in the community, to encourage the individual development of each student's physical, intellectual, and emotional strengths, and—as far as possible—to strive to compensate for their weaknesses. The school thus respects the uniqueness of each individual while using diversity to support and enrich each other.

In Germany, inclusion is still often seen as a voluntary option. However, local authorities are under pressure to act: the German government's ratification of the UN Convention on the Rights of Persons with Disabilities sets clear standards: every child has the right to collaborative learning.

The transition to an inclusive school system in Germany will take a long time, as it involves profound changes in teaching practices and in the role of teachers in multi-professional teams. The entire learning process will no longer be shaped solely by the traditional class structure but will be increasingly guided by individual learning needs. Methods and materials for internal differentiation and individualization of more goal-differentiated instruction, as well as cooperative learning, need to be developed, and learning guides must be trained in their use. Multi-professional teams consisting of teachers, special educators, social pedagogues, and educational staff need to be established. The role of the teacher is shifting from that of a classroom instructor to that of a learning guide and facilitator of diverse individuals.

Mainstream schools cannot, in principle, refuse to admit people with special educational needs—even if the reality in Germany often still tells a different story. Other countries are already demonstrating that it is both practical and sensible not to exclude anyone and to ensure that support systems are available close to home when needed. Strict case-by-case assessment must ensure that mainstream education, which the UN Convention considers to be the most effective form of support, can be made accessible for as many children as possible.

Architecture can support the pedagogical idea of supporting all learners in heterogeneous and inclusive groups by providing sufficient, well-organized, well-equipped, and sufficiently large rooms and spaces. Classrooms need to be complemented by differentiation and retreat spaces—some integrated into the learning space, some separate from it. The increased space requirements that, for good reason, were available to the former special needs schools must now be proportionately included in the future spatial planning of mainstream schools: inclusion is neither a cost-cutting model in terms of space nor staff. However, with the creation of inclusion areas in mainstream schools, such spaces no longer need to be maintained in special schools. As cooperation between different learning groups becomes even more important through inclusion, the corresponding models must also be reflected spatially—further underscoring the spatial hybrid models already outlined, such as Classroom-plus, Cluster, and Learning Landscape. Issues of individualization and differentiation gain additional relevance through inclusion and must be reflected in the spatial organization of the school.

In many places, the spatial implications of inclusion are still limited primarily to the barrier-free design of school buildings. On this point, it must be said: accessibility is an absolutely necessary but not a sufficient criterion for inclusion. On the one hand, it is a matter of course and laid down in a number of standards and guidelines; on the other hand, it is often a great challenge in everyday planning. The central question of accessibility in its various levels of meaning can rarely be answered unambiguously, especially when it comes to reconstruction projects, and can only yield good results through an intensive assessment process with those involved.

Pragmatically, two levels of inclusion can be identified in terms of their spatial implications. On the one hand, there is the concrete issue of accessibility, which can be defined by very specific requirements: circulation areas, movement areas, door and window dimensions, guidance system, control elements, etc. On the other hand, there is an abundance of soft criteria for supporting heterogeneous groups that are directly linked to the overall pedagogical debate. The previously outlined demands for adaptability, openness, and differentiation (e.g. through cluster formation), as well as for exchange and communication, gain additional and compelling justification here, as the spectrum of learning formats is significantly expanded in inclusive schools. At the same time, retreat spaces close to the classroom or learning zone are needed, which can only be made available across all learning groups and in a networked approach.[38]

The specific spatial requirements resulting from inclusion are not different fundamentally from the »standard« needs of general education schools. Rather, they complement and extend them. The list of requirements includes the following aspects: integration of differentiation areas for special educational needs—such as additional quiet and movement rooms—into the general learning areas; shared workspaces for all teachers; additional counseling and therapy rooms, if necessary; additional barrier-free sanitary facilities, etc.

38
Cf. Kricke / Reich / Schanz / Schneider (2018)

THESIS 6

Cultural and aesthetic education must be conveyed through pedagogy and architecture.

In today's research on teaching and learning, learning is no longer seen as a one-dimensional linguistic-logical or mathematical-operational process. It also includes expansions toward musical, kinesthetic, emotional, and spatial-creative learning. The more cognitive learning content can be linked to other domains, the more effectively different learners retain knowledge. Unlocking these additional fields of learning is a vital foundation for all forms of creativity.

However, this cultural dimension should not be seen merely as a supportive element to what is often considered »real« learning. Music, dance, art, and movement are far too important to appear in schools primarily in such functionally subordinated contexts. Rather, the cultural dimension must constitute one of the essential cornerstones of education in its own right. Even if so-called »core subjects« like to deny the importance and value of »soft« secondary subjects, it is precisely the latter that can make a significant contribution to the development of students' personalities.

Especially against the background of increasing medialization, the children's own acting and dancing, singing and designing, physical movement and physical challenges in all their forms should play a central role—in practice, not in talking about it. The ongoing shift toward all-day schooling makes this demand even more urgent. This learning-by-doing approach requires an activating learning environment—one that consistently allows students to try out and experiment for themselves with what in other subjects often remains mere theory.

Schools are places that create culture. As such, however, they are generally unable to serve all cultural disciplines with the same quality but must develop focal areas. For example, not all schools can provide high-quality programs in drama, music, dance, or physical activity in one building. However, each school should develop its own profile to achieve a particular quality in that area.

Schools are public buildings and, as such, strongly reflect the architectural production of a society. They document the importance of education and manifest themselves in ever-changing contemporary aesthetic expressions. As buildings, they are places that shape culture: over the course of the 12,000 to 15,000 hours of a normal student's life, they can directly unfold a daily cultural and aesthetic influence that goes far beyond any art history lesson. School buildings serve as role models and showcases of architectural culture that illustrate a sustainable built environment on a 1:1 scale.

The building as a »machine of perception« makes space in all its dimensions directly tangible to its users. Materiality, light, colors, proportions, connections, details, and much more are part of an everyday experience in which aesthetic and architectural education take on concrete meaning. Architecture has an impact on our well-being, our performance, our behavior, and our activities. Transparency creates visual relationships, ensures lighting, and establishes a connection to the outside world. High-quality materials characterize the value of the building and thus the status of the people in it. They also allow different sensory experiences. Proportions, dimensions, and shapes of rooms enable and inspire activities. The attitude of a school can be implemented through architecture. A high degree of transparency and visual connections in a building lead to more communication. Wooden steps immersed in plenty of daylight invite people to sit down. Areas flooded with light are ideal for spending time in. Thick wooden window frames with deep reveals offer spaces to retreat and take a break.

Architecture only reveals itself aesthetically and functionally in use. Thus, the true merit of architecture becomes primarily apparent in how it performs over time when it is subjected to changing receptions and evaluations. Through changing interpretations and types of use, architecture is thus in a constant process of appropriation and thus also of »demolding.« The relationship between architecture and its users is similar to that between literature and readers: when reading, texts are produced in the text through one's own interpretations. Likewise, architecture cannot define a real final state.

The starting point is not the (static) image of the built environment, but rather the question of the choreography of everyday life and the interaction between users and physical space. What spatial constellations, atmospheres, and settings can accommodate the various learning scenarios and usage requirements? In this allocation of meaning, other types of buildings may also be suitable for defining what schools is and can be—today and in the future: Ideally, creative appropriation and renewal can arise from the dissonance between the architectural shell and traditional usage patterns. Beyond predefined models of representation—»a school just looks like a school«—the design and use of a school building must be understood as an ongoing process of appropriation. Just as interpretations of what is considered beautiful and ugly change over time, so too do the uses of school buildings and their spaces. This is also true given the fact that school construction always involves school reconstruction—therefore calling for the definition of a design strategy for dealing with what already exists.

THESIS 7

Learning with a focus on health and movement takes place in stimulating environments.

Learning is not just a matter of the mind. Learning, brain, and health research has demonstrated in many ways that the brain needs the whole body to learn. With the coronavirus pandemic and the challenges of a world dominated by digital media, the issue of mental health among schoolchildren has also come to the fore. The term »well-being« plays an important role today—as a link between physical and mental health. Meeting basic physiological needs is a prerequisite for successful learning and students' health.

First and foremost, this means such seemingly simple things as being able to »hear properly,« »see well,« »breathe properly,« and »move sufficiently.« Existing school buildings, however, are often characterized by inadequate lighting, poor air quality, overheated rooms, and cramped classrooms. These factors are among the most avoidable stressors that prevent learning or at least make it very difficult. The size of the group in a room must therefore allow for sufficient opportunities for movement, and the size of the group per teacher must still allow for respectful relationships, sufficient opportunities for support, and intensive learning contacts in different learning scenarios. Successful school systems have a standard size of 20 students, or even fewer when pursuing truly inclusive education.

Schools—especially all-day schools—need to be »active schools« to counterbalance periods of quiet and concentration and to mobilize new energy. Some schools try to do this by scheduling an hour of sports or physical activity each day. Others take a broader approach, incorporating child-, teaching-, and learning-oriented rhythms throughout the day, active and independent learning, dynamic breaks, participatory and thus health-promoting organizational structures—right up to opening the school to the outside world in the sense of networked thinking. The demand for quiet zones and calm periods is therefore just as important as the movement aspect.

The school's outdoor space should provide a varied and physically challenging environment. Where possible, it should be integrated into the school day as a place for sensory experience of nature and ecologically conscious behavior. Indoor spaces also need to be stimulating and spacious enough to facilitate periods of work and rest.

The quality of the canteen is central to the regeneration phases, not only in terms of healthy and tasty food, but also in terms of the important communicative and cultural function it can play. Children, teenagers, and adults should want to spend time there. The catering area must also be part of a school's educational concept—nutritional education is health education. Nutrition is gaining importance in the concept of salutogenesis. Food and its production and preparation can be a direct part of the learning concept.

The requirement for a healthy environment also applies to the teaching staff. In an all-day school, all teachers and staff need to be able to work in the building—with meeting and retreat areas. These measures can help to significantly reduce the alarmingly high rate of sick leave—teaching is one of the most vulnerable professions—and at the same time create the conditions for establishing team-oriented forms of work. This involves a change in spatial organization models, moving away from the traditional image of the central teacher's room with individual desks, and establishing contemporary work environments.

Health and exercise are reflected in space on many different levels.

New school buildings are generally built to high norms and standards, which can ensure that the learning environment is designed with care and students' basic physiological needs are met. However, these standards are often not aligned with new pedagogical requirements and contemporary spatial organization models. Many existing buildings lack adequate quality due to a significant investment backlog and a lack of maintenance.

The motivation and cognition of both learners and teachers are directly dependent on the physical qualities of the building—on air quality, acoustics, lighting, and indoor climate. Noise reduction, lighting design, tolerable air and temperature conditions are therefore central aspects of school (re)construction projects and must be addressed as part of integral planning concepts. It is also important to consider what should be controlled by technology and what should be regulated by people.

Healthy schools also mean healthy working conditions. With about 1.5 square meters per person, teachers often have to work under completely inadequate conditions. In all-day schools, spaces previously designated as break rooms are now becoming formal workspaces. The space requirement increases to six to eight square meters per full-time teaching post. This also applies to work and recreation areas for special and social education teachers and educators in multi-professional teams. Adequate space for individual preparation, meetings, and informal exchange must be provided in appropriately designated areas. Orientation toward the conference situation—the teachers' lounge is large enough to accommodate the entire staff—is no longer the central criterion. Decentralized team stations are often combined with a central communication point, such as a cafeteria. Conferences are held in multi-purpose rooms.

The cafeteria plays a key role in regenerative phases in all-day schools—also in terms of its atmospheric qualities. The cafeteria should be more than just a place to eat; it should also be a place to communicate, learn, and spend time and, where possible, be complemented by quiet and social areas. The dining area should not be limited to lunchtime use. Its potential for other types of events should be explored. In most cases, this multiple use comes at the expense of a »feel-good« atmosphere, which is why some school authorities choose to prioritize comfort and quality of stay.

School outdoor areas used for physical activity are a classic area of tension in open space design, especially in inner-city locations. The desire for near-natural landscaping and extensive outdoor facilities often competes with high usage pressure and intensive use in central locations. The functional use of limited outdoor spaces on school campuses is always high, and multiple uses are the rule: the schoolyard also serves as a sports field and a playground. The near-natural outdoor areas demanded by educators are often rare. In some places, development concepts in high-density urban areas move the schoolyard to the rooftop in order to provide outdoor space at all. In other cases, opening up the school to its neighborhood and a nearby city park can provide additional recreational and movement areas that cannot be created in the same variety on the limited school site.

The environmental goals of urban development and the provision of outdoor spaces for a school are often in conflict. Schoolyard design reflects the full spectrum of current approaches to open space design—from artificially elevated and topographically modulated urban squares to almost dreamlike natural gardens. Sports facilities play an important role in the design of outdoor spaces. Here, too, the emphasis is on flexibility, as the traditional principles of open space planning need to be reconsidered in inner-city locations and under climate adaptation criteria.[39]

39
Cf., e.g., Professorship of Sport and Health Didactics TUM School of Medicine and Health, involved in the feasibility study for the school campus project »Luitpoldpark«; Stadt Frankfurt am Main (ed.) (2023a)

THESIS 8

Democratic learning requires a democratic school.

Democracy »on a large scale« is based on the separation of powers, political equality, and the unconditional respect for the dignity of all people. It is enshrined in the democratic constitution and guaranteed by law. Democratic action by individuals »on a small scale« is essential for living together in successful communication and conflict resolution, and for experiencing and shaping community. Such action cannot simply be learned as theoretical knowledge—it must first and foremost be available as an example for children and young people at school—and ideally also in the family and living environment—to be understood and practiced. Only in this way can democracy ultimately function on a large scale.

Acting democratically means accepting the difficulty of having to negotiate one's own opinions and interests with or against those of others. It also means having the opportunity to experience the appreciation of one's own point of view during such negotiations. It is important to have a voice and to hear and respect the voices of others. In this way, children and young people are not only empowered to develop an awareness of themselves and their interests. They also learn to perceive others with their interests and points of view and to deal with conflicts in a solution-oriented way.

Democratic education in schools also means teaching children and young people about their own agency and capacity to influence outcomes. The more comprehensively learners are able to determine what is relevant for them to learn, the more self-determined they can make the learning process. The greater the scope for self-directed activity, the more independent, free, and potentially ambitious the design of such a learning process can be. Self-determination in the sense of »non-authoritarian« ideals is not possible within the framework of school life—however, the goal remains to give students as much age-appropriate self-determination as possible, also about content and the participatory design of their learning process. A reflective approach to digital media (including combating fake news) and mastery of basic cultural and communication techniques are important building blocks in creating this »space of opportunity.« By providing democratic education, schools must also help counteract forces in the lives of young adults that may pose a threat to democracy.

A democratic culture develops and manifests itself in the public life of the school and in its surrounding community. It exhibits, celebrates, and presents its results. The school as a democratic place must be open—to the municipality and its public. This has benefits for schools, both internally and externally. It creates learning situations that demand social skills, a sense of community, the ability to integrate, and personal responsibility. And in a knowledge society, with its demand for lifelong learning, it seems obvious that further education and training opportunities are made available in the district, for which the school premises should also be used. This opening of schools to the neighborhood reflects a broader concept of education—summarized under the phrase »education is more than school«—that has been the subject of professional debate for many years. It expands the circle of users to include adults and youth from the neighborhood. Campus management is essential to ensure that intensified use is successful.

Building a school is the first litmus test of a democratic school. Within a clearly defined framework, the school itself must be involved in the planning and negotiation processes of its architecture—an opportunity it can often use to raise its profile in terms of content.

Communication is at the heart of the current pedagogical debate about ever-changing learning formats. Creating the spatial conditions for fostering communicative settings is therefore a central requirement in school construction. The pedagogically required »individualization of teaching« must be balanced by areas of activity in which joint learning and school life can unfold. Central to this is the »heart« of the school, which offers enough space to host an assembly of the entire school community, to perform plays, and to make music together. In many cases, a combination of foyer, forum, and school hall provides an ideal solution for this »heart.«

Democracy »on a small scale« thrives on the interaction of the different meeting spaces available in everyday school life:

— adequately sized indoor and outdoor spaces for school-wide gatherings to actively shape school life through celebrations and joint events;
— areas for informal exchange of ideas with a high quality of stay;
— spaces for student councils, peer mediator training, student tutors, information boards at key points, and exhibition areas distributed throughout the school grounds, both indoors and outdoors;
— school intranet and Internet access, available at all times both on-site and remotely, with dedicated access and storage space for students and staff;
— (parent-teacher) meeting rooms or even a »parent café.«

Once again, formal and informal communication spaces overlap, elude final definition, and evolve through patterns of use.

In the future, schools will play an increasingly important role in municipalities and neighborhoods. While it was primarily cultural buildings that served as symbols of an active urban society in the late 20th century, it will (once again) increasingly be educational buildings that are seen as expressions of a democratic society in the future. An open and vibrant school can also compensate for deficits in neighborhood infrastructure. School can be a place where learning and knowledge production are public events and the school constitutes democracy. This, in turn, facilitates the task of enabling social integration and equal educational opportunities.

THESIS 9

School is a role model in dealing with the environment, materials, and technology.

Environmental education in its broadest sense has become a central issue in education. Schools must promote a positive relationship with nature and an understanding of the function and impact of technology. The sustainability debate has fully arrived in the discourse around schools. UNESCO's Global Action Program on Education for Sustainable Development (ESD) sets the national education agenda. The global sustainability goals (United Nations, Sustainable Development Goals) give the concept a universal significance and an practical application, defining the objectives and measures of the international community for sustainable education until 2030.[40] The wide range of issues covered by the 17 SDGs—including no poverty, affordable and clean energy, and responsible consumption and production—can be addressed primarily through a focus on education. People around the world need not only knowledge, but also skills and values that enable them to act responsibly. This is also the goal of the international ESD program.[41]

The range of educational activities addressing these topics is broad. Models of resource conservation can be practiced in the school itself: energy monitoring tasks, waste separation and recycling, student-run fair trade initiatives, canteen meals using regional produce, reduction of food waste, etc. There are also experimental areas, from the workshop to the laboratory, where students can apply and deepen their theoretical knowledge through hands-on investigations. Plants, aquariums, and the like can complement the indoor environment.

Outdoor areas should also be included in the daily school routine to promote a sensual experience of nature and ecologically conscious behavior: for example, designed outdoor areas with different activity zones, an area where experiments can also be carried out, school gardens and biotopes, or projects beyond the boundaries of the school grounds, such as tree and stream sponsorships. All of these broaden the field of experience and allow students of all ages to acquire a positive approach to the environment, which expands to an ecologically conscious attitude. The relevance of these projects is also reflected in the high level of public support they receive—regionally, nationally, and internationally.

In order to nurture a mindset that incorporates sustainability meaningfully into all major everyday and professional decisions, it is important to make complex functional relationships somewhat tangible. Many, perhaps most, of the technical processes created and influenced by humans are today only barely visible, their principles of operation are not recognizable, and their economic interdependencies are hardly comprehensible. These relationships are therefore an important subject for education. Simply displaying the measured values of the photovoltaic system on the school's roof in the entrance hall is not enough. It is crucial to actively explain the processes to the students in an age-appropriate way through small- or large-scale experimental projects.

The principle of simplicity and user-friendliness should take precedence over complex high-tech installations. This applies not only to the school's science facilities but also to the technical systems of school buildings. Changing requirements do not necessarily call for technical solutions, they can also be solved through organizational measures.

40
United Nations (2015b)

41
Deutsche UNESCO-Kommission (2021)

The requirements for sustainable construction in both new buildings and refurbishment projects are high. The German Government[42] and the German Sustainable Building Council (DGNB)[43] have developed certification procedures with numerous planning criteria. The sustainability categories are comprehensive: ecological quality, economic quality, social and functional quality, technical quality, process quality, and site quality. At the same time, however, it must be ensured that the sustainability ambitions of a school building are aligned as closely as possible with educational objectives.

The architectural challenge of enabling »educating for sustainability« through the direct example of the school building itself is great. The goal of making the building's energy-related functions visible and tangible to the users is often hampered by the fact that, for example, the climate control system appears too complex and not immediately comprehensible.

In recent years, comprehensive measures for ecological renovation have been implemented in school construction in Germany, although often from a purely energy efficiency perspective. Requirements such as recyclability and reusability of building products are gaining significance, as are overarching climate adaptation measures. However, the changing pedagogical usage requirements also play a role in terms of the sustainability criteria of »social and functional quality.« The key development opportunities for future-proof schools can only be realized through the integration of technical refurbishment, pedagogical and organizational restructuring, design renewal, and forward-looking site development. This requires transdisciplinary collaboration between educators, architects, and specialist planners in integrated planning processes.

Given the complex demands of use, it is clear that sustainable design and user behavior must be coordinated. For example, individual ventilation patterns must be coordinated with the air conditioning and ventilation concept. Learning processes in handling the new technical systems must be initiated during commissioning. For this reason, many school authorities pay special attention to the initial familiarization phase. The sustainable use of school buildings also requires that users are fully involved in the spatial concepts and the desired spatial-pedagogical appropriation, and that they understand and implement the pedagogical potential (»Phase 10«).

Issues of sustainability also arise in special areas such as science rooms. Here, comprehensively equipped room concepts compete with makerspace concepts that follow the principle of »space over equipment.« In many cases, a continuously usable experimental area is more effective for teaching than a fully equipped lab that has to be cleared after every use.

In many cases, the design of outdoor spaces is a starting point for hands-on, site-specific environmental education in existing buildings. The extent to which sustainability criteria can conflict becomes particularly apparent when choosing a school site: on the one hand, the integration of outdoor areas close to nature is an important criterion—often favoring locations on the outskirts of the city; at the same time, schools should ideally be located as close as possible to residential areas—with the consequence of a high building density and limited outdoor space resources in central locations. This illustrates that sustainable planning is always a process of weighing priorities and must consider the surrounding environment. Networking opportunities can create synergies, for example when the nearby park is also used as a schoolyard.

Life-cycle considerations play a key role in school design and construction—because construction costs typically account for only about one-fifth of total costs over a 50-year period, with the rest coming from operational and disposal costs. This also means that school buildings should be designed with medium- and long-term adaptability in mind, allowing for future expansion, modification, or repurposing.

42
BMWSB (Ed.) (2017)

43
DGNB, dgnb.de

THESIS 10

The school opens up to the city—the city opens up to the school.

The school is not a closed system that can provide all the necessary resources on its own. The transition to an all-day school focused on competencies and individual potential—in the sense of the previous nine thesis—requires an opening both outward and inward. For all age groups, the boundaries of the school must be temporarily abandoned and learning fields outside the school must be made accessible in an age-appropriate manner. This is the only way for children and young people to connect in-school and out-of-school, formal and informal learning through practical experience. Such opening processes can be practiced in small steps from preschool onward: from museums to city forest, from theaters to stadiums, from youth centers to cooperation partners in the trade, from dance groups to sports clubs.

It is equally important to bring in people from outside, from the »real world«—as experts, supporters, or critics of the own results. Students' learning products can be documented and presented both internally and externally.

At the same time, a school—as part of an educational landscape—can open some of its spatial resources to the local community: auditorium, library, canteen, gymnasium, playground, etc. can extend and complement local infrastructure. This benefits both students and local residents—and reduces costs for municipalities.

Collaboration with youth services within the framework of all-day schooling enables new partnerships: from providing individual support for children and young people in difficult situations to improving the quality of professional educational programs that exceed traditional teaching routines. Such services should be strengthened to reinforce the educational role of the school in socially disadvantaged areas and to provide pedagogical support to teachers. With all-day schooling, the school becomes a kind of second home. The interweaving of formal and informal learning makes the boundary between public space and the classroom, between school building and city more permeable. In the context of collaboration with other educational professionals, this broadens the view of schools: understood this way, schools truly become inclusive all-day educational institutions.

School becomes part of an everyday context. The connection with the environment and the neighborhood is of fundamental importance not only for the school but also for the community or city around it. Campus management should be used to organize and coordinate cycles of use, define interfaces, and resolve conflicts. Despite all openness, it is also important to consider the school's need for protection: as much openness as possible, as much seclusion as necessary. Not all areas are suitable for unrestricted public access. A good school provides a home for the children and youth in its care—and a cultural focal point for the neighborhood.

Central functions of the school must be positioned in such a way that their location and an efficient orientation system allow for shared, semi-public use in the community context (forum, library, workshops, playground, sports facilities, canteen/cafeteria, entrance area, and parking lot, etc.). However, certain equipment-intensive specialized spaces—such as science, technology, and computer labs, music rooms, etc.—offer attractive opportunities for shared use outside school hours for adult education centers, youth music schools, and other partners. These spaces must be easily accessible. They then serve as an important interface between school and community.

School premises are unused for about half the year—if weekends, holidays, and school breaks are included. Additional capacity is available in the evenings. As a public facility, an open school can therefore be an important component in neighborhood development—especially in districts with inadequate infrastructure or specific development needs. For many years, school gyms have been used by local clubs after 5 p.m. and on weekends. Today, some cafeterias are being opened as neighborhood cafés, and community-run school and district libraries are being established.

When schools function as part of shared municipal infrastructure, the spectrum of school building typologies changes fundamentally. Two trends can be identified. On the one hand, there is the concentration model, in which various public service providers are brought together under one large roof, and the school is housed in one building along with other educational and counseling facilities. On the other hand, there is the dispersion model, which focuses on the intensive networking of different, often pre-existing educational components to form a municipal educational landscape. A school is then often no longer limited to one location but has several sites in the neighborhood. Resources are shared with other educational, youth, and social institutions without all being housed in one complex.

In both cases, the legitimate interests of the educational institutions on the one hand and the needs of the neighborhood on the other must be reconciled in order to achieve a balance that benefits both sides.

Outdoor spaces are a central planning issue for the interlinking of school and neighborhood. As transitional areas between the school and its surroundings, they take on an important mediating function. Attractive outdoor spaces make the anchoring and opening of the school in the community or district visible. Well-frequented areas are the best protection against vandalism—this also speaks in favor of a targeted (partial) opening of schools so that they can also be used in the evening, at weekends, and during vacations.

3

PRACTICE
Users and Their Spaces

Pedagogy defines models for the acquisition of skills and knowledge—architecture creates spaces within school buildings that support these processes. Both disciplines must meet a large number of subject-specific criteria, each of which influences the other. These interactions need to be described to jointly develop a qualified spatial program. The following questions arise:

1. What are the activity patterns of the different user groups in a school?
2. How can spatial requirements be deduced from the pedagogical needs of the users?
3. What are the consequences for spatial design?

The answers to these questions describe the cornerstones by which the educational user concept of a school can be »mapped« and translated into a resilient organizational and spatial concept. By linking pedagogical and architectural issues, the following chapter provides background knowledge for the start of collaborative planning process.

1. ACTIVITIES

WHAT ARE THE ACTIVITY PATTERNS OF THE DIFFERENT USER GROUPS IN A SCHOOL?

Over the last 50 years, the needs of the various users of a school building have changed fundamentally. This makes it even more important to describe their respective activities in detail so that the school building can provide the appropriate and supportive framework for them. The general objectives of a school program alone are not sufficient as a basis for sustainable building design. Identifying the specific activities, their patterns, their intensity and frequency, their importance, etc. creates the necessary basis for planning. Such a description can only be done on a project-specific basis. The key points are outlined here to provide an overview of the current users of a school building:

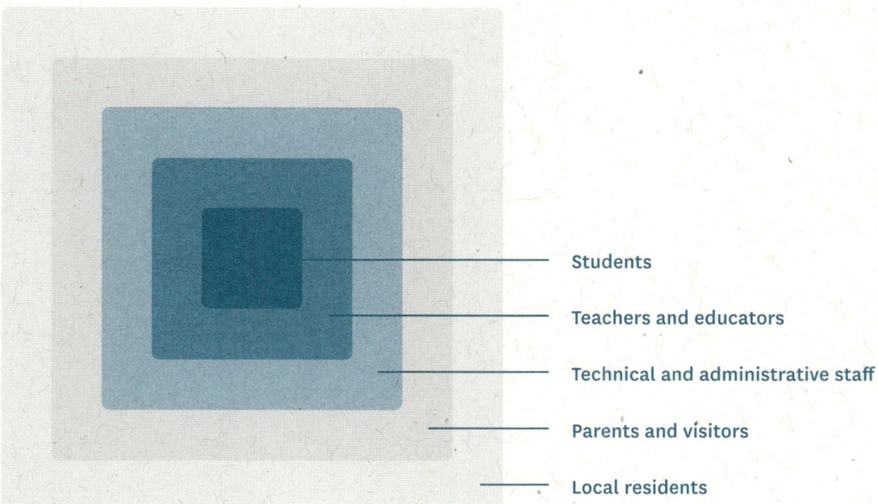

STUDENTS

Students are the main stakeholders and the largest user group. For them, the school is primarily a social place: they want to meet friends, exchange ideas and engage in discussions, feel comfortable, and be active on the sports field. For many of them, educational aspects such as acquiring knowledge, learning and working in peace, experiencing new things, reading and experimenting are often secondary.

New activity patterns

From an educational perspective, activity patterns have changed in recent years and decades: School used to be characterized—to exaggerate—by listening and answering, reading and writing.[44] Today, the list of pedagogically relevant activities reflects a greater openness and diversity in order to involve all the senses and the whole body, with rest and movement in constant alternation: experiencing, inventing, discovering, trying out, designing, researching, understanding, questioning, creating, acting out, painting, presenting, listening, watching, singing, making music—and also (especially in all-day schools) romping, chilling, playing, eating, drinking, arguing, relaxing, etc. Five activities are particularly important when we look for basic patterns of active learning in an active school:

44
Cf. also Seydel (2023)

1. The desires for interaction, communication, and dialogical conversations fosters a culture of participation and togetherness—in learning, in understanding, and in joint and individual development.
2. Participation in decision-making processes, such as in student and class councils, is an important activity for understanding and reflecting on one's experiences. In all learning scenarios it must be possible to switch to a circular form as directly as possible.
3. Concrete action manifests through play, movement, and other forms of self-expression.
4. Research activities in the investigation and exploration of things, facts, and problems, as well as experimental behavior are essential for learning.
5. Expressions and presentations, striving for expression, aesthetic design, combined with communication and construction, and also wanting to explore how things work.

These activities alternate in different ways and with different emphases throughout the day:

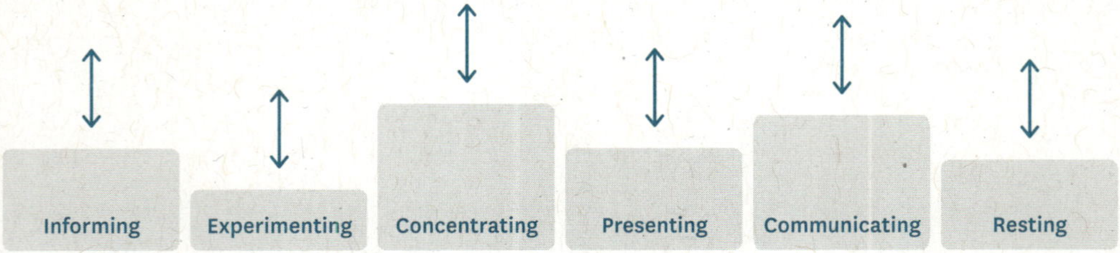

Phases of the school day

In the future, the school day can ideally be divided into seven phases, each usually varying in duration from 20 minutes to 2 hours:

— *Arrival* at school during individual flextime, during which students work independently or in small spontaneous groups: reading, consolidating, practicing—but also talking, playing, dozing off
— *Instructional lessons,* complemented by quiet individual work, small groups, and presentations; frontal and active forms of work alternate
— *Relaxation* and *mealtimes* organically embedded into the educational daily rhythm
— *Interest* and *aptitude groups* with differentiated offerings, some tailored to different performance levels
— *Physical activity periods* integrated into the educational daily rhythm
— *Interdisciplinary projects* or *presentations* that can involve several classes or grades
— *Departure* from school during a second flextime

Accordingly, the daily schedule, although clearly structured from one school day to the next, is varied and non-linear. The students no longer remain permanently grouped together in a single classroom, course room, or schoolyard; instead, their movement patterns resemble a dynamic ebb and flow—dispersing and regrouping.[45]

45
Zenke (2019) speaks of a »jellyfish principle« using the example of the Laborschule Bielefeld.

Social organization

In the past, learners were generally viewed as a largely homogeneous group with similar interests and dispositions. Current concepts of learning increasingly emphasize diversity and individuality. Instead of a stable class unit as a basic formation, students now move fluidly between different configurations: working individually, in pairs, small group, class units, large groups, by year groups, school level, or as part of the school community. As we respond to the needs of different age groups or learning needs, various concepts have emerged to define the social »home base« of individual students. The following examples show some of the most common current models:

Self-organized learning

In the context of competence orientation, current pedagogical concepts increasingly provide formats for self-organized learning. Opportunities for individualized learning can be mapped spatially in different ways. Personalized workplaces do not always have to be available.

Table group

Over long phases of a school year, sometimes even over several school years, the table group remains a stable unit with a maximum of 6–7 learners. It is composed according to the criterion of maximum heterogeneity, from students with special needs to gifted students. It is the core structure of all activities in and sometimes beyond the classroom—sometimes even extending to »table group parents' evenings.«

Tandem classes

Two classes work together in pairs and share a common room, e.g. in the Classroom-plus model.

Year-group team

All classes in a grade (e.g. 5a, 5b, 5c, 5d) form a socio-spatial unit in a cluster structure or learning landscape.

»Learning House«[46] or Learning Family

In multi-grade learning groups, students from different year groups are taught together—for example, Years 1–3, Years 4–6, and Years 7–9 form mixed-age learning groups.

46 The City of Munich, for example, has based its entire school construction planning on this concept. Cf. Landeshauptstadt München (2015)

Departmental structure

A cluster can also break away from the traditional classroom-based organization of a school. In this case, all subjects—not only science, but also English, mathematics, history, etc.—form a socio-spatial unit in a cluster structure.

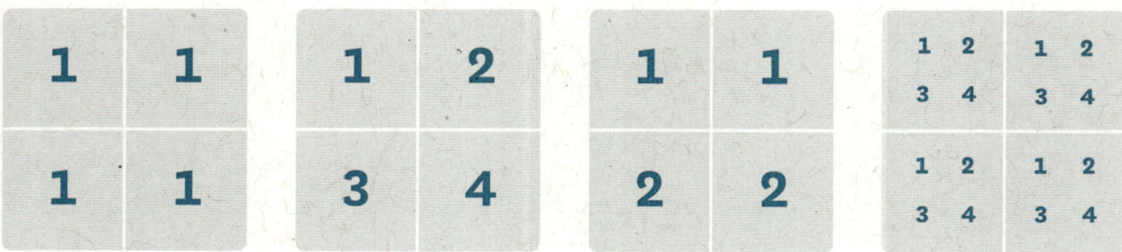

Year-group team | Learning House | Mixed form | Cross-grade team

Each of the forms described here, and others that are conceivable, offers advantages as well as certain challenges and conditions for success that must be carefully weighed according to the school's pedagogical profile.

Despite all the necessary variability in learning arrangements, one question remains of particular importance: how and where is the stable »home base« created for each student—through an individual workstation, a table group, the class group, the year group? The school's educational program must provide clear guidelines to which the spatial concept can respond.

Inclusion

There is a growing demand for effective educational provision for extremely heterogeneous learning groups. To prevent the exclusion of students with learning difficulties and disabilities while also supporting high-achieving students, it is necessary to offer additional differentiation and support programs. This further expands the range of activities:

— In so-called »practical classes« or classes for »productive learning,« temporary learning groups outside the regular class or home group are taught in a career-oriented, interdisciplinary, and subject-linking manner. Teaching takes place in well-equipped workshops using clear hands-on tasks.

— Schools address the lack of concrete opportunities to gain work experience by setting up student-run businesses: for example, students from each class take turns running the school cafeteria according to a set schedule.

— The necessary clothing is cleaned by a student-run initiative within the school; cleaning equipment such as washing machines, dryers, etc. is located within the school.

— Peers-to-peers support: For children and adolescents from similar backgrounds or in similar stress situations, temporary experiences in shared learning environments—especially at the lower secondary level—have also proven to be a supportive measure.

— Students who have difficulty maintaining concentration over longer periods because they are exposed to particular or psychological stress in their social environment (e.g. because of parental separation, relocation due to parents changing jobs, death in the family, or specific needs due to physical impairments) often require so-called »stop« or »time-out« periods.

— For students with specific disabilities, physical therapy may be necessary in their daily lives.

☞ Chapter 2, *Thesis 5*, pp. 34 ff.
Chapter 6, *Thesis 5*, pp. 195 ff.

In all of these cases, it is important to avoid exclusion and only temporarily interrupt collaborative learning when there is a demonstrable need to do so. At the same time, however, it has been shown that measures aimed at providing appropriate temporary support for all students ultimately benefit everyone, even if their circumstances are very different. This is one of the key success factors of the Finnish school system, where more than 25 percent of students receive some form of temporary support during their time in school.

TEACHERS AND EDUCATORS

The changing profile of students' activities at school corresponds to a fundamental change in the role of the teacher: from a teacher working alone to a learning guide in a multi-professional team.

Teachers ...

...as a learning guide

Teachers become facilitators in a »prepared environment,« encouraging the activity of the students. While there are still phases of instruction, they no longer take up the majority of the timetable. They are replaced by advisory support for individual learners and smaller groups. One visible sign of this shift is the changed positioning and equipment of the »teacher's desk«: formerly positioned centrally in the classroom—sometimes on a raised platform—it is now commonly placed at the side or even outside the classroom as a fully equipped workstation—complete with storage compartments, presentation materials, PC, and printer.

... as a »team worker«[47]

Many schools have realized that effective staff collaboration in small, stable teams is key to improving school quality. Everyone can benefit from the collective experience of the teaching staff. There are many forms of collegial collaboration in a school:

- grade-level teams, that support the same group of students over several years, dedicating most of their working time to this group;
- subject teams grouped around core disciplines such as German, mathematics, languages, social sciences, etc.;
- workshops for joint lesson planning;
- cross-disciplinary projects to restructure core teaching content;
- peer observation teams for mutual reflection on teaching;
- alternating tandem teaching (»co-teaching,« which is becoming increasingly important in the context of inclusive schooling concepts, e.g., by including special education professionals as a second teacher in mainstream lessons);
- steering groups responsible for preparing, monitoring, and reorganizing school development processes;
- multi-professional teams of teachers and educational specialists working together in all-day schools.

... as educational staff in all-day schools

The distribution of lessons and learning group times across a rhythmically structured all-day school routine and the requirement for common attendance times for teamwork on site change the working habits of teachers and staff. German all-day schools are currently developing in two different directions:

In the separation model, two or more half days are added together—»strict« academic instruction in the morning, »soft« supervision in the afternoon. After lunch, students are often handed over by teachers to educational specialists or, in some cases, to lay pedagogical staff.[48] This

47 According to data from the Deutsches Schulbarometer, Germany lags behind internationally when it comes to teamwork, see Deutsches Schulportal, deutsches-schulportal.de/bildungswesen/deutsche-lehrer-liegen-bei-teamarbeit-und-fortbildung-international-weit-zurueck/

48 Cf. Danner et al. (2023)

model—as an organizational consequence of the »open all-day school«—is currently in place in many German schools: Students—respectively their parents—can choose whether or not to attend. The choice is then binding for the school year. As a result, there is no guarantee that all students will be present in the afternoon, so that the additional time resources of the all-day school can hardly be used through a shared concept for the whole class. Especially with the change to inclusion, such a separation model must evolve into the direction of a bound all-day school.

Chapter 2, *Thesis 3*, pp. 28 ff.
Chapter 6, *Thesis 3*, pp. 201 ff.

For the consequences for space requirements planning, see Chapter 6, *Thesis 3*, p. 188

49
See also the project »Ganztag und Raum« by the Montag Stiftung Jugend und Gesellschaft

In the integration model, the whole day is rhythmically structured in phases that are optimal for learning physiology: concentration and relaxation, quiet and active periods alternate throughout the day. Teachers, social pedagogues, educators, and pedagogical assistants form a team. As a rule, this model presupposes that the all-day program is largely bound: all students are present. It is only through such an integrative model of a bound all-day program that the pedagogical potential as well as the personnel and spatial synergies of all-day schooling can truly be harnessed.[49]

Educational professionals

Successful inclusive all-day school systems show that, given a high level of student heterogeneity, additional staff is needed to provide professional support for social inclusion, health-related and psychological diagnostics, and counseling. These include special education teachers and social pedagogues, educators, school psychologists, vocational counselors, as well as extracurricular program leaders and special educational and one-to-one aides (»inclusion assistants«). They also provide low-threshold counseling services, for example, to support families with poverty backgrounds, migration issues, or other challenges. In most cases, responsibilities within the multidisciplinary team are increasingly split between individual counseling and group support (extracurricular groups, open sessions, teaching assistance). On the organizational level, the previously separate areas of morning and afternoon organization are thus merging into »inclusive all-day educational facilities.«

The requirements differ depending on the type of all-day concept a school follows: In the integration model, the educational professionals are integrated into multi-professional teams; in the separation model, they often work separately in terms of time and space and have to coordinate separate handovers. The integration model is better equipped to meet the need for collaboration than the separation model. In any case, the workplaces of educational staff need to be considered; in addition to teachers, all groups need to be involved.

So-called »third parties«

»Third parties« refers to external individuals who are a temporary part of the school team in the context of specific projects. For example, schools increasingly involve computer experts, sculptors, craftspeople, musicians, engineers, actors, and professionals from many other fields. In many cases, retired professionals are also integrated on a voluntary basis. While the involvement of these external »experts« is often seen as a stop-gap solution to staffing shortages, it can also have the effect of deliberately opening up the school. Besides their professionalism, the decisive factors for the qualification of third parties are their personality in their professional role, openness to new situations, confidence in the strengths of children and young people, and their willingness and ability to work together with students and teachers on real-world projects and to take on responsibility. In this way, young people's interests and strengths, which cannot be assessed by the school system, are brought to light and can be promoted. When working with third parties, it is important to clarify responsibilities, as external experts are often funded by external institutions or project sponsors.

Due to the current shortage of teachers, many schools are now permanently integrating lateral entrants as specialists for school tasks. Qualification measures for these individuals vary by region.

Teacher trainees and student teachers

As part of their training, student teachers now complete significantly more school-based internships than in the past. Teacher trainees and interns, as temporary users, need their own space in the school. Some schools work closely with universities and colleges, benefiting both the training and the school.[50]

50
See experimental schools in Hesse and Heliosschule in Cologne

TECHNICAL AND ADMINISTRATIVE STAFF

School office

With the expansion of all-day schooling, the requirements for school offices are also changing. Their role as a central point of communication becomes significantly more extensive. At the same time, as schools gain more autonomy, their administrative workload increases, and office staff need designated times and spaces where they are not disturbed by constant in-person inquiries.

Kiosk, canteen, cafeteria, kitchen

All-day operations bring new tasks and functional areas for staff working in kiosks, canteens, cafeterias, and kitchens. More and more schools now involve students and parents in these activities in a variety of ways, such as student-run businesses, internships, special support associations, and the like.

The library

As libraries today are often combined with a café or a self-study center, the role of the library staff is changing. Increasingly, libraries are also serving as district libraries or media centers for the district.

Building services

With increasing technology and medialization levels, the demands on technical staff are growing—tasks are clearly shifting from the traditional janitor role to building and facility management. Even if it is not formally include in their employment contract, technical staff often have a direct educational impact—for example, in the respectful handling of furniture and walls and by helping manage the sometimes complex requirements for heating and ventilation. In many municipalities, technical staff are not under the direct supervision of the school, but rather employed by separate organizations that manage public buildings.

Cleaning

Cleaning staff in schools are generally no longer employed directly by the school. Instead, services are usually outsourced and governed by external contracts.

SCHOOL LEADERSHIP AND LEADERSHIP TEAMS

The school leadership usually consists of the principal, vice-principal, and, depending on the size of the school, additional department heads responsible for grade levels or subject areas (school leadership team). They play a central role in shaping the school's pedagogical profile and are responsible for representing the shared mission statement developed with all stakeholder groups, both internally and externally.

In many German federal states, there is a trend toward increasing the autonomy of individual schools—including greater responsibility for personnel and budgets. As a result, the actual responsibility of school leadership is expanding, requiring additional management and leadership skills. Another change in the definition of leadership, and thus in the role of the school leadership and its management structures, results from the needs of all-day school development. Successful all-day schools have established management committees for the entire institution, usually consisting of the school leadership and the all-day program coordinators. Even in smaller school units, these are often structurally complemented to form extended management committees—similar to what is already common in the large systems of comprehensive schools or grammar schools with grade management—by one representative each from the teaching staff and the all-day program staff, and, in some cases, also by members of steering groups. The shared responsibility across the various professional groups means that these leadership bodies define common procedures, rules for collaboration, and coordinated decision-making processes.

PARENTS AND VISITORS

Parents are increasingly involved in day-to-day school life: as »breakfast moms and dads« running the school kiosk during breaks, as supervisors in the library, or as experts contributing to special projects. The requirements vary depending on the involvement model. In all cases, the creation of a designated »parents' area« as a point of contact and communication should be considered. In schools located in challenging social environments, regular »parents' cafés« and »parents' schools« are established in cooperation with social service organizations.

Parents—as well as other visitors from outside the school—need quick and easy orientation: Where is my child's classroom, the school office, the faculty, school leadership, the parent-teacher conference room, the events area?

In view of the increase in pick-up and drop-off traffic in front of many schools (»parents' taxi«), innovative school route concepts that encourage walking and cycling (e.g., the »walking school bus,« children walk together to school from certain stops) should be considered, as well as sufficient parking spaces for bicycles on the school grounds.

LOCAL RESIDENTS

In addition to a clear orientation system, there are special requirements for the (semi-)public use of school buildings: The library, sports facilities, school hall, café, and often specialized rooms, such as those used for evening adult education courses or by clubs, must be accessible without requiring access to the entire school building. The aim is to open up the school while maintaining a certain territorial integrity of the »internal« areas.

☞ Chapter 2, *Thesis 10*, pp. 49 ff., Chapter 6, *Thesis 10*, pp. 213 ff.

These spaces must be inviting and easy to find. A cafeteria (e.g. as a parents' café), shared school and district library, the integration of a youth center, or the establishment of a workshop (bicycle workshop, repair café) can play a special role. Multiple use of facilities is becoming increasingly important in the various campus projects throughout Germany but requires appropriate organizational safeguarding through active campus management.

2. SPACES

What are the implications for spatial design and equipment? The following section outlines the changes for the various areas of use and their spatial organization.[51] Historically, many of the associated requirements are not new. At the beginning of the last century, various educational reform movements anticipated many of these ideas, and some of them were implemented during the post-war period of renewal. The school building boom of the 1970s and the inclusion movement for integrated teaching from the 1980s onward also dealt intensively with the implementation of the following topics. It is only in recent years, however, that a change in thinking has become apparent and is being implemented on a broad scale and in public policies.

51
For all space and planning topics in this chapter, see www.schulbauopensource.de, the online platform of the Montag Stiftung Jugend und Gesellschaft

FROM CLASSROOM TO LEARNING ENVIRONMENT

In order to meet the pedagogical demands that represent a fundamental paradigm shift, modern school buildings must satisfy two critical pedagogical requirements in their learning / teaching areas:

- Variability in the use of different forms of learning and materials, and
- enabling students to engage in a variety of methodological activities of their own.

From an architectural perspective, appropriate conditions must be created: sufficient space and rooms that can be used in different ways and, above all, can be combined with each other.

Three prototypical organizational models for the general learning and teaching areas have emerged from today's functional requirements.[52] Variants and hybrid forms are possible—the actual implementation always depends on the specific requirements and conditions of each project and its location:

52
Cf., e.g., Schneider (2012); Schneider / Seydel (2013a)

- Classroom-plus: The classroom is noticeably enlarged and / or extended with an adjoining group room; corridors are activated wherever possible through a modified fire safety concept.
- Cluster: Several classrooms, differentiation and retreat rooms, and the associated enlarged circulation areas as a multifunctional common »center« are combined into one spatial unit, along with associated team rooms, storage areas, and sanitary facilities. Decisive for the use of a cluster are zoning, transparency, acoustic and fire safety optimization, as well as the creation of a clearly identifiable spatial identity.
- Open Learning Landscape: A large learning area is shared by a group of classes. It is structured by zones for group work and instructional phases.

In all three cases, the aim is to develop a basic layout that meets the demands of future-oriented teaching and allows a rapid transition between different social formats (individual work, small group, large group) and methods.

A school will usually choose one of these models based on its educational program, but it can also combine several approaches in different areas and develop them further to meet its specific needs.

The use of digital media plays an important role in all models, supporting both individualized work and spatial flexibility.

Classroom-plus

The need for multi-optional learning and teaching spaces can be met by enlarging, connecting, and rezoning basic rooms or classrooms. Starting at 72 square meters, occupancy of the room with up to 25 students results in significant improvements in flexibility of use for different learning activities in the room—prompting some school construction authorities to expand the learning space and create immediate differentiation options.

Chapter 7, *Examples, #Classroom-plus*, p. 217

If two adjacent classrooms can be connected by a (double) door, a glass wall, or a flexible partition, this results in additional usability when one class of them is not occupied.

In many instances where an additional group room is assigned to a learning room, but not directly connected to it, these rooms are often used only as storage areas. When two classrooms are assigned a shared group room, preferably located in the middle, that both learning groups can use for differentiation, the partitions are often equipped with doors and windows and / or large areas of glass. Despite acoustic separation, this creates a spatial continuum: multiple activities and learning formats can take place in parallel in the learning and group rooms without losing (eye) contact. The rooms usually have multiple entrances. Access from the corridor is either directly into the classroom or via the shared group room. The spatial tandem solution also allows for appropriate team development between the teachers of the two learning groups.

In all variants of a Classroom-plus model, the learning and teaching area can optionally be extended into the circulation areas. The walls facing the circulation areas should allow for ample visual connections, as should those toward the group room. A corresponding fire safety concept must be considered.

Movable partitions in the classroom should be as easy to handle as possible, which often conflicts with the need for good sound insulation. Curtains, which can also be acoustically effective, offer an optional solution for adaptability and separation of learning areas.

The guiding principle for choosing a Classroom-plus model is still the individual class unit as the main organizational form.

Cluster

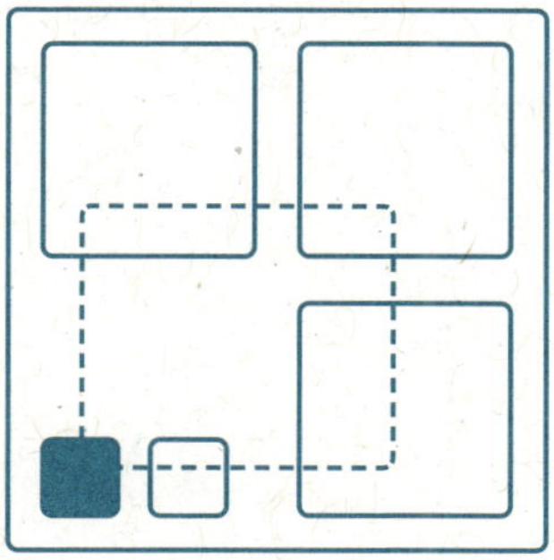

Chapter 7, *Examples, #Cluster*, p. 217

Clusters are groups of rooms in which several learning and teaching rooms are combined with associated differentiation, recreation, and regeneration areas to form a clearly identifiable unit. The circulation areas are extended to form a pedagogically qualified »common center.« Decentralized team rooms for educators (teachers, special education teachers, and pedagogical staff), sanitary facilities, storage and ancillary rooms, and an entrance area with a cloakroom must be included. Separate access to the outdoors or a balcony is desirable. As a rule, three to a maximum of six classes are grouped in a cluster to form a socio-spatial unit; if more are included, there is a risk of significantly overburdening the common center. If the number of parallel classes is higher, a double cluster with partial separation is recommended.

Clusters make it possible to offer a variety of different spatial situations in the immediate teaching environment—intimacy and openness, introversion and extroversion, individuality and community. Cluster structures can be adapted to changing usage requirements thanks to their wide range of spatial combinations. They allow for pedagogical flexibility in the use of different learning formats and create spatial synergies: shared-use classrooms, adjoining group rooms with visual connections, communicative circulation and recreation areas, balconies, etc. expand the range of available spaces, especially for small-group and individual work, as well as for space-intensive forms of teaching such as station work, simulation games, etc. The size and arrangement of the clusters can also be adapted to changing pedagogical needs.

The size and layout of a cluster depend on the number of classes it accommodates. Its structure is determined by the school's pedagogical concept and the architectural conditions of the site. Inclusion and all-day areas are (largely) integrated. The shared use of the rooms in a cluster means that all classes it accommodates have extensive possibilities for adaptation. This also applies to future uses, such as changes in the number of parallel classes.

The cluster model is based on a cross-class organizational concept. Clusters are formed either for several parallel classes of a single year group or for several consecutive learning groups across year groups. Hybrid models (e.g. two learning groups from two different year levels) are also possible. Alternatively, subject-specific clusters (e.g. for languages, mathematics, science, social studies, etc.) can be formed.

Open Learning Landscape

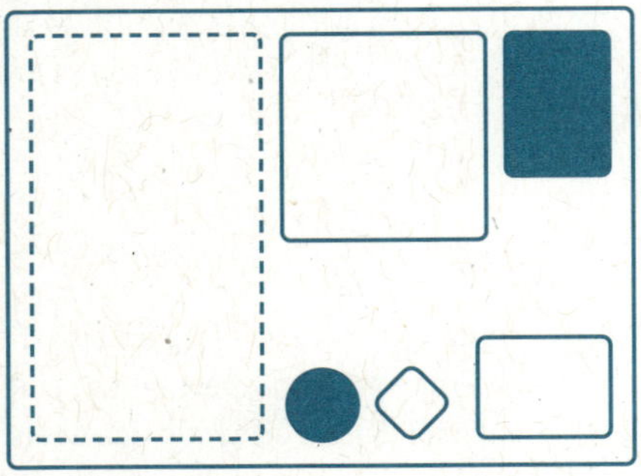

The model of the (partially) open learning landscape moves away from the learning and teaching areas structured in conventional classrooms, instead creating multifunctional learning zones that span classrooms and allowing for individualized and small-group learning as well as concentrated periods of instruction. The degree of »openness« may vary depending on the concept. Current implementations usually differ from the radically open variants known, for example, from the Laborschule Bielefeld.

Chapter 7, *Examples*, *#Open Learning Landscapes*, p. 219

In this organizational model, too, spatial units of three to four classes are usually formed, which serve as a »home base.« These spatial structures can accommodate different learning situations with maximum flexibility. Separate functional rooms are typically reduced to a minimum in the learning landscape, while circulation and common areas are directly integrated into the learning landscapes as communication or working zones.

In open learning landscapes, teachers and learners choose their own places for individual or group work depending on the situation. The learning zones are usually internally differentiated—for example, with designating areas for input phases, open learning, individual workstations, tea kitchens, and group rooms. Depending on the project, different areas and zones are created, sometimes with fixed walls or glazed partitions, sometimes with moveable partitions. Students and teachers »construct« spatial situations as needed.

Special spatial solutions for individualization and self-organized learning

With the increasing implementation of new teaching and learning models aimed at opening up instruction, which support the independent learning of students from the outset, appropriate spatial-architectural solutions need to be developed. Common examples include:

Study Hall / Self-study center: Central offering

In a central location in the library or in a dedicated »study hall« (or similar), a limited number of non-personalized individual workstations are provided for use by all students at different times. Support through appropriate furniture is important to provide visual screening and some level of acoustic insulation.

Learning Office

The learning office or learning studio is a learning area that provides personalized or non-personalized individual workstations, depending on its size. This can be the cluster center itself, a dedicated corridor zone, or a separate room, the »learning office«[53] that complements the classrooms. If the workstations are personalized, they are usually equipped with their own storage space or shelf.

53
The term »learning office« can describe various pedagogical as well as spatial scenarios. See also Seydel (2023), p. 71, p. 179, p. 216

Alternatively, personalized individual workstations with storage space are created for each student in each classroom, usually grouped into two to four workstations. This grouping can then be used as a starting point for forming small groups as needed. At the same time, an area of the learning space must be kept free at all times so that a circle of chairs can be formed during input or discussion phases. The advantage of this solution is that it is possible to move quickly and flexibly between individual work, small groups, and large groups.

The learning office can be the cornerstone of a spatial model instead of the classroom. In addition to the learning office(s), rooms for group work and instruction are planned.

Activating circulation areas

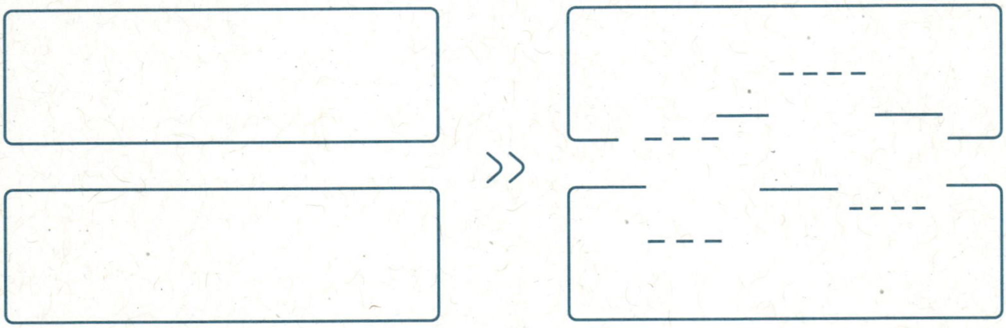

Activating circulation areas—greater permeability and recreational areas

Chapter 7, *Examples, #Corridors as educational spaces*, p. 218

Regardless of the organizational model, the activation of circulation areas is always a key resource for the sustainability of school (re-) construction projects. Contrary to popular belief, corridors offer design potential—they do not have to be »wasted spaces.« By modifying fire safety concepts, corridors and classrooms can become single fire compartments, transforming corridors into fully usable educational spaces. When the previous categorical distinction between »teaching« and »non-teaching« becomes less clear, transitional zones emerge that need to be defined and designed based on their use in everyday school life. Measures of inclusion and appropriation range from the always-open classroom door or a classroom with two doors and a glass slit, to wide glass walls and spatial »airlocks« that reinterpret the relationship between classroom and corridor, through to completely open spatial structures inspired by the image of a »street in the city.«

Circulation areas can be used for a variety of purposes, ranging from individual conversation niches and recurring seat/table combinations to lounge-like design approaches throughout the entire building. In the future, pure circulation areas will only be needed in areas with a very high »traffic density«—for example, in the main entrance area, which visually and acoustically separates the school from the outside and gives it its identity, or in the stairwells. All other circulation areas can be used for learning and recreation, provided they are appropriately designed and classified as educational areas regarding fire safety.

Locked doors are a particular issue to the use of circulation areas and the integration of corridors. There are still schools that insist on fitting classroom doors with a knob on the outside so that they can only be opened with a key. This is motivated by arguments such as protection against vandalism and frenzied attackers. On closer inspection, however, this protection is an illusion: neither vandals nor gunmen are likely to be deterred by a locked door.[54] Conversely, successful schools—especially those in socially challenging neighborhoods—demonstrate that doors can always be open, both before and during classes. If a culture of teaching can be established along the lines of »This is our space, which we have

54
See also recommendations for amok protection in Baden-Württemberg: Expertenkreis Amok (2009)

created together,« a strong willingness to take responsibility emerges. Classes start more organically because there is no crowding at the door, an »open start« is possible, and transitions between work and break times can be made fluid, depending on the process.

Sanitary facilities

In many schools, centralized sanitation facilities for the entire school are almost impossible to manage pedagogically and are perceived as intimidating spaces by many students.[55] Therefore, toilet facilities should be smaller in scale and decentralized—preferably within the clusters or learning landscapes—so that the »occupants« of these spaces can clearly take responsibility. In Finland, a simple solution to prevent vandalism and bullying in toilets has proven successful: rather than shared facilities, there are only self-contained individual toilet rooms with integrated washbasins, which are assigned to the learning and recreation areas in clusters or learning landscapes. In many projects, the importance of quality design is particularly evident: it enables these spaces to be appreciated and protects them from neglect. Involving students in the design of sanitary facilities also increases acceptance. Moreover, there is a growing demand for gender-neutral toilets in schools.

55 Cf. German Toilet Organization e. V. (Ed.) (2023)

Movable versus fixed furniture

In the past, furnishing concepts focused on equipping rooms with tables and chairs in line with the learning setting of front-of-class teaching. Today, the focus is on enabling smooth transitions between different learning and teaching settings. The interaction between loose furniture (various table sizes, sofas, beanbags, stand-up tables, stools, etc.) and fixed furniture (seating niches, seating steps, window sills as worktops, kitchenettes, etc.) is particularly important. Both fixed (built-in) and freestanding furniture must be included in the planning.

A balance must be struck between flexible furniture in the form of movable furniture and usage-specific furniture. Furnishings with movable elements allows users to freely adapt the rooms by rearranging the furniture and quickly adapt them to the necessary teaching and learning settings. Use-specific furniture provides users with defined options for teaching and learning settings. Depending on the setting, the location is changed rather than the layout of the furniture.

Both furnishing options, movement and flexibility, are important. In addition to multifunctional areas with adaptable furniture, clearly defined spaces are also needed that can be interpreted in different ways and stimulate new uses.

Lighting, air, and acoustics

Good lighting and indoor air quality must be just as self-evident as appropriate acoustic conditions. Many existing buildings still lack sufficient quality in these areas.

For educational and sustainability reasons, as many areas of the school building as possible should be naturally ventilated. The concept of natural ventilation in school buildings is strongly influenced by architecture and spatial planning decisions. Open-plan concepts, such as learning landscapes, provide ideal conditions for effective air circulation due to the contiguous volumes and generous ceiling heights, benefiting both the well-being of the occupants and the required air exchange.

It is imperative that lighting systems in school buildings exhibit a high degree of flexibility and adaptability to accommodate diverse and changing uses and educational requirements. Lighting should not only be functional but also contribute to creating a pleasant atmosphere for learning and spending time. This involves planning for different light intensities and color temperatures, which must also be adaptable.

Acoustics in learning environments, especially in open or semi-open spaces, must be carefully planned to ensure good speech intelligibility and a pleasant working and learning environment. This requires a differentiated approach that considers the various zones within a space and their specific use, as learning activities—and therefore acoustic requirements—may change.

Fire safety

Opening up spaces and integrating circulation areas place new demands on fire protection. Traditional school construction guidelines, such as the current Model School Construction Regulation (Muster-Schulbaurichtlinie), which specify fire safety requirements for general and vocational schools, and the Model Building Code (Musterbauordnung), are still based on the »corridor school« typology where conventional classrooms are lined up along a central circulation axis. However, numerous built examples show that open spatial structures and fire safety are by no means contradictory. In response to current developments in school construction, various new recommendations have been issued: Individual municipalities, as well as the Working Group of the Heads of Professional Fire Services (AGBF Bund) together with the German Fire Brigade Association, have already published recommendations that address the spatial models of open learning landscapes and clusters.

The results of the study »Brandschutz im Schulbau« (Fire Safety in School Construction)[56] demonstrate, for example, that clusters and learning landscapes of up to 600 square meters are permissible. There are no fire resistance requirements for partitions within the cluster or learning landscape. A high level of transparency within the cluster or learning landscape is a requirement. If there is a lack of transparency, appropriate early fire detection measures must be considered. The number of exits depends on the size of the cluster or learning landscape.[57]

56
The study was carried out by the Department of Structural Fire Protection at the Technical University of Kaiserslautern in cooperation with the Bund Deutscher Architektinnen und Architekten BDA, the Montag Stiftung Jugend und Gesellschaft, the Unfallkasse Nordrhein-Westfalen, and the Verband Bildung und Erziehung (VBE) and was financed by the Deutsche Bundesstiftung Umwelt (DBU).

57
See the conversion measures of the five pilot projects »Ganztag und Raum.«

Circulation areas can be used as learning areas without restriction, and can therefore be freely furnished, provided they are not designated as »required corridors« from a fire safety perspective. In such cases, there are no specific fire safety requirements for walls and doors within the learning area. The goal is to define circulation areas as part of the learning space in terms of fire safety, and to divide the building into sections or functional units based on this combined learning area, rather than separating it into rooms and corridors.

In any case, it is advisable to involve the relevant authorities in all new construction and reconstruction projects from the beginning. Even in existing buildings, openings from classrooms to the corridor and the unrestricted use of corridors as learning space can be achieved through modified fire safety concepts.

FROM SEGREGATED TO INCLUSIVE SCHOOL

☞ Chapter 2, *Thesis 5*, pp. 34 ff. and Chapter 6, *Thesis 5*, pp. 195 ff.

To start with, students with special educational needs do not require fundamentally different spatial conditions than other students. There is no such thing as »exclusive inclusion rooms,« except for very specific therapy rooms. The same criteria apply to »successful inclusion« as to a »good school.« It is essential to avoid reproducing the old logic of segregation in a new form within mainstream schools by creating a new, covert special needs school through the corresponding spatial separation.[58]

58 See Kricke / Reich / Schanz / Schneider (2018)

A literature review reveals that many requirements of an inclusive spatial environment appear to be commonplace and represent a fundamental improvement of the sometimes far-reaching shortcomings not only for students with special needs, but for everyone in schools. This can be illustrated by three examples:

Students with special educational needs—like all students—have a need to retreat. These periods may be more frequent and more immediate for them than for others. It is therefore important that there is a possibility to withdraw close to the classroom. How this is achieved must be determined locally—the spectrum of possible solutions ranges from a pop-up tent or a window niche, which in some cases may already satisfies the need for separation within a room, to separate rooms.

Improved acoustic conditions are the basis for successful learning, especially for students with special educational needs. At the same time, the poor acoustic conditions in many school buildings are one of the reasons for the widespread phenomenon of burn-out among teachers. In principle, any student can unexpectedly find himself or herself in a difficult personal situation (divorce of parents, loss of a relative, etc.) and then make use of counseling services. In particular, the combination of all-day and inclusive schools offers numerous synergies for planning and equipping rooms and spaces.

Collaboration in peer groups plays a central role, especially in inclusive schools. Sufficient additional space must be provided for learning groups to work together temporarily.

Many spatial requirements of inclusive schools can only be addressed across learning groups. This also applies to staffing. That's why appropriate space contingents are needed that can be used flexibly. Whether the rooms listed below need to be provided in addition depends primarily on the type of support required.

— Therapy: rooms for therapeutic work, e.g., for physiotherapy or rhythmics.
— Hygiene: special sanitary facilities for students with severe disabilities and an increased need for assistance with personal hygiene; if necessary, additional nursing room requirements beyond the installation of a toilet for the disabled, rooms with a washing machine and dryer.
— Medical care: medical staff room and first aid station for safe storage of medication for children with special medication needs, possibly also to be used as a school social center or health care room, e.g., if medical staff are present at set times.
— Technical assistance: adequate parking for wheelchairs or other assistive devices in front of classrooms, specialist rooms, and other highly frequented common areas such as the cafeteria, school hall, self-study center, and library.

However, every limitation also means exclusion. Instead of setting up specialized schools with a focus on disability, the »Zero Limit« concept should be preferred wherever possible: it provides for the inclusion of every student, no matter how severely disabled, as part of the mainstream school. Numerous examples have emerged, demonstrating the efficacy of such neighborhood-based schools in terms of content and concept, staffing and resources, as well as spatial and functional design.

#Zero limit concepts are already being implemented in Canada, Norway, and Italy, among other countries. However, individual German schools such as *#Fläming-Grundschule* and *#Sophie-Scholl-Gesamtschule* in Berlin have also been practising this approach for many years.

FROM HALF-DAY TO ALL-DAY SCHOOL

From the 2026/27 school year, every child of primary school age in Germany will have the right to a place in all-day care and education.[59] The transition to all-day schooling is currently taking place in Germany, sometimes with considerable differences in organizational structure. There are several levels to consider, all of which are related to the spatial level.

59
BMFSFJ (2021); as discussed above, all-day school is usually not really the whole day long in the sense of the working world, it ends often at 2 p.m.

Chapter 2, *Thesis 3*, pp. 28 ff.
Chapter 6, *Thesis 3*, pp. 201 ff.

Degree of obligation

— *Fully bound* form (all students take part in the all-day program)
— *Semi-bound* form (not all classes are part of the all-day program, only one or several).
— *Open form* (students decide at the beginning of the school year / semester whether they want to participate in the all-day program, possibly only on specific days).
— *Half-day schools with compulsory afternoon classes and a wide range of project groups* (these schools—especially many grammar schools—are »disguised« all-day schools: formally, they are not recognized as such but must effectively fulfill many of their functions).

Time structure

- *Rhythmically structured all-day schools:* Fully bound all-day schools have the opportunity to introduce a daily schedule that distributes quiet and active phases, as well as periods of concentration and relaxation throughout the day.
- *Afternoon activities:* Open all-day schools generally maintain a strict separation between traditional instruction in the morning and a homework and activity program in the early afternoon.

Staff structure

- *Multi-professional teams:* The educational program of bound, rhythmically structured all-day schools is usually run by multi-professional teams that include educators, social workers, and supervisory staff alongside teachers.
- *Supervisory staff:* Many open all-day schools with a qualitative separation of morning and afternoon activities also separate responsibilities. The mornings are the responsibility of the teachers, while the afternoons are organized by an external organization on behalf of the municipal authority.
- *Cooperation partners:* In both cases—multi-professional teams and shared responsibilities—many schools additionally involve cooperation partners: music schools, sports clubs, scout groups, youth centers, artists, craftspeople, and others.

Spatial structure

The discussion about spatial organization models for all-day schooling can be roughly divided into the basic dispositions already described: the separation model and the integration model.

- The *separation model* is based on the basic understanding of all-day schooling, in which the day is divided into morning lessons and afternoon supervision, each under separate responsibility, and dispenses with the introduction of a consistent educational daily rhythm. Learning and teaching areas and all-day care facilities are largely housed in separate rooms; depending on the organization, they are only used interchangeably to a limited extent.
- In the *integration model,* the concept of a rhythmically structured all-day school forms the organizational foundation of spatial planning. Accordingly, there is no categorical separation between teaching and all-day care areas—(almost) all rooms are used for both lessons and all-day activities. Differentiation and recreation areas in the learning and teaching zones are therefore available throughout the day. Centrally located communication zones outside the immediate learning area not only serve as lounges for those arriving early in the morning or leaving late in the afternoon, but can also be used as »specialist« rooms, e.g., for physical activities. Low-threshold craft rooms, open student labs, robotics stations, theater stages, etc., which are important components of the all-day program, can also be activated for regular teaching.

This multiple use unlocks far-reaching possibilities, because all-day areas (in combination with differentiation and inclusion spaces) activate considerable space resources. The basic requirement: there must be sufficient storage space to keep the materials for the various activities available on site. Whereas in the separation model, the team rooms for all-day and school staff were also separate, the integration model combines these spaces, as the students are supervised by mixed teams consisting of teachers, social workers, educators, and other educational staff.

Separation model: all-day area in an annex

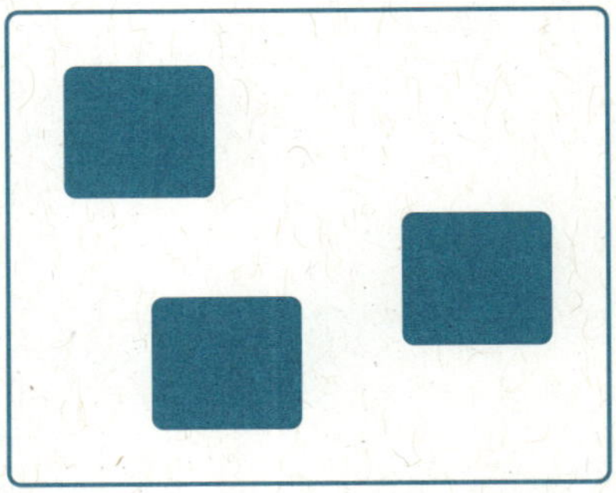

Integration model: all-day areas within learning spaces

The separation model is still applied in many schools today—partly because it accommodates the still widespread »open all-day schooling« approach, and partly because it follows the traditional (but no longer up-to-date) role patterns of teachers, social workers, and other specialists. However, a future-oriented school needs the direct cooperation of all those involved. Another major disadvantage of the separation model is that all rooms are largely empty for half the day. Since there are no mixed teams, different team areas need to be created accordingly. In addition, if in this model, which is typically implemented as an »open all-day school,« not just a minority but a large number of students were to participate in the all-day program in the future, the additional space requirements would be immense and financially unfeasible. There are already examples of how a separation model can be cost-effectively transformed into an integration model in terms of space, organization, and pedagogy.[60]

60
See Montag Stiftung Jugend und Gesellschaft (Ed.) (2023/2024)

In the long term, only an all-day concept based on a bound all-day program with a rhythmically structured schedule and managed jointly by multi-professional teams, including teachers, will be sustainable. Such a concept also offers considerable synergies and savings in terms of space requirements, since there is no categorical separation between teaching and all-day areas. The decisive argument in favor of the integration model is ultimately pedagogical: not only the obvious spatial synergies (using all rooms »all« day), but above all the pedagogical experiences of recent years are decisive. Only when these framework conditions—integrating all components—are in place, when both intentional and non-intentional learning are given equal importance in school, when all students are involved, can the hoped-for pedagogical »added value« of all-day schooling over the half-day model be achieved. This applies in particular to the compensatory function of all-day schooling with regard to the demand for »equal opportunities.«

Comparing the models shows how far-reaching the pedagogical decisions made during the initial »Phase 0«—before planning even begins—are for the spatial organization of the all-day school: Concentrating all all-day areas in a separate wing, for example in the form of an all-day annex, is a fundamental decision that is difficult to revise. Even if a school prefers an open all-day format due to parental demand and other circumstances at the time of planning, a school authority with an eye on the building's long-term use should strive for a spatial solution that will allow for consistent integration of these areas.

User needs and functional areas in all-day schooling

The space available in a school must be adapted to the expanded needs of the users. The main objective is to cover a variety of functions in terms of quality. Many solutions are conceivable within a flexibly interpretable constellation of spaces; not every function must be assigned to a dedicated room. Typical functions are listed below as examples. They relate to a field that has been largely neglected in both conventional pedagogical school development and in school construction planning: »non-intentional learning.« All of the functions mentioned here offer valuable learning opportunities—especially with regard to social learning, but also far beyond. Against this background, every half-day school should also fulfill these functions.

The following list is not about specific »all-day spaces,« but about expanding the pedagogical spaces of a school, which should be more than just a »place of learning.« It must also become one of the key »living environments« for students, both indoors and outdoors, with outdoor spaces taking on additional importance in all-day schools.

Many of the listed areas are not additional all-day rooms but are also used multifunctionally for the regular teaching program.

The following overview presents typical activities with examples of associated functional areas that are essential not only in the afternoon, but also in the morning:

Eating and drinking

Indoor: multifunctional student restaurant with different areas and atmospheres, preparation kitchen, staff lounge for kitchen personnel, storage and cold rooms, waste disposal room, toilets, cloakroom, student kiosk, drinking water dispenser, etc.
Outdoor: covered seating areas, kiosk with covered forecourt, drinking water dispensers, etc.

Meeting up with other students

Indoor: cafeteria, Internet café, room for lending and playing board games, etc.
Outdoor: covered zones (rain / sun protection), cafeteria area, barbecue area, seating areas, seating steps, toilets accessible from the schoolyard, etc.

Being physically active

Indoor: areas for physical activity games, fitness / exercise room, etc.
Outdoor: covered zones (rain / sun protection), storage room for outdoor equipment accessible from the schoolyard, play areas that are also used for physical education classes, project and active playground for primary school students, etc.

Retreating, resting, doing nothing

Indoor: library, reading niches, room of silence (meditation room), quiet zones, window niches, etc.
Outdoor: lawn for sunbathing, walking paths, various seating options (to see and be seen), etc.

Experimenting, making, creating

Indoor: workshops with storage rooms, instrument practice rooms, makerspace, student lab, school band room, etc.
Outdoor: school garden, pond, petting zoo, aviary, construction playground, etc.

Presenting, exhibiting, performing

Indoor: school hall, stage that doubles as a theater rehearsal space, open seating staircase, foyer with display walls, cloakroom, restrooms, lighting and sound control room, chair storage, props and scenery room, makeup studio, puppet stage, etc.
Outdoor: seating stairs, open-air stage, sculpture trail, storage boxes, etc.

Celebrating

Connection between canteen and school hall, disco room, moveable grandstand furniture, etc.

Seeking help

Social worker's office, school counselor's office, infirmary, mediation room, student council room, parent-teacher counseling room, etc.

Meeting with educators

Consultation zones or rooms, individual team workstations (with storage compartments, network and printer access, meeting areas), informal meeting places for teachers and school staff, etc.

FROM SPECIALIST SUBJECT ROOM TO MULTI-PURPOSE ROOM

For specialist subject rooms—as for all teaching areas—the overriding question is how teaching and experimental processes can be designed to support a variety of learning formats. Individualization and group work also play an important role here. New curricula increasingly call for more flexibility in the use of different forms of learning and sufficient space to allow students to engage in their own activities using a variety of methods. These two requirements also apply to specialist subject rooms, which require special equipment. In the future, even more emphasis will be placed on hands-on activities: practical exercises with demonstrations and experiments, examination and processing of learning materials and samples, project work, and communication in learning groups of various sizes. It is foreseeable that subject-specific profiles will evolve and that cross-disciplinary, integrative teaching content will become increasingly central. This can already be seen, for example, in Education for Sustainable Development, in subjects like »natural phenomena,« and STEM (science, technology, engineering, and mathematics). In many cases, independent experimentation with simple materials (school laboratories, makerspaces) provides a much more effective introduction to scientific and technical issues than expensive and less robust high-tech equipment. The issue of thematic networks also raises the question of how to make spaces available to as many users as possible, so that they are rarely vacant.

☞ Chapter 7, *Examples, #Specialized learning and teaching areas*, p. 221

☞ Chapter 2, *Thesis 9*, pp. 46 ff.

Multifunctional science rooms

Science classrooms that are either multifunctionally equipped or combine specialized laboratories with general learning spaces provide the basis for the broadest possible education.[61]

Multifunctional science rooms: Lecture hall seating is outdated, as are fixed desk layouts. A »multifunctional workshop« is preferable to a »dedicated room with laboratory pretensions.« Individual and group work should be made possible, especially when student experimentation alternates with instruction and evaluation phases as a standard form of science teaching. High-end equipment is by no means always required—current experience shows that even in chemistry up to high school level, teaching content can be conveyed without using hazardous substances. When planning specialist subject rooms, the increasing importance of laboratories, workshops, and storage areas for project groups must be taken into account, where students can set up, temporarily store, and carry out experiments (e.g., project group »Jugend forscht« (a German youth science contest)) largely independently (student laboratory) over a longer period of time.

61
Cf. Stadt Frankfurt am Main (Ed.) (2023b); Schneider / Seydel (2019); Seydel (2023), pp. 88 ff.

Grade-specific requirements

Science classrooms are subject to grade-specific requirements that increase with students' age from primary level to upper secondary level. At the primary level, there is generally no need for specialist science rooms; the focus of teaching is on comparatively simple student experiments. In a pilot project, the city of Münster has set up exemplary »research workshops« in several primary schools, which use simple means to encourage curiosity and the joy in discovery while supporting children in finding their own solutions.[62]

Laboratory carts are used not only in primary schools but also in some lower secondary schools (grades 5/6).[63] They enable science and technology lessons, which in some federal states are no longer based on subjects but on cross-disciplinary topics, to be held in standard classrooms or in multi-purpose rooms if these are large enough. By contrast, especially at the upper secondary level, advanced equipment requirements apply.

62
The project ran from 2004 to 2007.

63
Cf. inter alia PIB (2009)

From traditional specialist subject room to workshop

Understanding theoretical scientific models on the various nature and technology topics on the one hand, and a practical experimental approach on the other should complement each other equally. This requires an in-depth study of the various scientific methods offered by the individual subjects—physics, chemistry, biology, and engineering. At the same time, a variety of interdisciplinary perspectives should be made possible: The world we live in is not organized by subjects but presents challenges that need to be solved »holistically« (cf. key objectives of Education for Sustainable Development, ESD). The combination of theory and practice, the understanding of the specifics of each individual subject as well as the overarching interrelationships are a particular didactic and methodological challenge.

The spatial planning of the science and technology area must also take into account the following aspects:

— safety requirements for hazardous substances, electricity, gas, etc.;
— increased space requirements for experimental workstations and storage;
— small group sizes for practical instruction in laboratory classes (supervision issue).

Against this backdrop, new spatial concepts are currently emerging for the fields of science, technology, and crafts. On the one hand, this involves connecting the collections—in some cases in the form of genuine »show depots« that are transparent toward the circulation areas; on the other hand, an expansion of multifunctional and subject-independent experimentation areas for students should be considered. Unlike in Germany, schools in other parts of Europe—especially in the Netherlands and Scandinavian countries—are now much more »willing to experiment.«

Variants for organizing science rooms: subject area or function?

An increasingly important aspect, especially at the upper secondary level, is the provision of spaces that pose no safety risks and thus allow groups to work largely independently, for example in the context of youth science competitions (such as *Jugend forscht*), robotics clubs, and the like. Additional storage space should be provided for long-term projects.

Specialized individual rooms – separate collections

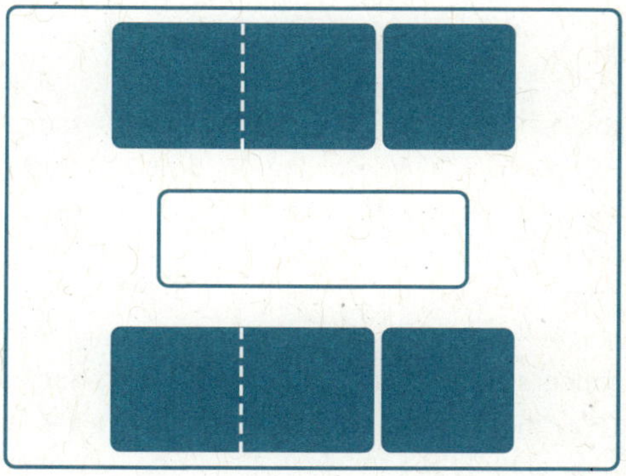

Specialized individual rooms – integrated show depot

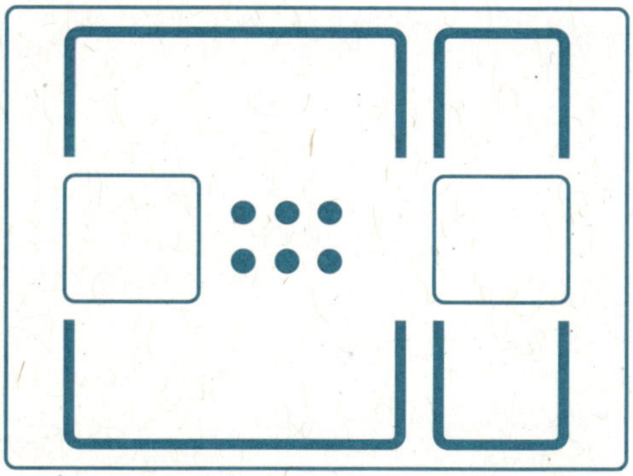

Open center with experimental workstations

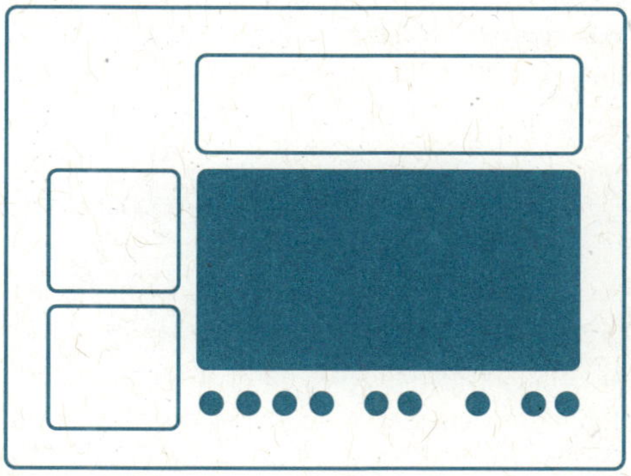

Experimental hall

External resources

In view of the declining popularity of scientific subjects in recent decades—physics and chemistry have been among the least popular subjects in Germany for years—opportunities to strengthen and raise the profile of science education in schools are currently being pursued intensively. This includes projects and initiatives in STEM subjects (science, technology, engineering, mathematics) and makerspaces. Therefore, the use of external resources and cooperation with partners outside the school is becoming increasingly important. At the same time, some schools are significantly upgrading the standard of their laboratories and specialist subject rooms by making them available to non-school users in the evenings. In some large cities, upper secondary schools are now developing distinct specializations, each with a focus on different, technically complex scientific topics. High school students then move between these high school centers depending on their current subject focus, just as they might attend the Chinese course offered as part of a special language program at the neighboring high school. Networking with existing external »student labs« and »makerspace initiatives« also plays an important role in this process.

Other workshops and studios

Dedicated rooms will continue to be needed, despite the trend toward multi-purpose specialist rooms. Examples include a music room with special soundproofing or technical workshops with specific equipment for working with wood, metal, ceramics, and electronics. In the context of all-day schooling and inclusion, these rooms take on additional importance.

For grades 0/1 to 6/7—especially in small all-day schools—the school's program will have to set a clear priority: should dedicated rooms (e.g., music room, arts and crafts room, science and technology lab, gym, quiet room, etc.) be given special consideration, or should these areas be allocated proportionally to each learning area so that there is always enough space for flexible, student-active teaching during normal operations? In view of the requirements of all-day schooling (increased formation of interest-based groups across year levels), the question of the territorial integrity of learning areas must be considered.

FROM TEACHERS' ROOM TO TEAM ROOMS AND STAFF WORKPLACES

The traditional »teachers' room« has always been conceived as a break room and had to combine a variety of functions for a large number of adults in a small space for a short period of time: filing, individual and collaborative lesson preparation, team meetings, phone calls, photocopying, informal exchanges, recreation during breaks between classes, conferences, and more. Clearly, a single room cannot meet these competing demands in today's all-day schooling. What is needed instead is either a work/relaxation area in a central location with dedicated zones for different uses, or alternatively, a centrally located communication hub with decentralized team bases. These can be structured differently, depending on the pedagogical concept—for example, as team bases by year group or subject department.

The department-based principle need not be limited to traditional subjects such as music or science. All other subjects can also be assigned to a dedicated department area: German, mathematics, languages, social sciences, etc. Unlike the classroom-based principle, where teachers go to students, this model has the students go to teachers.

Another model for organizing the workplace is the »teacher room« principle: here, too, there are no longer any classrooms. Instead, there are rooms, in which teachers (alone or in pairs) have their »own« fixed space they can personalize. The great advantage is that there is no diffusion of responsibility when it comes to the question of who is responsible for design and order. However, unlike in primary schools—where the class teacher usually covers a wide range of subjects and classroom and teacher room are essentially the same—this concept has two major disadvantages in secondary schools: collaboration and team building are not promoted, and retreating to »lone wolf« status tends to be encouraged. In addition, it is extremely space-intensive and results in significant underutilization if implemented in a »pure« form. Another problem is that all students are constantly »on the move« and have no »home base.«

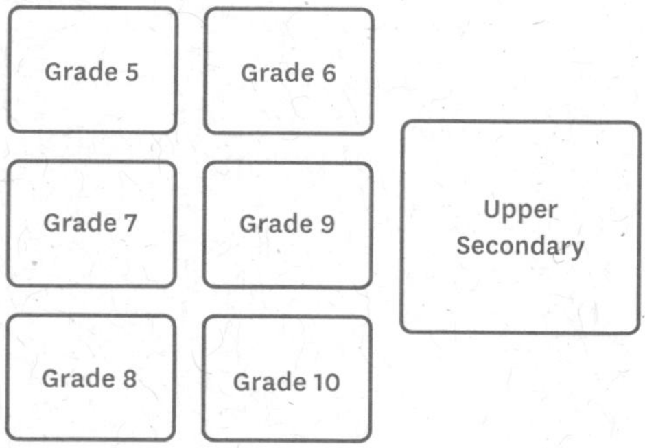

Spatial organization by year group teams

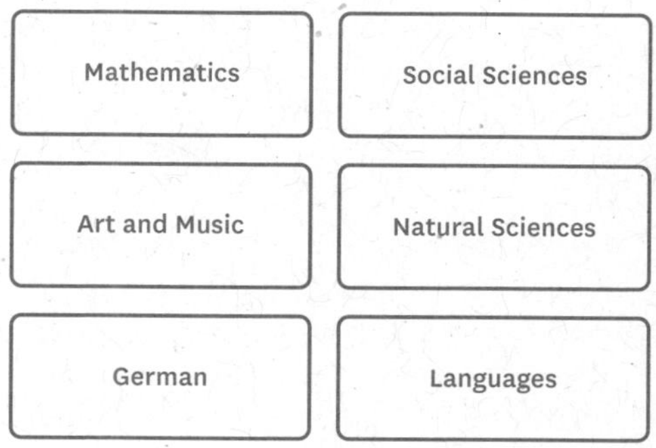

Spatial organization by specialist subject rooms

With all-day schooling, the question of workplace quality within schools becomes fundamental. This requires new working hours and shifts in on-site presence. Research on schools has shown that team schools are more successful from an educational point of view and at the same time offer much better conditions for maintaining the health of teachers than the previously common »lone wolf« constellation.[64] Workplaces therefore need to be created not only for teachers but also for school social workers, pedagogical specialists in the all-day program, special education teachers, therapists, interns, and other staff. The principles of integrated all-day schooling and inclusion must also be reflected in the integration of workplaces—only then can multi-professional teams emerge.

Successful teamwork in an all-day school definitely requires different working conditions than those previously provided in staff rooms conceived as break rooms. The outdated habit of »my seat in the staff room« is replaced by a »workplace« in a decentralized team base or in a central team area.

Depending on the size and internal organization of the school, two different spatial models have proven successful for the organization of workspaces. Both solutions require a structural differentiation based on six functions, which can be implemented in different spatial configurations:

1. *Communication:* In a central location, a communicative lounge, cafeteria, or similar space should be available, where teachers can meet and talk informally during breaks or free periods. Ideally, this common area should have access to an outdoor space such as a balcony or terrace.
2. *Meetings:* There should be a space for meetings of four to six people, either in a central meeting area or in decentralized team bases. A separate enclosed meeting room is needed for confidential discussions (e.g., with parents).

64
Cf. among others the series of the German School Award: Fauser et al. (Eds.) (2007)

3. *Individual work:* In all-day schools, space must be provided for undisturbed work; this can be achieved through a pool of freely available, non-personalized workspaces in a central location, or through workspaces located within team bases integrated into the year group or cluster of specialist rooms.
4. *Storage:* An area with personalized lockers (cart, if necessary) and pigeonholes must be designated.
5. *Retreat:* A quiet area can make a significant contribution to recovery in a school day that can be stressful in phases.
6. *Conference:* A dedicated room for general staff meetings is not required. Instead, a multifunctional space can be used, which is otherwise available for teaching or other gatherings. The daily need to communicate up-to-date information that must reach everyone is met, for example, through the intranet and »digital bulletin boards.«

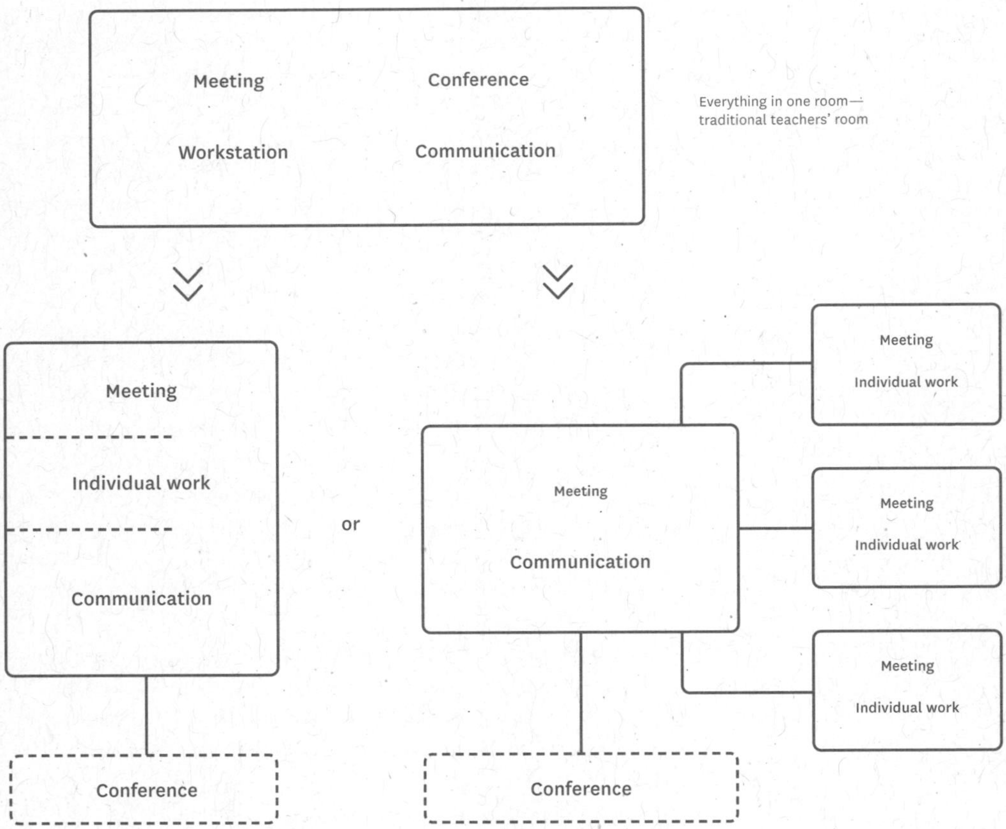

Everything in one room—traditional teachers' room

Separation of functions in a central teacher area

Separation of functions in a central communication area and decentralized teacher bases

There are also ancillary rooms such as sanitary facilities (possibly with a shower), cloakrooms, copy rooms, and materials storage. All these functions can be centralized or decentralized. The decision depends on the school's pedagogical concept and size—whether there is a class- or course-based organization, year-group teams, subject-based room allocation, open learning landscapes, or other formats.

For this reason, schools must make three organizational decisions prior to the planning stage when arranging workspaces:

— decentralized or centralized location
— proximity or distance to student areas
— personalized or non-personalized workspaces.

A particular question arises regarding the location of areas for school counselors, school social workers, and student councils. In general, these spaces should be centrally located and easily accessible, especially to students, but not be directly visible.

Another aspect needs to be considered in workplace design: Several scientific studies show that an appropriate workspace actively contributes to the health of educational staff and can significantly reduce absenteeism.[65]

65
See, for example, the Potsdam study on the mental health of teachers 2000–2006 (for results see Schaarschmidt (2006)

As regards space requirements for staff outside the learning areas, it is essential to consider the fundamental shift from break room to workspace that must take place in German school construction if the aspirations of the current development of all-day schools are to be aligned with reality. Earlier space requirement calculations—unlike those in, for example, Scandinavia—did not adequately address the topic of »workspaces for teachers in schools.« Current planning frameworks and school construction guidelines now take this into account. Depending on the school's concept, the space allocation for the individual work areas will vary.

In many cases, it is still assumed that teachers have an external workspace at home. Workspaces for other educational specialists in all-day and inclusion programs are also often not included in the calculation of space requirements. However, the aim should be to create appropriate working conditions throughout the day for everyone working in schools.

The aim here is to take up and evaluate the comprehensive findings from the development of work environments in the office and service sectors.

COMMON AREAS

Every school needs its »heart,« a central common space for communication, encounters, presentations, and performances. The more teaching is individualized or organized in small groups, the more important this component becomes. The school community needs to be experienced with all the senses, e.g., in assemblies at the beginning and end of the week, in presentations and discussions, in drama and music projects, and so on. This is the mission of social learning in a democratic community.

The heart of the school can be divided into different areas that are positioned and used depending on the spatial situation. What is definitely essential, however, is the concept of interconnection—combining various functions to concentrate sufficient spatial capacity and ensure flexible, shared use. Common areas are made up of different modules: forum, foyer, canteen / cafeteria, library / self-study center, retreat area, sports / exercise areas, outdoor areas.

☞ Chapter 2, *Thesis 8*, pp. 43 ff. and Chapter 6, *Thesis 8*, pp. 205 ff.

From school hall to forum

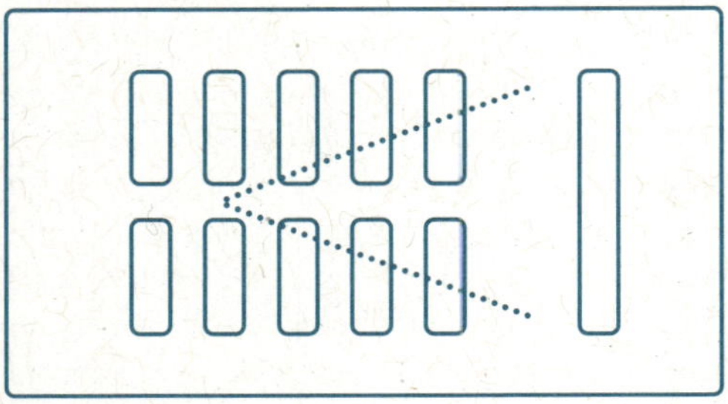

From stage-centered school hall with a festive aura ...

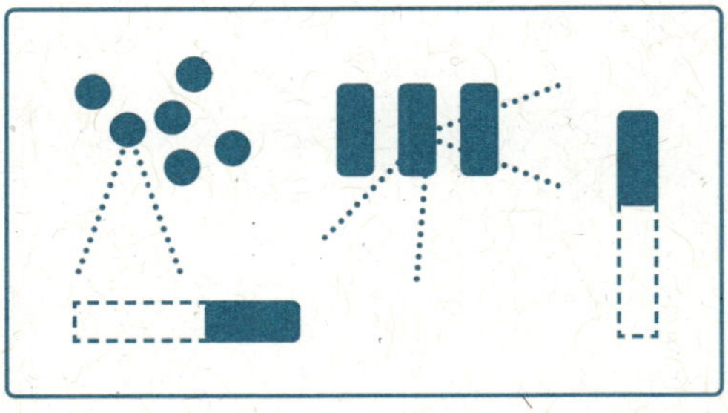

... to a multi-purpose meeting and market place.

A »forum« is essential to the social life of a school. Given the relatively short periods of use, the construction of a separate »classic« school hall is often dispensed with today. Instead, a common event and presentation venue can be created through intelligent multiple use, e.g., by designing the »foyer« accordingly or central circulation areas with stepped seating, by expanding the canteen with a stage, or by linking it to the music hall—including the necessary access routes. However, very large schools (with more than 800 students) will rarely have the possibility to design a space in the school building where the whole school can gather. They will have to limit gatherings to subgroups (grades, etc.) or, for large events, use suitable external venues. In school centers, where common areas are shared by several schools, there may be other appropriate solutions. The important thing is that a school gets its center—its »heart.«

The stage is of great importance in multifunctional solutions; it can act as a link between two rooms and be used from both sides (e.g., music room / foyer or canteen / sports hall). Ideally, it should be acoustically and visually separable by means of movable wall elements and should only be open for performances, thus reducing conflicts of use. If necessary, stages should also be used independently, e.g. as dance and movement spaces. For this, a separate access should be provided. Since drama has become a central educational tool in many schools for all age groups, the stage must be able to be organized in such a way that it is »suitable for performances« (lighting arrangements, backstage area, scenery storage, etc.). The event area should be usable for both internal and external uses and therefore include a separate entrance for use outside of school hours. This also applies to the assigned stage, storage, sanitary, and cloakroom areas. Particular attention must be paid to interface planning, especially if there is no separate, enclosed school hall. Fire safety and the German »Versammlungsstättenverordnung« (Ordinance on Places of Assembly) must be observed.

From entrance area to foyer

☞ Chapter 7, *Examples, #Foyers, auditoriums, Cafeteria*, p. 218

The »heart of the school« is often directly linked to the entrance area. This is the »face« of the school. It is the access point, meeting place, and a space to linger. This is where information is shared and the »janitor's lodge« is located; ideally, the administration and school social work offices are directly accessible from here. Depending on the school's size, the foyer can accommodate exhibition and seating areas. Together with the forum, it serves as a recreation area during breaks with niches for various activities and as a learning space for work assignments, project work, and presentations, or as a place for communication. Depending on the all-day concept, large schools in particular need a dedicated meeting place, usually adjacent to the foyer or cafeteria: games circulation desk, waiting area after school, etc. Rooms for mediators and student representatives should also be as centrally located and as closely linked to the foyer/forum as possible.

From dining hall to cafeteria+

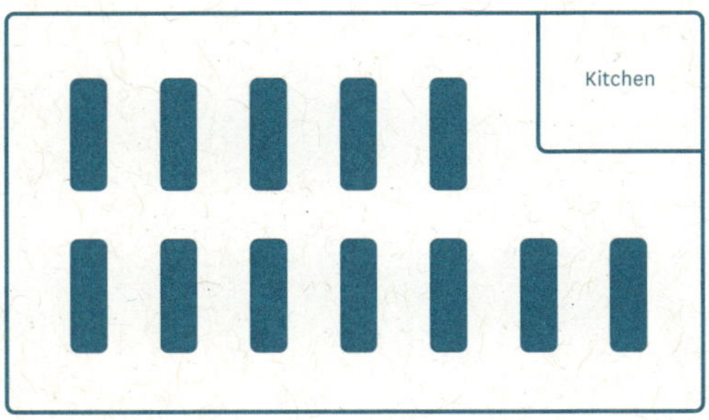

From cafeteria as a place to serve food ...

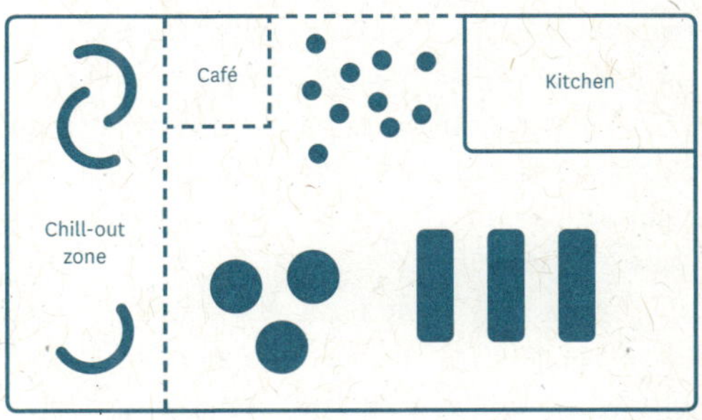

... to the cafeteria as a meeting place with a differentiated food offer, various seating areas, cafeteria, chill-out zones...

The cafeteria plays a key role in both health education and social life. It is not only a place to eat, but also a place to meet, relax, and regenerate, especially in an all-day school. Accordingly, the area should be linked to the foyer and the event area. The dining and lounge areas should be spacious, acoustically softened, and inviting. It should be possible to divide the actual dining area into different zones (quick meals, café corner, group dining zone, etc.), with an attached (shaded) outdoor area, if possible. Food is served at stations, either at a counter or at serving islands.

Chapter 2, *Thesis 7*, pp. 40 ff. and Chapter 6, *Thesis 7*, pp. 203 ff.

There are different organizational models and catering systems, which impact the respective spatial concepts. The way in which »cooking / eating / nutrition« is integrated into the school's educational concept also shapes the required spatial program (e.g. involvement of students in the organization and preparation of meals or decentralized organization of meals, etc.). The planning of the kitchen should be based on a catering concept that takes future development goals into account.

Lunch is typically served in shifts to reduce the space required for the school cafeteria. As a guideline, the German Nutrition Society (DGE) and regional school meal networks recommend approximately 1.5–1.8 square meters per seat. While earlier models assumed that a maximum of 50 percent of students would eat in an open all-day school, successful cafeteria concepts offering high-quality, fresh food and a variety of meals can now achieve significantly higher utilization rates (up to 100 percent). Such a development is desirable and should be anticipated in the architectural design. It must also be noted: The values vary considerably depending on the age of students and the school environment.

A cafeteria with its own kitchen includes necessary ancillary rooms (pantry with cold room / refrigerators, dishwashing area, staff rooms) as well as a dedicated delivery and disposal zone. Depending on the operating system, kitchen space requirements range from 0.25 square meters (heated meals) to 0.8 square meters (frozen / cook & chill) to 1.0 square meter (fresh food) per diner.[66]

66
Cf. BMEL (Ed.) (2014)

As snack catering becomes more important, an area for corresponding offerings (sandwiches, salad bar, etc.) should also be provided; this can easily be combined with a cafeteria that can be used outside of the main meal times (and in which students may also be involved).

For possible evening use of the cafeteria by external groups, it makes sense to provide a »mini-kitchen« (»communal kitchen«) in the cafeteria area for preparing food, so that the actual school kitchen can remain closed.

The core component »lunch« can be expanded to include additional use modules, provided that the all-day functions are not integrated into the general learning areas: counseling room for youth services, open game room, cafeteria and recreation area, etc.

Library / Self-study center

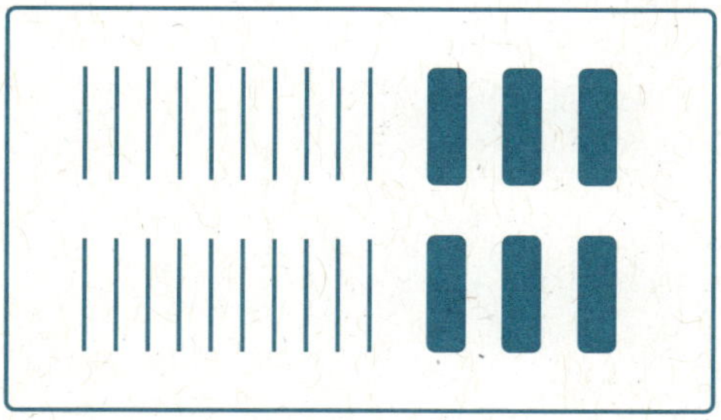

From a traditional library with shelves and reading areas ...

... to a diverse self-study centre with a variety of media, reading areas and places to linger

☞ Chapter 7, *Examples, #Libraries and self-study centers*, p. 219

The school library is an information, reading, learning, and documentation center that serves as a place of work and research for individual learning and, if necessary, for work in smaller groups. The lending function of books is now of secondary importance. In some schools, library functions are integrated into the teaching areas in the form of reading corners or »learning offices.« In any case, the library has an important additional function: it is one of the most important places where undisturbed and focused individual work is possible.

The internal structure of a school library should include an entrance area, an information area, and a media area, as well as defined spaces for quiet work (preps) and work in small groups (acoustically separated workspaces). If necessary, a lockable storage room for textbooks (with circulation desk) can also be connected to the library. Workstations must be connected to the media, and an appropriate number of workstations should be available for research and information retrieval.

The library should be centrally located and easily accessible; the required room size depends on the media stock, the number of users, the integration of the library as a place of work into the school's educational concept, and the availability of individual and group workstations in the school's general learning and teaching areas. The combination of a school library with a district library creates additional synergies and potential uses. When a school library is combined with a district library, additional criteria determine the size of the library; in this case, the library must have a separate, clearly identifiable entrance for use outside of school hours.

Flexible-use rooms

To allow for future spatial needs of the school or its local partners, additional multi-purpose rooms should be included, if possible, whose use has not yet been determined. Such buffers are not a »luxury«: a vibrant school is constantly evolving, external requirements are redefined, occupancy levels fluctuate, etc.

From gym to movement center

Sport and physical activity are essential to the physical, mental, and emotional well-being of students. Lack of exercise, declining physical fitness, increasing numbers of overweight people, and rising rates of chronic diseases among children and adolescents have been a growing concern among experts and the public for years. Programs such as »Bewegte Schule« (Active School) use this as an opportunity to initiate far-reaching efforts to integrate movement in everyday school life. Due to competing leisure activities and a lack of incentives to be physically active in their everyday environment, many young people are becoming less and less motivated to exercise. Even popular trend sports typically only reach a small proportion of young people. Informal forms of exercise and sport are gaining in importance. This also means changes in school sports.

That is why every school still needs a gym: it is used for team sports and as a space for exercise and training in a variety of ways. In large schools, it is sometimes supplemented by a dance studio, a psychomotor activity area, a climbing wall, or circus equipment—sometimes even by a low-threshold fitness room for extracurricular activities during extended school hours.

Sports halls can be used for a wide range of sports. For the »big solution,« bleachers can be optionally extended and otherwise recessed into the wall. Gymnasiums have long been used for extracurricular activities: sensible use by sports clubs in the afternoons, evenings, on weekends, and during school holidays is in many cases a well-established practice, as is the use by different schools. As a result of all-day schooling, changes are taking place. Students spend more time at school and less time in clubs. In some places, clubs are therefore directly involved in all-day programs, while in others, the range of activities on offer is fundamentally changing.

From schoolyard to living environment

Outdoor areas on school grounds are important learning and living spaces in everyday school life: as places for physical activity, social interaction, quiet retreat, sport, nature, and circulation. These functions are associated with very different, sometimes even competing, usage requirements. The spectrum of design concepts is correspondingly diverse, ranging from multifunctional platforms inspired by urban plaza typologies to sports and play areas with swings, climbing frames, table tennis tables, basketball hoops, beach volleyball courts, and soccer fields, to school gardens or naturally designed biotopes with a stream or pond.[67] A sufficiently large covered area for protection from rain and sun is just as important as plenty of seating—which does not necessarily mean benches. Sufficient drinking water dispensers and storage for training equipment and furniture should be provided in the outdoor area, as well as in the indoor recreation zones.

67
Cf. www.gruen-macht-schule.de

☞ Chapter 7, *Examples*, *#Outdoor spaces*, p. 220

In view of increasing demands for densification, innovative sports areas[68] must be developed that adapt to the location and often diverge from standardized dimensions required for competitions. From a climatic point of view, large sports facilities with a traditional layout also need to be reconsidered: these often lack both shade and rain shelter.

68
Cf. Stadt Frankfurt am Main (Ed.) (2023a)

It is important to define usage distributions and activity patterns for outdoor areas. These can be based on the following system. A school's outdoor space must serve three very different functions: outdoor spaces for instruction, areas for communication and recreation, and areas for retreat, as well as zones for sport and movement. In addition, the entrance area in particular—because it is directly visible from outside the school—serves as a kind of »calling card« for the school.

From a planning perspective, there are two categories of outdoor spaces:

Teaching-related zones

— Themed work areas (e.g. school garden, »tree nursery,« rock trail, etc.)
— Flexible-use project areas (work areas in front of the art/technology room, experimentation and research areas, open-air stage, presentation path, etc.)
— Water and power connections and storage for outdoor materials must be provided

Age-appropriate activity and recreation areas

— Age-appropriate play and activity facilities (table tennis tables, swings, climbing wall, etc.), as well as activity areas that—unlike those used for physical education—are freely accessible as part of the all-day program (soccer pitch or cage, streetball, beach volleyball, etc.)
— Common areas for sitting and »chilling out« as well as for seeing and being seen (rain/sun shelters, worktables)
— Accessible sports facilities on or near the school grounds.

An open zoning of the recreation area according to lower, middle, and upper school levels is desirable, depending on how the outdoor space on the site is designed. It is critical that the design of these physical activity and recreation areas reflects all four »quadrants« in terms of age-specific needs.

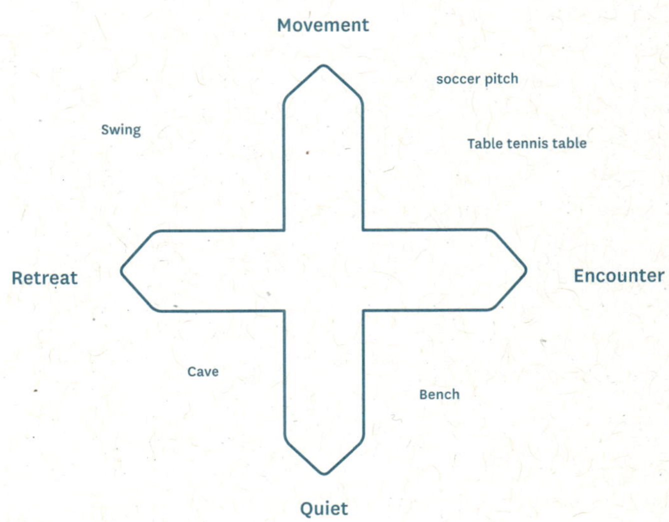

Technical functions

The access and entrance areas not only serve as an important orientation function—they are also the school's calling card. Covered seating should also be provided here, allowing students, parents, or visitors to meet before the school opens in the morning.

In addition to their »educational« functions in a broader sense, outdoor spaces are also linked to a number of other requirements that need to be coordinated through integrated planning: secure bicycle parking, safe access, a limited number of car parking spaces for staff and visitors with charging stations. Safe transportation (safe routes to school, bus stop, Kiss & Ride area where required, bike and pedestrian paths) must ensure that the school is easily accessible. Waste disposal and delivery to the kitchen must be organized, as well as emergency assembly points, fire department access, and escape routes.

The outdoor space is particularly important in terms of sustainability and climate adaptation. The criteria range from issues of biodiversity, climate and recycling, rainwater management and degree of sealing, and participation through to quality of use and landscape.[69]

Integrating outdoor spaces into teaching is also desirable from a pedagogical perspective—not only when a school garden is included. At some schools, students and teachers are even responsible for the entire maintenance of outdoor areas. The importance of this planning task can be seen in the broad support it receives from the public sector: design competitions are held, advisory brochures are published, and special municipal advisory teams are formed.[70]

69
Cf., e.g., Schuhmacher (Ed.) (2010); Stadt Frankfurt am Main (Ed.) (2023a)

70
Pedagogical advice center »Grün macht Schule« of the Senate Department for Education, Science and Research, Berlin; working group »Forum Schulhöfe,« Frankfurt am Main

The school as an urban learning environment

In view of the common recommendation of five square meters of break area per student, it should be noted that many inner-city locations currently do not meet these requirement—this figure does not even include sports facilities. The goals of sustainable urban development and sustainable outdoor space design on school campuses are in direct competition. Reconstruction or extension projects often involve the threat of densification, which is problematic in terms of outdoor space requirements. Today, schools are built in highly built-up areas—in some cases, schoolyards are even relocated to rooftops, or public parks are included as outdoor space. This overlapping of functions is unfamiliar to many stakeholders. The idea of clearly separated outdoor areas is still firmly anchored in the public opinion as well as among students and teachers. This is justified not only by supervision duties and safety or liability considerations, but also by the desire for a clearly defined and identifiable territory for schools use.

However, this concept is at odds with the lifestyle habits of today's children and young people, who move around the public spaces of a city or community as a matter of course. It is simply a matter of balancing interests: Will space be gained for the students' urge to move that would otherwise not be available? After all, it is not uncommon for dual-use spaces in inner-city areas to be repurposed because they have reached the end of their useful life and thus trigger a willingness to invest. Potential disadvantages can be offset—for example, by setting clear usage times for schools, by having trained educational staff supervise outdoor spaces, or by cooperation between schools and the district, etc.

Shared outdoor spaces are a central component of a municipal educational landscape that helps schools connect with their surroundings.

Shifting boundaries—beyond the fence

Schools in inner-city contexts are increasingly concerned with the shared use of public spaces that also serve as recreational areas for students. The idea of a school's own outdoor area for exclusive use is no longer viable or meaningful in densely populated areas. New open space typologies are emerging that function both as outdoor school spaces and public squares or parks.

☞ Chapter 2, *Thesis 10*, pp. 49 ff.
Chapter 6, *Thesis 10*, pp. 213 ff.

In the design of school sites, adjacent public open spaces are taking on an increasingly important key function—because they are used as areas for movement that are not available within the school grounds; because they create (show) stages for »seeing and being seen;« because they represent the necessary open-air counterpart to a schoolyard on the rooftop; because they serve as extended learning environments in the course of digitalization, etc. This aspect is directly related to how educational landscapes are physically shaped and perceived within a district.

The reverse is also true: expansive outdoor spaces on school grounds are increasingly being opened up and used as a resource outside of school hours. They become important steppingstones in a network of public open spaces. Even though this opening up can be problematic (vandalism, etc.) if there is a lack of social control, the interweaving of school and public open spaces in urban areas is irreversible. This calls not only for innovative design concepts but also for modified management and stewardship strategies that lead to sustainable structures. Successful examples in both rural and urban settings demonstrate the broad potential this development offers.

New hybrid forms are emerging in the planning discussion—the school square, the educational park, the learning plaza, the school terrace, the classroom lawn, ... the urban educational »landscape« as a composition of interlinked open spaces.[71]

71
See Bildungslandschaft Altstadt Nord in Cologne: *Klingelpützpark is not only used by schools and children's and youth facilities, but also by the district.*

These spaces are characterized by their public-educational »hybrid character«—and it is precisely in this supposedly diffuse »in-between« that they represent contemporary fields of learning par excellence, because they are open to interpretation and not conclusively determined. If school is to become a living environment, then it must be part of (public) life—formal places of learning and informal places of education intertwine. Open spaces thus also reflect a shift of content-related, pedagogical, and conceptual boundaries—as a departure into the zones beyond the fence.

FROM SCHOOL TO EDUCATIONAL AND NEIGHBORHOOD CENTER

Schools are a natural and increasingly vital part of municipal education networks. In the future, they will become even more closely intertwined with other educational and leisure offerings. Whereas in the past it was only the adult education center that used classroom, or the sports club that used the school gym, the future will see even more collaboration between the school and out-of-school educational institutions, as well as with actors from urban and village communities. Key focal points of these connections in school buildings are spaces such as the library, forum, canteen, and sports hall. Depending on the educational concept, different areas take precedence alongside the sports facilities. For example,

— the cafeteria is also used by local residents;
— the library also serves as a neighborhood library;
— the forum is also used by external local amateur theater groups, music ensembles, dance groups, the town council for information evenings, etc.;
— external experts are also integrated into the extracurricular science clubs;
— examination rooms are also used as venues for events organized by local clubs or as polling stations;
— and so on.

For this semi-public use of school areas, it is essential that they are independently accessible for external users and that there are clear boundaries between public and purely school use. The necessary boundaries must be considered: as much openness as possible, as much separation as necessary. Several spatial prerequisites support the success of a constructive neighborhood cooperation:

— separability of the »internal« school areas from »public« ones;
— access to sanitary facilities from public areas;
— lockable cabinets in public-use areas;
— signage system both outside and inside the school building.

Conversely, all-day schooling also means that schools are increasingly opening up to the outside world; external places of learning in the immediate vicinity of the school are being opened up for cooperation. Schools are therefore increasingly integrating youth centers, libraries, makerspaces, museums, zoos, theaters, craft workshops, city forests, etc. into their own curriculum in a structured and systematic way.

From closed school …

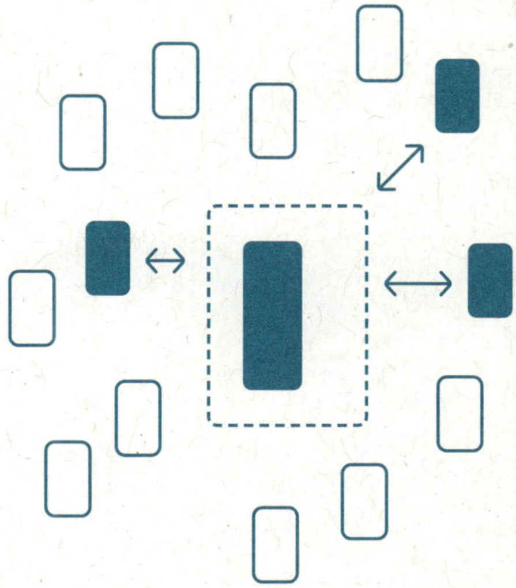

… to interconnected school and educational landscape

Across Germany, the associated opening is gaining in importance, especially in areas where schools take on far-reaching tasks beyond traditional knowledge transfer. We have noticed that schools in »neighborhoods with special development needs« are becoming increasingly relevant and are often the driving force for change in the surrounding area. Provided that they are adequately staffed and sufficient space is available, educational institutions can play an important catalytic role and become a resilient anchor for structural improvements. Increasingly, educational facilities are being incorporated into integrated development strategies and are essential to securing and maintaining the value of housing stock. Funding programs such as the nationwide »Startchancen-Programm« respond to this situation and call for integrated spatial and educational planning processes.

4

PROCESS Stages and Stakeholders

Following the overview of topics and areas of action, we now turn to the process itself: What factors come together in Phase 0? Who are the key players and decision-makers? And how can the process be designed from the beginning to lay a solid foundation for all subsequent steps? This chapter provides the necessary background information for well-coordinated collaboration. It outlines the most important planning steps and frequently refers to the modules of a Phase 0 process presented in Chapter 5, highlighting its importance as the starting point for a successfully implemented school building project.

1. PLANNING AND PARTICIPATION

STANDARDIZATION AND INDIVIDUALIZATION

Over the past 100 years, school construction has been characterized by continuous growth. The development took place in waves, with peaks in the 1950s and 1970s. School buildings were generally not conceived as unique structures, but rather as optimized serial products. This concept was accompanied by the idea of a universal and transferable requirement profile, in which school buildings only differed according to the type of school. The concept of generalizable serial products, on the one hand, and a multitude of regulations and standardized space allocation plans, on the other, were mutually dependent—validating each other's raison d'être. Both the federal financing of school construction by West German states and the national financing model in East Germany required a generalizable and transferable basis. Standardized space allocation plans thus had and still have a dual function in many cases: they are the basis for planning and for allocating funds to cities and municipalities. Educators and architects have criticized this situation for 50 years—school construction and the determination of space requirements have primarily been administrative acts. Although there have always been outstanding examples of school architecture, stereotypical solutions have dominated—school buildings as mass products.

This tradition continues to have an effect today, although significant changes have taken place over the past 25 years: in many places, school construction is both a growth model and a transformation task due to changing demographics. Today, the focus is equally on new construction, adaptation, and reconstruction, with significant regional differences. At the same time, all schools are expected to have an individual educational profile.

The associated school-specific differentiation of pedagogical concepts requires a needs analysis for each location—both spatially and pedagogically. The extent to which these development perspectives can differ was described in Chapter 3. As schools become more individualized and specialized, the planning process must also evolve: in addition to standardized space allocation plans and reference projects, a precise needs analysis—both quantitative and qualitative—must be carried out at the beginning. Based on this, the foundations for how a particular school can and should develop in concrete terms can be defined in Phase 0.

☞ Chapter 3, pp. 52ff.

The aim must be to define a reliable and recognized framework through guidelines and recommendations, while still allowing room for individual interpretation and prioritization. In this context, municipal responsibility and the need for expertise beyond standard concepts and guidelines at the local level will increase. This calls for a shift of attention from the enforcement of general standards to the individual planning of specific locations.

PROCESS STRUCTURE AND PARTICIPATION

Administrative regulations alone do not make a »good school.« It cannot simply be »decreed.« If specific needs are to be identified, users must be invited to the planning table. While this may sound self-evident, it is far from standard practice. To this day, many schools are still being built and converted without real user participation and without a specifically coordinated space allocation plan.

The following outlines the planning process with a special focus on the early stages of project development—as is now common practice in almost all fields of planning, from office and residential construction to large cultural buildings and infrastructure projects. Precise user analyses and an accurate assessment of the urban planning situation are just as indispensable for the success of a building project as specific space requirements planning with a clear cost framework.

When teachers, students, and parents are not involved in the planning and decision-making processes of a school construction project, this is usually due to concerns on the part of administrators and politicians. They are afraid of being confronted with supposedly unrealistic demands that cannot be met. However, recent experience in this area shows that when municipal school authorities involve local users on an equal footing in a clearly structured process of rethinking school structures, the result is often higher quality of and greater identification with the outcome. If the framework is transparent for all involved, schools generally make reasonable demands. User participation enables the development of a precise, project-related space allocation plan within an appropriate and predetermined space budget, which strengthens the sustainability of the investments made—a benefit that also extends to the operation of the property. Considering the life cycle of a building, this is an increasingly important aspect of investment projects.

Participation makes planning decisions understandable for local stakeholders. Building can become a personal experience—with responsibilities that can be assigned and that allow direct influence through one's own actions. Goals can be made readable and measurable in a clearly formulated development framework.

The basis for effective participation is a solid project structure and good process management. This requires additional financial and human resources at the beginning of the planning process—an investment that quickly proves worthwhile and cost-efficient when considering the long-term economic viability of planning and construction decisions. If there is no appropriate management capacity at the municipal level, this role should be taken on by external consultants.

PEDAGOGICAL CONCEPT

The involvement of a school and the definition of its specific needs and space allocation plan must be based on an individual pedagogical concept. This concept must describe the central functional processes in everyday school life—both for the present and, as far as possible, also for the future. Experience shows that when educators and planners enter into dialogue, a step-by-step process of understanding and clarification begins. Patterns of use are reflected and concretized in the planning questions. The necessary planning decisions help shape the educational concepts, which often deal with many fundamental aspects.

Particular attention must be paid to the spatially relevant components of the pedagogical concept. This raises questions such as »How is teaching organized and what spatial conditions are needed to support it? How important is differentiation? How is the all-day program organized? What is the relationship between phases of work, communication, and recreation? What are the team structures for teachers and educational staff? What is the role of communal areas?« And so on.

☞ Chapter 5, *M2 Site and Building Assessment*, pp. 165 ff.

Even if many schools already have a pedagogical concept in place, it is evident that this often requires substantial refinement and expansion for the planning process with regard to spatial developments. In most cases, changes to a school's physical structure are accompanied by a revision of the pedagogical concept as part of a self-assessment process.

In the school construction discourse, the notion of »space as the third educator« is often given special attention and appreciation. As welcome as this attention is in principle, it is equally important to point out that »good architecture« alone does not make a »good school.« Architecture can provide a supportive framework, but it cannot replace educational content or a school concept. The more precisely and specifically user requirements are defined, the better architecture can respond to them.

Practice shows that this specification can often only be achieved through a dialog between pedagogy and architecture. Ensuring architectural quality in school construction therefore means, above all, creating and maintaining a structured and qualified process of exchange between these two disciplines.

EXTERNAL PROCESS SUPPORT

Based on our many years of experience in various school development and planning processes, we are convinced that addressing pedagogical and spatial development needs separately along traditional sectoral lines will not lead to sustainable solutions. The necessary dialog between schools, architecture, planning, and administration is usually not established and not easy to achieve: counting classrooms and thinking in terms of outdated standardized space allocation plans often stands in the way of individual, needs-based planning. At the same time, those involved must adapt to new, unfamiliar communication and decision-making structures.

☞ Chapter 4.3, *Phase 0*, pp. 106 ff.

To achieve the necessary translation between the various disciplines, it is advisable to involve external school construction consultants. Their role is to structure, facilitate, and manage the needs assessment process. This includes translating educational concepts into functional spatial programs and documenting the results of Phase 0 in a report for future reference throughout the planning and implementation process. This is essential to the implementation of the requirements agreed upon by school authorities and schools. A crucial prerequisite is that school construction consultants have both educational and architectural experience and expertise.

The early involvement of external school construction consultants in project development and subsequent project management is recommended, particularly for larger, more complex building projects.

CONSTRUCTIONAL REQUIREMENTS

Construction measures in schools are often triggered by purely technical considerations. Changes in fire safety requirements and energy efficiency upgrades are among the most frequent drivers of spatial restructuring. Despite their importance, inadequate lighting, ventilation, and acoustics are rarely the reason for renovations. More and more often, surveys reveal that the building fabric of a school is in such poor condition that it requires a full-scale refurbishment—or even demolition and replacement. Against the backdrop of the current sustainability debate (»demolition memorandum«), a broad rethinking toward the transformation and adaptive reuse of existing buildings can be observed.

As school authorities are obliged to ensure the structural safety of buildings, technical renovation measures are often uncontroversial because they are objectively necessary and required by law. This makes it even more important to use these interventions for the school's future-oriented development in terms of content and structure.

MUNICIPAL DEVELOPMENT PLANNING

Demographic shifts have created a need for municipal school development planning that covers all school sites and goes beyond the question of how much additional space will be needed at each site and when. Rather, an overall strategic development plan is required, in which many factors play a role: from educational provision and urban development to the sustainability debate. The development of local education is thus increasingly intertwined with urban development policy. Questions such as which school site should be expanded and with which profile, and which in turn should be scaled back or even closed, can only be answered in an integrated planning process that involves local decision-makers. In this sense, school development planning should no longer only address pure provision demands, but also become an important strategic management tool at the municipal level.

Chapter 5, *Municipal Baseline Assessment*, pp. 161 ff.

To safeguard the educational mandate and to contribute to sustainable urban development, traditional school development planning with its purely quantitative methodological approach is currently undergoing major changes. The demands of lifelong learning require a strong integration of the various educational sectors—from primary and secondary education to adult, family, and extracurricular education. The quality of the interfaces and transitions between the different types of schools and educational institutions is becoming a central development criterion for successful educational careers. All-day schooling and the call for inclusion require an expanded concept of education—one that can no longer be achieved at a single location, but only within a wider municipal context. Informal educational processes are becoming increasingly important, and a successful integration policy is also largely depend on the provision of broad educational opportunities. The aspects outlined above make it clear that a contemporary and successful school construction process is not possible without a socio-spatial assessment and without the integration of school development policy into the neighborhood- or district-level urban planning.

2. STAKEHOLDERS AND DECISION-MAKERS

The stakeholders involved in the process of basic analysis and project development are quite diverse. Their roles are shaped by a traditional understanding of their tasks and often subject to preconceived notions that, however, can be overcome through a well-structured planning process. One objective of Phase 0 is to establish an organizational structure that is understandable to all those involved and to clarify responsibilities.

(Re)construction processes in schools are usually triggered by changes in the structural and pedagogical framework, but they can also simply be the result of changes in the number of students.

Both the public »school« and »building« sectors are governed by complex administrative, evaluation, and decision-making structures. A similar structure can also be found among major providers of private schools, such as churches. While they are therefore not fundamentally different from public school authorities, politics and administration generally play a much smaller role in the independent authorities and their decision-making structures are less complex.

When a school is being renovated, modernized, remodeled, or newly built, the parties involved usually articulate clear requirements for the joint project, fulfill specific tasks, and are subject to certain hierarchies and constraints. As a rule, they operate within distinct frameworks of argumentation and sectoral rationales.

Chapter 5, *M1 Platform Formation*, pp. 124 ff. and *M3 Dialog*, pp. 158 ff.

Four key stakeholders can be identified in the development process of school construction:

Planning: municipal planning officials and architects and planners commissioned by them

School and educational community: students, teachers, and educational staff, as well as school leadership and parents; extracurricular partners are becoming increasingly important within the network

Administration: The local administration is primarily responsible for the municipal obligation of school construction. However, its actions are also determined by the state and, to a limited extent, by the federal government (e.g. profile of funding programs)

Politics: urban society and its political representatives

Planning

Commissioned architects and planners, potentially also municipal planning authorities

School

Students, teachers, school leadership, and parents

Politics

Urban society and its political representatives

SCHOOL CONSTRUCTION

Administration

Primarily the municipal level, but also the state and, to a limited extent, the federal government

SCHOOL COMMUNITY

Schools as users are made up of various interest groups. The goals of students, teachers, school leadership, and parents often differ significantly and require internal coordination.

Since a school's educational concept is often revised and specified during the planning process, key points must be formally adopted by the teachers' or school conference—ideally with active involvement of the ideas and interests of students and parents. Precisely because school stakeholders are usually not experienced in building matters, it is advisable to set up a school project group »construction« to consolidate and communicate user needs. If it is also to take on quality assurance tasks in coordination with the administration, the project group must have decision-making authority.

It is also advisable to involve extracurricular educational and cooperation partners in the planning process from the outset, and to involve them directly where appropriate.

POLITICS

The commissioning body and client for public school buildings is the local authority or municipal corporation. It is represented by the municipal council—usually a school committee. This body is supported by the administration, in particular the departments of education and construction.

Considering the high priority given to educational policy, school development and construction are key areas of political profiling at the municipal level. Innovative, participatory school construction processes bring new responsibilities for municipal elected officials. At the same time, there remains an expectation that guidelines should be issued by the state capital. However, the previous practice of deriving local requirements directly from state ministry guidelines can no longer be maintained. Today, standardized space allocation plans no longer provide precise spatial specifications but rather define area allocations for functional zones within which variations can then be made. For example, the total area for learning and teaching spaces is specified but not the layout of classrooms. Local parliaments must therefore develop a corresponding understanding of the importance of controlling school construction processes.

ADMINISTRATION

»School construction« is a municipal obligation. Accordingly, it should play a central role in municipal administration. Unfortunately, inadequate staffing and limited financial resources often set clear limits to municipal action. Since educational sovereignty lies with the federal states, responsibilities often become blurred—in extreme cases to the point where each party shifts the responsibility to another.

Administrative rules vary by federal state. Nevertheless, across the board, it is evident that recent restructuring within public administration has opened up new opportunities for action at the municipal level.

The federal level acts through legislation and corresponding funding programs and initiatives with clearly defined scopes, e.g. the current »Startchancen-Programm« with a strongly integrated planning approach. The individual states also offer a wide range of funding programs for school (re)construction projects.

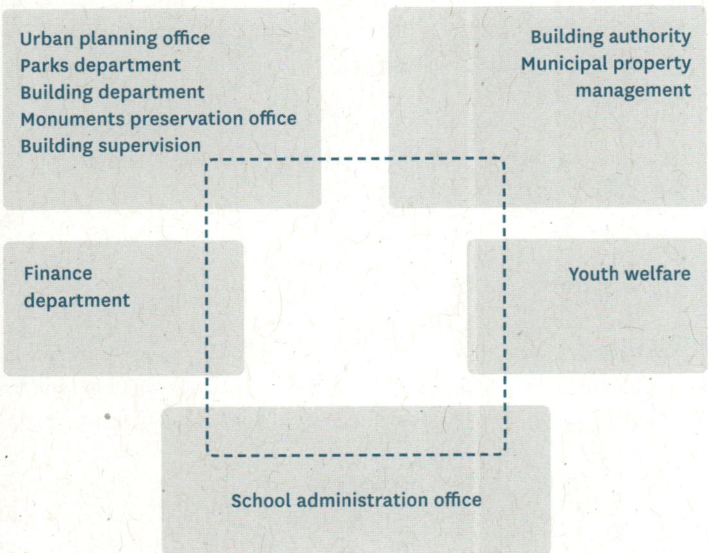

Trends toward deregulation

While some federal states have deregulated school construction measures to a relatively large extent, and funding is provided via lump sums, others continue to rely on project-based funding structures. The scope for action of municipal authorities varies accordingly. In North Rhine-Westphalia and Hesse, a school construction lump sum has been introduced, and the municipal school authorities can in principle decide on their investment priorities largely independently—as long as they do not neglect their duties as school providers. At the same time, however, it should be noted that the school construction lump sums often »dissipate« in the municipal budget and are frequently insufficient even for the upkeep of existing buildings. It is not uncommon for school construction to depend on »co-financing« from broader programs such as urban development or neighborhood development initiatives. In other states, however, funding is still project-based. Submitting applications to the state ministry ensures quality criteria but also tends to perpetuate traditional structures and delegate responsibility. Consequently, it is difficult to hold specific actors accountable. Depending on state regulations, funding for school construction measures can be applied for either on a case-by-case basis or through the so-called »school lump sum.« In both cases, the launch of a new, temporary funding program creates an enormous impetus for change.

☞ Chapter 1, *Funding Programs*, p. 19

The fact that cities such as Cologne, Frankfurt, Herford, Berlin, Munich, and the district of Darmstadt-Dieburg have now drawn up their own school construction guidelines and planning frameworks is evidence of the strengthening of municipal responsibilities. Despite this development, signs of overload are also becoming apparent: municipalities struggle to find permanent and competent staff, land is scarce, and financial resources are tightening. As a result, some municipalities no longer make full use of design and decision-making powers in school construction—to the extent that the obligatory municipal task is being transferred to private providers due to excessive demands, who are also expected to provide a plot of land.

☞ *See bibliography*, pp. 240 ff.

The relationship between state and municipalities is regulated by the school supervisory authority. This body is subdivided into the highest school supervisory authority (ministry) and the lower school supervisory authority (state education authorities); in many federal states, there is also the upper school supervisory authority (district government / regional authority) as an intermediate level. The task of the school supervisory authority is to encourage the school providers to fulfill their duties and to promote the interests of local self-government in the schools. Recently, authorities have often been supported by external evaluation groups in assessing educational processes. For this reason, advisory functions in school management are becoming more important than supervisory functions. In many states, there are school institutes that deal with fundamental issues of school development and contribute important groundwork—though this must always be actively integrated into local pedagogical models. In some cases, there are specific advisory services for school construction.

Role of municipal administration

In the territorial states, the municipality has the role of school authority for public schools.[72] It is responsible for external school matters. Municipal building authorities, municipal real estate companies, or property management companies are responsible for the maintenance, renovation, and modernization of school buildings on behalf of the municipal authorities. Many cities in Germany have decided to transfer municipal building construction to a company-like institution or to organize it as an independently managed municipal enterprise. This means that specialist departments are no longer maintained, but replaced by economical, semi-autonomous units with their own properties and business plans (profit plans, asset plans including investment strategies for construction measures, medium-term financial plans, etc.). Accordingly, their actions are strongly driven by purely financial considerations. Some local authorities carry out parts of their new school construction and maintenance projects through so-called »public-private partnerships« (PPP procedures) in cooperation with private developers and general or total contractors.[73] Others rely on their municipal housing associations, commissioning them to build and operate school buildings.

In all organizational models, the building authority is usually the commissioning body for planners and architects. Ultimately, it is responsible for ensuring that a functional, cost-effective, climate-resilient, and, above all, user-friendly building is delivered. It is also responsible for coordinating requirements related to heritage preservation, landscape conservation, urban planning, fire safety, and building supervision. At the municipal level, it is primarily the school administration office that determines whether new space is needed or whether there is a surplus—based on the most recent school development plan. For a long time, this was assessed using statistical projections of how many students can be expected at which locations in the various school types over the next few years. With the individual profiling of certain schools, greater freedom of school choice, and the growing importance of school development planning as a strategic control instrument of education and location policy, this process is becoming increasingly complex and less predictable in the form of a linear projection.

School administrations are usually also responsible for equipping schools. All movable furniture not directly related to construction is applied for and approved by the school administration within the limits of available funds. Increasingly, schools are provided with small budgets to purchase furniture independently.

The school administration—sometimes also the building authority or municipal property management—is also responsible for school secretaries and janitors. Unlike teachers, they are, with a few exceptions, municipal employees. Depending on the local decision, the rosters and schedules are organized per school or for several schools at the same time via a staffing pool.

72
There are positions advocating for a further development of the organisational structure of school sponsorship—for example, the German Association of Cities (Aachen Declaration, Munich Declaration). The focus is on expanding decision-making powers and supplementing school development planning with qualitative elements, i.e., aspects concerning the internal role of the municipal administration.

73
The experiences with the PPP model in the Offenbach district over the past 20 years, alongside the City of Essen's recent initiative to launch new PPP projects, highlight the different assessments of the development potential associated with the model.

In addition to the building authority, the municipal property management, and the education authority, many other authorities are involved in school construction projects. Because of its strategic importance, the urban planning office must be involved. For existing buildings, it is often necessary to involve staff from the monument preservation office. In all cases, the local fire safety authorities are an important partner in understanding the possibilities and limitations within the construction process. In many all-day schools, there are numerous interfaces with youth or social services departments. Integrating schools into their neighborhoods requires careful consideration of open space and traffic planning.

In addition, there is cooperation with municipal institutions that are not officially called »offices,« but are also run by the municipality or are considered by the municipality to be partners. These include continuing education institutes, adult education centers, libraries, museums, swimming pools, sports clubs, theater groups, and shared sports halls. If municipal companies, such as housing associations, are to take over the project management for new construction or reconstruction, they should also be involved at an early stage.

School construction processes require intensive coordination and management due to the large number of decision-makers and project participants. This task is usually coordinated by the administration through the appointment of a municipal steering group. However, the complexity of the planning process is one of the reasons for the excessive backlog of renovation work. Some municipalities are therefore currently restructuring their »school services,« pooling resources, professionalizing planning processes, appointing responsible »caretakers,« and establishing special sponsorship models for school construction.[74]

74
Cf. among others: Hamburg: Schulbau Hamburg; Berlin: HOWOGE; Duisburg: Schulbau Gesellschaft Duisburg mbH, etc.

PLANNING

The client is usually represented by the municipal building authority or by a municipally owned entity (property management, real estate management, etc.). External architectural firms are often commissioned with the design and planning through to completion. Due to staff shortages in public administration, these tasks are less and less often handled by municipal building departments.

Regardless of who is responsible for the planning, a reliable requirements profile and space allocation plan are essential foundations. To profile a project brief for the respective school, it is advisable to involve an interdisciplinary team of a pedagogue and an architect as school construction consultants in the project development and management. In a dialogical planning process between pedagogy and architecture, between school, administration, and politics, which is described below as an example, the requirements and potentials of use can be defined.

3. PHASE 0

BASICS

Phase 0 is the beginning of the planning process. It is during this phase that key decisions are made, which determine the course for the entire project.[75] The term »Phase 0« refers to the classification of service phases according to the German Fee Structure for Architects and Engineers (HOAI), which previously provided for service phases 1 to 9—but not for integrated advance planning (Phase 0) or planning services beyond commissioning (Phase 10). Phase 0 differs from conventional requirements planning in that it includes not only quantitative but also specific qualitative specifications. Phase 0 and Phase 10 are now increasingly recognized as key factors in the successful planning and implementation of efficient school buildings. Crucial to this is not only the professional implementation of Phase 0 but also the seamless transfer of its results to the subsequent phases—especially the transition from Phase 0 to the established planning phases 1–5.

75
Based on this book, the Montag Stiftung Jugend und Gesellschaft has advised and supported 10 pilot projects on »Designing and Planning (Inclusive) Schools« during Phase 0. Cf., e.g., Montag Stiftung Jugend und Gesellschaft (Ed.) (2015a)

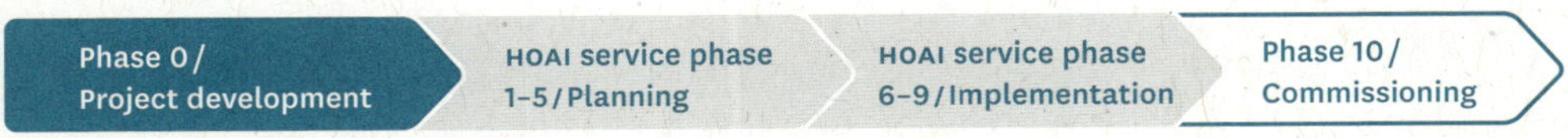

The goal of Phase 0 in school construction is to develop a sustainable concept and spatial framework in collaboration with key stakeholders at the interface of pedagogy and architecture. The pedagogical concept is specified and aligned with the architectural possibilities—opportunities and limitations are explored, which is of central relevance when converting existing buildings. The basic principles of the school organization are defined. A spatial organizational structure is developed and supported by a catalogue of requirements that is as detailed as possible. Organizational decisions are far-reaching and have a formative influence on everyday school life. In the end, reliable and realistic quality criteria should be formulated across all scales—from urban planning and spatial organization models to information on equipment, from the pedagogical mission statement to teaching structure. Finally, Phase 0 also defines communication and process criteria for the further course of the project.

Prerequisites and scope

The first project description must define the core objectives and identify the partners responsible for realization and implementation. The subsequent process must be described qualitatively, and a concrete time schedule and action plan must be established.

The willingness of the schools to participate in the planning process should be assessed as early as possible. Likewise, the general willingness of the school supervisory authority to support the process constructively is also beneficial. On the political side, support for the planning process—ideally in the form of a formal resolution—should be in place.

A comprehensive survey—in pedagogical, municipal, and architectural terms—then forms the basis for the spatial organization models, which are jointly developed in dialog (e.g., in workshops): for learning environments, subject teaching and all-day areas, team areas and administrative spaces, communal and outdoor areas, the integration with the neighborhood, etc.

Funding

Since Phase 0 is not part of the HOAI, it usually needs to be budgeted separately as a special service. However, many administrations have realized that this investment should not be seen as an additional cost, but rather as a prerequisite for a more efficient planning process and good usability of the building. With careful planning during Phase 0, school authorities can benefit from significant savings in the subsequent construction and operation of the school—or, conversely, avoid planning mistakes that are irreversible and may result in unforeseeable follow-up costs. Investing in Phase 0 generates added value not only for the school and the people who work and live in it, but also for the local area, which can benefit from an efficient educational building in a number of ways. By involving local stakeholders, their identification with the future building is strengthened from the outset.

PLANNING CONTEXT

The following sequence summarizes the function of Phase 0 in the context of a school construction project and the key development steps that follow this phase.

☞ Chapter 5, *Modules for Phase 0*, pp. 120 ff.

Phase 0: project development

Every project begins with a needs assessment: What is needed, and where? The initial report is usually the result of a collaborative effort: the school and its school leadership, the school administration, and possibly the school supervisory authority formulate a need for action. The specific needs of individual schools must be assessed in light of the broader municipal school development plan. Based on the needs reported by a school, a foreseeable need for action identified through municipal school development planning, suggestions from the school supervisory authority, or technical maintenance issues, the school and administration formulate an initial guiding question for a construction project.

The educational, planning, technical, and financial capacities available for the process must be assessed and described at an early stage. This is often not easy at the outset, as a large number of individual aspects and particular interests have to be taken into account. However, especially for complex construction and development projects, early coordination with local political bodies is an essential prerequisite for success. Based on the educational objectives—often only partially defined and therefore requiring targeted elaboration for the planning process—space requirements should be defined, and an initial space organization model should be developed. Although current standardized space allocation plans can be used as a reference, they should not be seen as blueprints. In any case, a site-specific concept tailored to the individual school is required. Any existing pedagogical concept must be refined and further developed regarding the spatial and equipment-related development criteria.

The spatial basis must first be clarified by means of a survey. A comprehensive assessment is especially important for reconstruction projects. Existing spaces must be examined for their conversion potential. Often, significant structural alterations to everyday school life arise from the need for structural renovation. A comparison of the occupancy plan and the standardized space allocation plan often provides important indications of the need for changes—both to state guidelines and local circumstances. These principles must be made transparent to all project participants and agreed upon as a binding common starting point. The requirements for structural studies must be defined—although these are not part of Phase 0, the resulting findings must be available.

After aligning the baseline conditions and identified needs, initial alternative spatial development models (usage scenarios, floor plans, atmospheric sketches, etc.) can be helpful in setting priorities and making decisions in a dialog between laypeople and professionals. These must then be condensed into a consistent synthesis.[76]

At the end of Phase 0, the usage requirements and development goals are summarized graphically and in text form in a project description—supplemented by a usage concept, which must be reviewed for feasibility and expected costs at an early stage, especially in the case of reconstruction. If necessary, these findings can then be examined in more detail as part of a feasibility study. Initial cost estimates are usually made using generalized space-based parameters (m^2/m^3). Based on this first synthesis plan, which should be as reliable as possible, a political decision must be made to determine the space allocation plan, costs, schedule, and procedure. The school community—consisting of students, teachers, other school staff, and parents—must be involved in the assessment of needs and target definition. This involves important translation work. Since development options are often difficult to imagine, a sketch-style visualization of the spatial organization in the form of alternatives is helpful. Only then will users be able to understand the consequences of their demands and decisions. It is recommended that the results of Phase 0 be bindingly adopted as a development goal by the school conference (the school's highest decision-making body, made up of staff, students, and parent representatives). This creates planning security for the school administration, even in the event of personnel changes, and underscores the binding nature of the process to municipal decision-makers.

76
Recently, it has become apparent that with the establishment of the term, more and more fields of activity are being integrated into Phase 0, which means that it often loses its specific role at the interface between pedagogy and architecture.

Planning (HOAI service phases 1–5)

The architectural design is developed in HOAI service phases 1–3. In the case of new school buildings, architectural competitions are often used to select the best design from several options. A jury decides on the winners according to defined criteria and recommends the implementation of one concept to the politicians. As an alternative to competitions, other selection procedures (in Germany known as »VOF-Verfahren«) are increasingly used, particularly for reconstruction projects, where the selection is based primarily on references, fee offers, and, if applicable, an initial design sketch. For investments of around two million euros or more, a public, Europe-wide tendering procedure must be held if the municipal authority is the commissioning body. A public tendering is not required if the municipality itself is responsible for the design. For smaller construction projects, three competing bids are usually solicited. The preliminary design (Phase 2) is then used to develop an architectural design proposal for the new or reconstructed building. Early cooperation with specialist planners in the sense of an integrated planning solution plays an important role—especially for reconstruction projects. In addition to structural engineering and building services, fire safety must also be considered. Once the design planning and cost calculation (Phase 3) are complete, the municipal authority usually decides on further implementation by means of a construction resolution. This decision is typically prepared by the relevant committees (finance committee, building committee, etc.) and then adopted by the city council.

Users must also be directly involved in design planning. It is often necessary to convince the administration and architects of this. However, such cooperative procedures have proven their worth in terms of both quality assurance and legitimization of political decisions and are increasingly being adopted.

Approval planning (Phase 4), the preparation of the planning documents for the building application, is followed by implementation planning (Phase 5). At this stage, all the necessary details are worked out, materials are sampled, and tenders are prepared for contractors. The design phase (Phase 3) should include a concept for the furnishings, which will be further developed in the implementation phase. Again, it is important to ensure coordination with the users, as many equipment-related decisions are only finalized at this stage. The involvement of the school in this planning step is urgently required, since daily school life is largely shaped by the alignment of space, equipment, and usage concept.[77]

77
Cf. Seydel (2023), pp. 24–27

Implementation (HOAI service phases 6–9)

Once the specifications have been developed, tenders for the construction work are solicited and contracts are awarded: either as a complete package to a general contractor or in individual lots to the various trades (Phases 6–7). During the subsequent project supervision (Phase 8), regular construction site meetings must be held and a constant, often tedious coordination process must be carried out. This makes it all the more important to use the construction site as a learning and teaching opportunity. The execution phase ends with the completion of a building or reconstruction.

The inauguration ceremony marks the (provisional) completion of the project. Commissioning is accompanied by documentation and an inspection to identify and correct defects (Phase 9). For the facility management team, this marks the start of the building's operation and maintenance phase, which, when considered over the full lifecycle, can account for up to 80 percent of a building's total investment.

Phase 10: commissioning

Like Phase 0, Phase 10 is not part of the HOAI. Nevertheless, it plays an important role. The commissioning process requires a period of review and optimization. Adequate monitoring can cover the first two years of a building's use, or optionally, it can be an ongoing process accompanying the users' appropriation, interpretation, and further development of the building to ensure sustainable and successful use of the facility. After all, a building comes to life with its users. And users need time to discover the spatial potential that supports educational activities. Needs, users, and local requirements may change. If necessary, it may be useful to establish a regular training program to help teachers make the most of the opportunities offered by the new spatial concept. The relationship between users and their environment, which was established in Phase 0, continues in Phase 10. This is an important prerequisite for strengthening the users' responsibility for the spaces in the long term. At the end of the first year of operation, a systematic evaluation of the building and its suitability for everyday use should be carried out: Is the building functioning as intended in Phase 0? Post-occupancy evaluation procedures, which are common in other construction projects, should also be applied to school construction in the future. The results should be shared with all those involved in the planning and decision-making processes. Possible improvements or adjustments to the use of space are identified. School authorities and school construction planners could use the results of such evaluation of Phase 0 and the subsequent planning phases for future school construction projects. It is important to ensure that adequate planning resources are available for Phase 10.[78]

78 Cf. Montag Stiftung Jugend und Gesellschaft (Ed.) (2025a)

PROCESS CONTROL

Quality assurance I: steering groups

An internal school project group »construction« should be established for the planning phase. This group should include the school leadership, teaching staff, and representatives from the various departments. Selective or continuous involvement of students and parents should be sought.

Managing a planning and participation process also requires transparency. Regular meetings between the municipal departments and the schools must be held from the start of the project until handover. This is independent of the planning meetings between the specialist planners. A steering group should therefore be established at the municipal level to work with the school project group »construction« through formalized coordination processes.

School construction consultants can ensure effective interdisciplinary collaboration. As external consultants from the fields of education and architecture they professionally manage and moderate the integration of specialist disciplines throughout the entire process.

Quality assurance II: procedures

Competitive planning processes—such as architectural competitions or multiple commissioning—provide the opportunity to reach an optimal decision by evaluating different planning proposals. They have proven to be an essential component of quality assurance. Cooperative procedures, which are not subject to anonymity, cover the participation requirements well and can be carried out in accordance with the guidelines for planning competitions (RPW 2013). Representatives of the user community and local politicians should be involved in jury meetings and site visits—not least to give them a better understanding of the relationship between quality and cost.

While the school department usually takes the lead in project development at the start of the project and drives coordination with other municipal departments, responsibility is usually transferred to the building department once the basic decision on the measures has been made. The opening of the completed building is then usually done again by the school department, possibly in cooperation with the building department.

Drivers in the process

Essential to the planning process is the role—usually not »formalized«—of the drivers, who

- set the process in motion and define goals;
- transfer the dynamics of the process to all stakeholder and decision-making levels;
- repeatedly provide energy, ideas, and resources to keep the process alive;
- keep an eye on the organizational and strategic implementation;
- stand for the realization of the project with conviction and passion.

The drivers of a process can come from all areas involved in planning: from administration, politics, planning or process control, school leadership, staff, parents, external architecture or project management offices. The role of the drivers should not be confused with that of project coordination in the planning process.

The stakeholders' understanding of time

Those involved in school planning often have very different perceptions of time. The rigid deadlines of a construction schedule and the open timelines of a pedagogical development process are often worlds apart. It is important to establish a direct relationship between the two and to create awareness among all stakeholders of different time and decision-making cultures with their specific necessities and constraints.

(Interim) school leadership

When setting up a new school, it is important to establish an interim school leadership team, supported by a small advisory group, during the planning phase to represent the future school's educational requirements and user needs during the development phase. A successful approach in this context has been to assign mentoring schools—existing schools that temporarily represent the interests of the future school. In the case of extensions, reconstructions, or renovations, the process is easier because the groups needed to work through the process are already in place.

DECISION-MAKING PROCESSES

Interaction between stakeholders and decision-makers

Ultimately, a construction project is decided by local politicians. Key political decision-makers must be identified in advance, and their involvement in the process must be well planned. It is important to give everyone a role that is conducive to decision-making. It is particularly useful to thoroughly brief political representatives on participatory processes in advance. To avoid partisan instrumentalization, all participants should commit themselves at the beginning of the planning and participation process to a fixed procedure and a timeline during which guidelines for further development in the interaction between education, administration, and architecture are defined. Intermediate results are communicated and exchanged. Ideally, the development processes of decision-makers and stakeholders are coordinated by a steering body that knows and understands the perspectives of all participants and is recognized by all. Well-prepared interim steps facilitate the decision-making process.

Decision-makers

Every school construction process has different phases, with decisions and resolutions required at the transitions between them. The more complex a project, the more complex the relationships and interdependencies between the decision-making stages. If the process is to run as smoothly as possible, there must be clarity from the outset about all the decision-making stages and the corresponding responsibilities. At the beginning of the project, it must be determined which stakeholders will be involved in making decisions at which project stage, and how the decision-making processes at the pedagogical, planning, and administrative levels will be coordinated and kept transparent for all parties involved.

The decision-makers are all those involved in the political decision-making process in the city council and in the committees—usually, for example, the urban development committee, school committee, youth welfare committee, building committee, municipal building management board, district council, and others. In many municipalities, this structure is leaner and therefore less complex. Other key actors include the mayor, the board of directors, department heads, and directors of departments or offices as representatives of the municipal administration. The school participation committees must make decisions in the context of construction planning that have an impact on the educational concept. In addition, the lower and upper education authorities may be involved in decisions. Compared to other countries, this situation is complex because it is specific to each school and very confusing. It does not correspond to the overall school approach proposed by the UN.

Factors for »good« decisions and resolutions

Decisions need to be made and coordinated at different analytical and operational levels:

— construction planning (of all decision stations and their sequences);
— participation process (of decision-makers, stakeholders, and the public);
— information (through meaningful, well-prepared reports and documentation, as well as targeted use of interactive media);
— facilitation (by neutral, competent experts recognized by all).

Information is everything

When decision-makers are involved in the process, the key is to provide them with comprehensive, efficient, and targeted information. Decision-relevant data must be easily accessible to all interested parties. Form is important: too much or incorrect information can overwhelm stakeholders or risk disengagement from the process. Interim information should only be provided when there is real progress and a new status.

Not a decision-maker, but a decision-shaping force: the public

The public, public opinion, the press, and the Internet are external factors that can have a massive impact on a decision-making process. There is a considerable public interest in matters of education—even from people not directly involved in the process but want to be stay informed about the progress of the project. This public has a right to be informed. The press must be taken seriously as an independent party from the outset, as it often has its own interests. If, despite good communication, there are misleading or even false reports in the press, it is all the more important that the project management, in consultation with the project and steering groups involved, has its own communication channels and strategies to answer questions from the interested public. The Internet has proven to be particularly effective for good communication: In addition to regular and well-coordinated information on the municipality and school websites, forums and blogs, live chats with municipal and administrative decision-makers, information via social networks, etc. are effective options. What matters most is that the needs and interests of everyone involved in the project are taken seriously. Well-prepared, objective information should always be available to everyone.

PLANNING LEVELS AND STEPS

There are five levels that come into play in any Phase 0 implementation: Steering, Pedagogical School Development, Municipal Planning, Site / Building Planning, and Dialog / Communication. The steps that take place at these levels vary depending on the project, and the sequence (and duration) is not always the same. The following are examples of typical implementation steps. They are not intended as a model but as a suggestion for the project management team to develop their own milestone plan for Phase 0. The most important prerequisite for a successful design is the realization that each Phase 0 must always be individually conceived and specifically structured to the requirements of each project.

Survey / analysis

Project management

Chapter 5, *M1 Platform Formation*, pp. 124 ff.

— Definition of project management / structure / coordination by the commissioning body
— Clarification of responsibilities and decision-making authorities
— Establishment of a municipal project group to coordinate the process at the operational level together with the school construction consultants (school / youth / social affairs and construction / planning / open space)
— Formation of a steering group with members with decision-making power (school / youth / social affairs and construction / planning / outdoor space)
— Establishment of a school project group »construction«
— Schedule (jour fixe for project construction group, e.g. every two weeks; steering group every six to eight weeks)

Chapter 5, *M2 Pedagogical Assessment*, pp. 135 ff.

Pedagogy

- Review and specification of the pedagogical concept
- Pedagogical potential analysis: team structures, all-day school program, cooperation / educational network, social tensions, etc.
- Establishment of a school-internal construction group, whose members should have insight into the specific concerns of individual areas of use
- On-site inspection
- Expert lecture
- Visits to other schools (»learning journey«)
- (Online) research
- Key interviews on the pedagogical concept
- Definition of pedagogical objectives and initial presentation of resulting space requirements
- Decision to hold an Educational Day

Chapter 5, *M4 Municipal Baseline Assessment*, pp. 161 ff.

79
The planning dimension »municipal planning« plays an important role throughout the entire planning process; questions about location and distribution arise time and again. However, as these decisions should be made as early as possible in the planning process, this category is only included in the survey phase.

Municipal planning[79]

- Alignment of needs report with school development plan
- Review of criteria for school development planning
- If not available, preparation / revision of the municipal school development plan
- If necessary, addition of qualitative criteria
- Evaluation of the location in the community context
- Decision on future development of the location
- Clarification of the need to involve additional experts

Chapter 5, *M5 Site and Building Assessment*, pp. 165 ff.

Site and building planning

- Spatial analysis of the existing conditions
- On-site inspection
- Key interviews on the initial spatial situation (individually with key stakeholders)
- Review of preliminary planning considerations (e.g. concepts, reconstruction plans), space requirement calculations / comparisons, status quo—guidelines
- Evaluation of existing building(s) on the basis of as-built surveys, potential refurbishment needs, reconstruction potential, repurposing options, analysis of individual spatial components
- Urban context analysis: education & neighborhood, open spaces, etc.
- Objective: development of a concept study on spatial allocation / organizational structure

Chapter 5, *M3 Dialog*, pp. 158 ff.

Dialog / Communication

- Clarification of the initial situation
- Presentation of the current state and planning needs
- Creation of a secure Internet platform for downloading documents (protocols, but also references and case studies)

- If applicable, informing local politicians (alternatively, establishment of a political working group to accompany the planning process)
- Contact with the education authority
- Press communication, if necessary
- Workshop 1 with the aim of clarifying the initial situation and mutual information (»everyone knows the same thing«); presentation of the results of the survey; preparation of all relevant information; discussion in working groups and summary in a plenary session; documentation of the workshop

Project and education scenario

Chapter 5, *M6 School Program and Space Allocation Planning*, pp. 172 ff.

Project management

- Definition of milestones in terms of time and content (in coordination with the commissioning body); information for municipal administration and politics
- Ongoing meetings of the municipal steering group (every six weeks) with clear decision papers
- If necessary, feedback from experts
- Review and adjustment of schedule

Pedagogy

- Statements on the spatial organization models; review of the implications for everyday school life and the main educational goals
- Early formulation of initial thoughts on the relationship between space and equipment
- Refinement of pedagogical organization models for further school development
- Identification of potential networks / collaboration opportunities

Site and building planning

- Presentation of the interaction between pedagogical and spatial design criteria
- Development of a requirements plan and an initial spatial organization model based on the results of Workshop 1 and the pedagogical organization model
- Building on this: elaboration of (three) development scenarios aligned with the pedagogical guidelines and within the framework of defined space requirements (e.g. year-group teams or specialist subject room principle, focus on experiential learning or cognitive approach, etc.)
- Definition of urban development and open space planning criteria
- If applicable, information on the building's atmospheric and furnishing qualities

Dialog / Communication

- Workshop 2: presentation of pedagogical guidelines and spatial scenarios; presentation of space requirements; discussion in working groups and summary in a plenary session
- Informing municipal politicians and the local public, if necessary

Optional (if required):
in-depth elaboration on individual modules

Project management

- Regular meetings of the project group (jour fixe)
- Meeting of the municipal steering group
- Completion of expert report
- Review of investment framework
- Review of project schedule

Pedagogy

- Definition of the pedagogical structure and organizational model
- Definition of functional sequences for individual spatial modules
- Initial specification of equipment and furnishing standards

Site and building planning

- Evaluation of the scenarios (including cost estimates), SWOT analysis
- Exemplary detailing of individual functional modules in the buildings, e.g., cluster formation, integration of all-day school activities, connection to outdoor areas, etc.

Dialog / Communication

- Dialog with stakeholders
- Further workshop if necessary: presentation of individual functional units and development components at different scales
- If necessary, consultation with education authority

Synthesis planning

Project management

- Regular meetings of the project group (jour fixe)
- Meeting of the municipal steering group

Pedagogy

- Considerations on suitable participation formats in the construction process
- Elaboration of the »pedagogical interpretation« of the synthesis planning with development goals and their implementation

Site and building planning

- Development of a synthesis plan—considering the scenarios and components
- Presentation of the space requirement calculations / investment estimate (»cost framework«)
- Optional: presentation of potential implementation / construction phases

Dialog / Communication

- Workshop 3: presentation of the synthesis plan, discussion in working groups, and summary in a plenary session

— Consultation / coordination with education authority
— Drafting of a resolution recommendation
— Informing municipal politicians and the local public

Final report, recommendations for action, construction resolution, and further steps

Project management

— Regular meetings of the project group (jour fixe)
— Meeting of the municipal steering group
— Coordination of recommendations for action
— Definition of cost framework and coordination of funding applications
— Check of the project schedule

Pedagogy

— Revision of the pedagogical concept taking into account spatial organization according to the results of Workshop 3, coordination
— Preparation of draft resolution for the school conference
— If applicable, elaboration of further tasks for school development

Site and building planning

— Revision of the synthesis plan regarding spatial aspects according to the results of Workshop 3
— Preparation of the final report and definition of the cost framework, overview of possible funding profiles
— Working out recommendations for action
— If applicable, drafting of the invitation for submissions for the subsequent competition or competitive procedure

Dialog / Communication

— Presentation of results to school committee / building committee / youth welfare committee; acknowledgement of results; decision on further planning procedure, if necessary
— Consultation / statement of the education authority
— Informing the public

Suggestions for the concrete implementation and design of the steps in Phase 0 listed here can be found in the next chapter.[80]

☞ *See bibliography*, pp. 240 ff.

80
Examples of concrete implementations are presented, among others, by the documentary »Fünfmal Phase Null und Phase Null – der Film,« both published by the Montag Stiftung Jugend und Gesellschaft

5

IMPLEMENTATION

Modules for Phase 0

If a school wants to change, it needs to define and decide on construction measures. What is the best way to start such a process? How do you ensure that everyone involved works together as effectively and constructively as possible? What methodological and strategic support is available to ensure that the process produces reliable and meaningful planning material?

The following modules provide a wide range of suggestions, guidance, and tips on how educators, architects, and administrators can work together to prepare for the implementation of their project during project development and Phase 0.

The composition of the modules (M1–M6) reflects the key needs in the early stages of a planning process:

- M1 and M3 help create a common platform for planning and dialog between the various professions involved.
- M2 provides suggestions for pedagogical stocktaking and for reviewing the pedagogical concept.
- M4 and M5 focus on the planning issues of the municipal baseline assessment, site assessment and—in the case of an extension or reconstruction—the building-specific survey.
- M6 outlines concrete planning steps for the development of a spatial organization model by directly interweaving the perspectives of pedagogy and architecture.

At first glance, the variety of modules and the corresponding time and cost may seem extensive. This impression is misleading. The modules represent he modules are a toolkit that, when used appropriately for each project, can save both time and money:

- Not all modules need to be applied to every project; the selection, sequence, and time required vary depending on the local context.
- The consequential costs of inaccurate planning in Phase 0 are higher than the costs of using a carefully selected set of modules.
- The later planning objectives are changed, the more expensive it becomes; Phase 0 saves resources and reduces costs in subsequent planning phases. A systematic review and implementation of all necessary work steps in this phase is the basis for an effective and resource-saving planning process.
- The proposed modules provide a secure foundation in the form of a checklist and a solid basis for subsequent targeted and smooth implementation.

M1 Platform Formation

- Clarification of interests/self-image and image of others
- Priorities and objectives
- Establishment of a municipal steering group
- Clarification of funding for planning and project development (budgetary funds, subsidies, etc.)

M3 Dialog

- Discussion of pairs of term

M2 Pedagogical Assessment

Inspiration and Information

- Setting up a school project group »Construction«
- Expert lecture
- Visits to other schools
- (Online) research

Review of Mission Statement

- Walk through/inspection of the own school
- 10 Theses as a checklist

M4 Municipal Baseline Assessment

- Forecast of student number
- On-site inspection
- Analysis of existing school concepts
- Coordination of municipal educational offerings
- Location decision
- Objectives of urban development

M5 Site and Building Assessment

- On-site inspection
- Key interviews
- Evaluation of area summary
- Occupancy plan / layout
- Comparison with model space allocation plan
- Coordination of technical assessment
- Location and relationship to neighborhood

M6 School Program and Space Allocation Planning

Workshop 1
Analysis of initial situation

- Presentation of assessment results
- (First) determination of organization models for instruction, all-day schooling, subject teaching, common areas, team structures

OVERVIEW OF MODULES

The modules for Phase 0 together form the planning process in the early stages of a school construction project. Module 6, »School Program and Space Allocation Plan,« is the goal and focus of this process. The other modules prepare for this step. Phase 0 lays the foundation for all subsequent HOAI service phases. The results are to be substantiated throughout the entire process, right through to operation (Phase 10) and beyond.

Workshop 2
Scenario Development

A) Overall scenarios
— Alternative organization models

B) Spatial components
— Specification of individual functional modules in the buildings on the topics of cluster formation, integration of all-day schooling, connection to open spaces, specialist rooms, workplaces, etc.

Workshop 3
Synthesis planning

— Development / presentation of the overall plan

Recommendation for resolution

Option: Feasibility study

M1
PLATFORM FORMATION

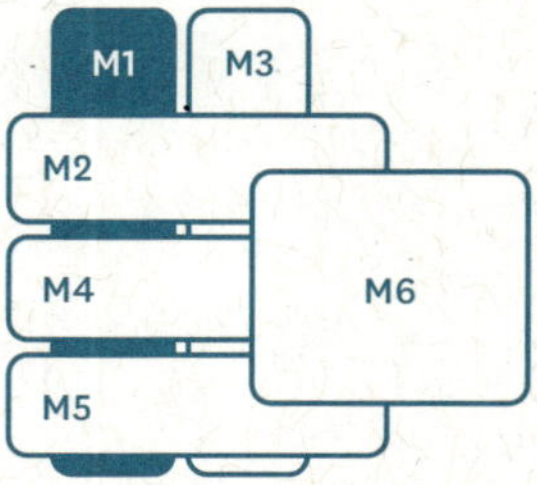

A successfully managed school construction project requires well-organized and well-prepared cooperation between the professions and stakeholders involved. It is therefore important to first establish a common platform: qualified and well-coordinated planning can only be achieved if people from all areas of responsibility talk openly, align their actions, and exchange ideas. Everyone involved should understand and take each other's perspectives seriously. It is important to establish reliable coordination structures, identify potential stumbling blocks, and work together to overcome them. This step serves to establish a common basis even before any content is discussed. As a result, even controversial discussions can lead to constructive solutions.

Experience shows that the following steps should be taken in preparation for the joint process:

— formation of a municipal project group to carry out the project work during the process, participate in workshops, and represent the various groups from schools, administration, and the neighborhood;
— establishment of a steering group in which municipal decision-makers make the necessary determinations for the planning process; it meets once during each planning stage;
— exchange about the different, sometimes conflicting interests that stakeholders, groups, individual factions, or opinion leaders of these groups bring to the process;
— raising awareness of and clarifying the mutual prejudices that may exist among the groups involved;
— definition of the different priorities of the groups involved and the order of the topics to be addressed during Phase 0.

M1.1: ESTABLISHING A MUNICIPAL STEERING GROUP

Phase 0 in the sense described here is not yet provided for in the fee schedule for architects or in the usual municipal planning procedures. To make Phase 0 possible, it is advisable to set up a robust organizational platform. The formation of a »steering group« has proven successful for this purpose.

Tasks

The municipal steering group should not and must not limit the decision-making powers of the various authorized bodies. Its main task is to provide a broad and constant flow of information to ensure a solid decision-making basis for these bodies, to coordinate the timing of the preparatory steps, to assign »homework« for the various survey and assessment processes, and to clearly define the project milestones. The process of defining the space allocation plan described in module M6 is consolidated in this committee.

However, the responsibilities of the municipal steering group do not end with the completion of Phase 0, i.e., the preliminary planning. There will always be a need for adjustments in the subsequent stages—from design planning to commissioning. Increased costs may make it necessary to scale back the original program. During construction, new possibilities may suddenly open up; and during operation, serious deficiencies may become apparent, etc. In such cases, subsequent coordination between all the parties involved will be necessary, especially when far-reaching interventions affect everyday teaching. It is essential to take into account the priorities that the school may have to redefine.

Composition

The number of participants and the composition of this steering group will vary according to the nature and size of the school building project and the communication processes already established in the municipality. Natural members are representatives

- of the school (usually the school leadership or delegates from the school project group »construction«);
- of the administration (school, youth welfare, and property management / construction management / procurement);
- of the education and / or district authority, if applicable.

The number of people and the differentiated roles with which these groups are represented depend on the local conditions. As a rule, the school and building committee and, if applicable, the youth welfare committee of the municipal council will not be directly represented in the operational business. However, it is important to prepare their decisions with comprehensive information provided by the steering group. The core of the steering group should not be too large (no more than eight members). Depending on the situation, it may be necessary to bring in additional expertise on a temporary basis—and in good time (!)—to address specific issues: from fire safety to heritage preservation, from residents' representation to landscape architecture.

The municipal project group prepares the relevant information for the steering group and condenses it into draft resolutions for the committee. It is important to incorporate existing administrative knowledge into the planning process.

At a glance	
What?	Establishing a municipal steering group
Why?	To secure the interfaces between school, administration, politics, and planning; to provide a basis for committee decisions
Who?	Varies depending on the size of the project; natural members are representatives from the school and the administration
When?	At the start of the planning process
How long?	Until one year after commissioning of the new building

Tips for implementation

— Binding membership with two representatives from each institution, who may substitute for one another if necessary; no alternating membership

— Binding schedule (jour fixe of the project group and well-prepared steering group meetings as milestones in each planning phase)

— Binding agreements on chairing meetings, minutes, etc.

— Creation of a common Internet platform for ongoing documentation

— If required: external facilitation (recommended for large projects)

M1.2: INTERESTS

The interests of those involved in the process can vary greatly. They relate to the direction and pace of change to the school associated with the construction project. The following module describes four different change scenarios. Discussing these scenarios makes it possible to raise awareness of different expectations and interests, to avoid narrow-mindedness, and to identify possible points of consensus.

Four change scenarios

Scenario 1: Everything should stay as it is

Many of those involved believe that all that is needed is new or additional spaces. They do not see a fundamental need for changes to the teaching and school processes or in terms of the architecture. The construction measures should be designed to preserves both the educational practices and the architectural structures.

However, the municipality, as the school authority responsible for construction, must not only focus on the current short-term interests of those involved. A school building must also allow for future developments, as the depreciation period is much longer than the now foreseeable period of use by the current teaching staff, and therefore also the ideas of today's users and decision-makers.

Discussion

— How can a school remain flexible in the face of changing requirements such as increasing or decreasing student numbers, new subjects, new teaching methods, or a new role in the community?
— How can significant rework costs arising from insufficient forward planning be avoided?

Scenario 2: We build the cheapest school and only for the next ten years

With empty coffers in almost all municipalities in Germany, the idea of looking for temporary solutions is an obvious one. They can provide relief for at least a few years and are the least expensive. Typical examples are container buildings or splitting the school across multiple locations—measures that were promised as temporary but often remain in place permanently and gradually deteriorate from year to year.

However, the community needs to think long term about the economic future. The quality of the educational offering is key to the competitiveness and social stability of a location. On closer inspection, therefore, school buildings are not a cost factor but a long-term investment. Given the growing awareness of the importance of quality education, parents, students, and teachers are generally opposed to short-term solutions. They may choose another school because pedagogical work always suffers under the pressure to save money.

Discussion

— What are the long-term benefits for the municipality of a sustainable educational offering?
— Which infrastructure measures—including school construction—should be prioritized?
— How can the construction project be divided into sensible phases?

Scenario 3: Everything should be radically different

Schools must be fundamentally reimagined. Alternatives are sought to contradict the status quo in every respect. By being different, the new school is to be fundamentally better than the old one.

However, while the call for reform is understandable given the shortcomings of the current school system, real-world conditions rarely allow for abrupt system change. In addition, radically »different« school buildings do not automatically change the expectations and routines of teachers (and parents) that have evolved over generations and can also overwhelm users.

Discussion

— What proven examples of sustainable school development can we learn from together?
— Which steps do we want to take now, which ones should remain open for the future?
— How could the teachers involved learn to truly use a new structural concept? Are they willing and able to engage in this learning process?

Scenario 4: We are uncertain about what and how to build

This scenario is the most common: questions about the use of space often cannot be answered by the school based on the existing school program, because the relevant interfaces between space and pedagogy are generally not defined.

However, given that it has not traditionally been standard practice to involve users of school buildings comprehensively in the building process, the uncertainty about what and how to build differently is understandable. Often, Phase 0 of construction planning needs to be preceded by a self-clarification of the school's educational program so that it can answer the planners' questions. In many cases, this clarification process can be coupled with a spatial analysis. The use of external process support has proven effective in obtaining reliable results within a reasonable timeframe.

Discussion

— How up to date is the school's existing educational program, and to what extent are the users reflected in it?
— What should the school's educational program look like in five or ten years? What are the main goals?

- What indications does the pedagogical concept provide for the spatial organization?
- How could a revision or a new development of the pedagogical concept be organized and designed?

At a glance	
What?	Preparing for the change process by discussing different types of change scenarios
Why?	To become aware of potential conflicts, to develop a sense of the conditions for success
Who?	College, municipal steering group, administration, politics
When?	At the beginning of Phase 0, during the survey / assessment
How long?	The use of the four scenarios and the time required for this will depend on the specific case

Tips for implementation

- It is important that the decision-makers in both the municipality and the school find out where the participants stand and how their interests differ. This understanding forms the basis for planning the next steps. This applies both within and between the groups involved.
- It may be sufficient to explicitly point out different scenarios, discuss the answers to the questions posed, and identify possible points of consensus in one of the first meetings of the municipal steering group.
- However, it may also be necessary to seek a reconciliation of interests with the help of external facilitation—either over a longer process or as ongoing support—in order to create the necessary foundation.

M1.3: SELF-IMAGES AND IMAGES OF OTHERS

The people involved in the school construction process come from very different backgrounds. They often know very little about the other groups involved. Nevertheless, they get an idea—often unconsciously—based on existing prejudices and stereotypes. The following module helps raise awareness of such perceptions. It addresses the difference between self-image and image of others, opening up perspectives on the specific potential of all those involved in the process.

Stereotype / Prejudice

Students
— have no desire
— treat equipment, the premises, and buildings carelessly
— do not adhere to rules

Potential

— like to join in if you let them
— identify with their school
— have many ideas about school as a place to learn and live

Stereotype / Prejudice

Teachers
— are lazy and only work part-time, are always on vacation
— just complain
— don't want anything new because it could involve extra work

Potential

— bring with them a wealth of knowledge and experience
— can contribute a great deal to the design of working, learning, and regeneration areas
— are open to new ideas if they are not left alone with the implementation

Stereotype / Prejudice

Parents
— only think about *their* child, they don't care about other people involved
— want to have a say in everything, even if they don't know what they're talking about
— are never satisfied
— seek confrontation, do not contribute to solutions

Potential

— are happy to get involved if everyone benefits
— are a diverse source of ideas, know-how, resources, and knowledge thanks to their professional and life experience
— bring in new perspectives as outsiders

Stereotype / Prejudice

Administrations

- only do what is necessary
- do not know what is really important for the school
- prevent rather than enable
- do not work transparently, do not like to pass on information
- like to show their power, especially when it comes to the budget

Planners

- feel like artists, want to express themselves
- only know school from the perspective of their own school days
- know nothing about modern pedagogy and how it should be translated into architecture

Politicians

- want to look good in public
- do not see the needs of the learners and teachers, but think in party-political terms
- are not interested in long-term developments
- must be urged to act

Potential

- know the guidelines and regulations and know how to turn possibilities into realities
- maintain an overview of the complex process
- ensure smooth processes and coordination with politicians

- translate user requirements into spatial arrangements
- get the best out of the available space
- identify room for maneuvers with limited financial resources and develop alternatives

- consider democracy important and give education a top priority
- have experience in municipal development
- are committed to municipal development—economic, social, and cultural—that can be achieved through good educational opportunities

At a glance	
What?	Discussion of stereotypes / prejudices and potentials
Why?	To raise awareness of differences between self-image and the image of others, focus on strengths and potentials
Who?	Everyone involved in the process / municipal steering group
When?	At the beginning of Phase 0, during the survey / assessment
How long?	The time required depends on the specific case

Tips for implementation

— A cartoon can help dispel prejudices and stereotypes among the stakeholders involved if it is presented and discussed at the beginning of the planning process in an appropriate setting as a humorous yet serious starting point.

— The material can also be used for a short role play, for example as a warm-up for the municipal steering group at the beginning of the process. The roles can also be swapped: teachers act as students, students as parents, administrators take on the role of teachers, etc. With the roles switched, the beginning of a fictitious planning process can then be simulated.

— If prejudices are too strong for a playful approach, external facilitation of the process is advisable.

M1.4: PRIORITIES AND GOAL ORIENTATION

The complexity of interrelationships in a school construction process is high. This makes it even more important for everyone involved to agree on priorities, responsibilities, and the order in which work should be carried out. The following module presents a series of key questions to help clarify the starting point for collaborative planning and agree on priorities and steps for Phase 0.

Key questions

1. What student numbers can be expected in the foreseeable future? How is the flow of students distributed among the different schools and school types in the catchment area? What does the municipality's current school development plan say about the school? Does it need to be revised? The school authority's clarification of the quantities is the basis for the entire planning process and is therefore significant.

2. Is there a milestone plan for Phase 0? How is the work process organized in the municipal steering group? Minutes, documentation, mutual information, follow-up checks, etc.?
3. Is there a school program that clearly specifies the interfaces between pedagogy and architecture? In particular, the school must make statements about

- forms of learning (ratio of student-active / independent forms of learning)
- department profiles (importance of specialist rooms / multifunctional rooms)
- social and active forms of learning
- team building in the classroom (individual class organization, year-group team, department-based principle)
- structure of the all-day program (separation model or integration model)
- new and old media
- inclusion concept
- aesthetic education (e.g., definition of focal areas)
- health education (e.g., »moving school,« outdoor space concept, canteen concept)
- democratic school (e.g., status of the assembly hall)
- sustainability
- opening the school / school and district

4. Is there a need for information on sustainable model projects in school development (e.g., schools that have won the German School Award, schools that are part of the »Blick über den Zaun« network)? Should expert discussions or visits to exemplary model projects be organized?
5. What is the influence of the state's school policy on the school? Are changes to the school structure expected that may affect the flow of students in the region?
6. What changes in urban development can be expected in the school's catchment area?
7. What external learning locations are potentially available to the school in its catchment area? What municipal needs might the school be able to meet in the future?

At a glance	
What?	Definition of key objectives and the process for starting planning
Why?	To narrow down issues, make people aware of alternatives, work out structures, define working rules
Who?	Municipal steering group with representatives of all groups involved, external consultants if necessary
When?	The tasks resulting from these questions must be defined at the very beginning of the process by the municipal steering group with representatives of all groups involved.
How long?	Half-day workshop

Tips for implementation

- The parties involved can agree on how to deal with these questions—a checklist can also be helpful, recording aspects such as »need for clarification,« »problems,« »responsibilities,« »deadlines,« etc.
- The outcome of working through these questions should clearly indicate: Who will do what and by when?

M2
PEDAGOGICAL ASSESSMENT

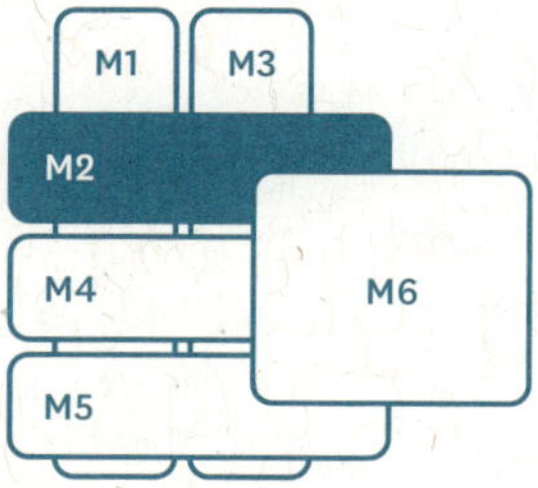

At the beginning of a pedagogical assessment, a school project group »Construction« is formed, which coordinates and consolidates all further steps within the school and coordinates with the municipal steering group.

There are many ways to get initial information and inspiration. Modules M2.2 to M2.4, grouped under the heading »Information and Inspiration,« present a number of proven approaches used successfully in many projects—including expert lectures, visits to other schools, and online research.

The next and central step is to review one's own mission statement, which will later form the basis for all building activities. In Module 2.5, a proposal is made on how this mission statement can be reviewed regarding future space requirements. If necessary, this can be further developed during one or more »pedagogical days« with external facilitation. The 10 Theses can serve as a checklist.

The appropriate approach and the number of these (and other) steps to be taken for the pedagogical assessment before actual planning begins will vary from project to project. Visiting other schools that have successfully completed building or reconstruction projects is highly recommended—ideally together with representatives from the municipal steering group.

M2.1: SETTING UP A SCHOOL PROJECT GROUP »CONSTRUCTION 1«

Preparing and supervising construction planning is not part of a teacher's typical responsibilities. Their core tasks are teaching and education, which normally consumes the time capacities of the teaching staff and school leadership. However, to include the urgently needed expertise of users in the planning process, it makes sense to set up a »Construction« project group within the school. This group can consolidate user concerns regarding the building on the part of the school and act as an interface between the various stakeholders in the planning process. Such a group offers the opportunity to reduce the workload of the school leadership, while also collecting and representing the wide range of experiences—and often conflicting interests—within the teaching staff and incorporate them into the planning process.

Tasks

Throughout the planning and construction process (i.e., not just in Phase 0), the school's »Construction« project group is essentially responsible for the following tasks. It

— delegates (usually two) representatives of the school to the municipal steering group for the school construction project and evaluates its results on an ongoing basis;
— ensures that the school, based on its educational program, formulates (and, if necessary, refines) its development goals in such a way that binding pedagogical requirements for spatial planning can be derived;
— initiates the process of goal formulation and definition required for this within the relevant school committees;
— ensures a continuous flow of information on the building project to all school committees—including students and parents—and takes up suggestions;
— evaluates the consequences of changes to the originally approved plan during the construction phase (Which changes might no longer be acceptable from an educational point of view?);
— evaluates the educational work after the completion of the construction project (Is there a need for structural improvement? Is it necessary to initiate further training measures to make use of the newly created potential? Does the school program need to be updated given the new conditions?).

Composition

The composition of this project group will vary depending on the size and organizational structure of a school. In small schools, these tasks will need to be taken on by an extended school leadership team or an existing steering group (which should then be relieved of other responsibilities during the construction planning phase). Larger schools will delegate these tasks to a specially set up group.

Depending on the size of the school, the »Construction« project group should comprise between three and seven members, with a maximum of ten. Depending on the school's situation, students and parents should also be involved. If it is possible to set up a dedicated construction group, its composition should be representative, based on criteria the school considers relevant for its specific case. In addition to curiosity about and connection to the topic of »architecture and school development,« the following criteria are possible:

— at least one member must be part of the school leadership team;
— if the school has different areas of responsibility in addition to the departments (e.g., all-day care, evening school, etc.), these should also be represented alongside the departments;
— including members of the staff council can prove very productive;

— a »healthy« mix of supporters and sceptics with regard to the upcoming pedagogical changes resulting from new spatial solutions is important for long-term acceptance. Members who only want to be obstructive are counterproductive;
— members should have expertise in specific thematic areas while being generalists with a holistic view of school and education.

At a glance	
What?	Establishment of a »Construction« project group within the school
Why?	To provide an interface between the school and the planners, usually through the school leadership
Who?	Varies depending on the size of the school: a dedicated new project group or an existing steering group
When?	At the beginning of the planning process
How long?	Until one year after the new building has been put into operation

Tips for implementation

To make it easier for the »Construction« project group to fulfill its responsibilities, the following steps have proved effective during the introduction phase:

1. The entire teaching staff is informed about the tasks (and defined »non-tasks«) of the »Construction« project group.
2. The composition of the project group is based on the above-mentioned criteria in a process that is transparent for the entire teaching staff.
3. The project group receives its assignment qua contract from the school community (e.g., from the general school staff conference, a school forum, or a school conference). This must be in writing and is considered an official commissioning.
4. An estimated time commitment is agreed upon (there may be relief hours).
5. A budget and timeframe for visits to exemplary schools (not limited to project group members) are determined.
6. The form of documentation and communication channels are agreed upon.
7. The project group members may prepare for their future tasks in an appropriate training course (e.g., basics of project management).

It is advisable to network and exchange ideas with »Construction« project groups at other schools within the same »educational region« at an early stage, at the start of planning phase.

M2.2: INSPIRATION AND INFORMATION I: EXPERT LECTURE

An expert lecture introduces the topic, raises participants' awareness of all relevant aspects, and can prepare them for possible stumbling blocks in advance of the process. For the suggestions presented in the lecture to be effective, it should take place as shortly as possible before the step of clarifying or creating the school's educational mission statement.

Contents

The expert lecture should provide insights into

- the broader cultural and social contexts in which school construction and new learning requirements can be seen;
- what it means to convert or construct a building that is also sustainable for future learning;
- the key contents to consider in a new concept;
- the necessary process steps and stumbling blocks to expect;
- the extent to which stakeholder groups can or must be involved responsibly, when and how.

At a glance	
What?	Expert introduction in the form of a lecture followed by a discussion
Why?	To introduce the topic and provide information
Who?	School staff, municipal steering group, representatives from politics and administration
When?	At the beginning of the process, during the assessment / survey, but before M2.5 (Mission Statement)
How long?	Evening event or half-day workshop

Tips for implementation

- Experts can come from the field of education or planning. It is important that they have already gained experience with school construction processes at the interface of pedagogy and architecture.
- One option that has proven successful is to present the above-mentioned content using the 10 Theses for the particular school and to support them with examples.
- Sufficient time for discussion should be planned after the lecture.
- During the discussion, activating methods can be used to encourage as many participants as possible to make their own statements or ask questions in order to identify concrete starting points for the following steps and to collect open questions.

M2.3: INSPIRATION AND INFORMATION II: VISITS TO OTHER SCHOOLS

Visiting schools that have already implemented new, forward-looking ideas is recommended for several reasons: old ideas about school buildings and classrooms are challenged and horizons are broadened. Ideas and suggestions from real school life are more convincing than any theory. At the same time, this is an important constitutive moment for the project and planning groups: those who travel to other schools and jointly search for further solutions create a valuable basis for a constructive process. For this reason, it is important to plan this step well and to involve all stakeholders directly. It is strongly recommended that as many representatives as possible from all the groups involved take part in this »looking over the fence.«

What should be considered when visiting a school?

Being confronted with a concrete example does not automatically have the desired effect. Nonreflecting reactions of school tourists can be quite inappropriate: ranging from uncritical enthusiasm to premature rejection, from lack of understanding to prejudiced unwillingness to know. Such »visual disturbances« are blockades to innovation that occur whenever an attempt is made to disrupt traditional images by presenting concrete alternatives. Four of these visual disturbances can be diagnosed using the criteria of »novelty« and »acceptance«:

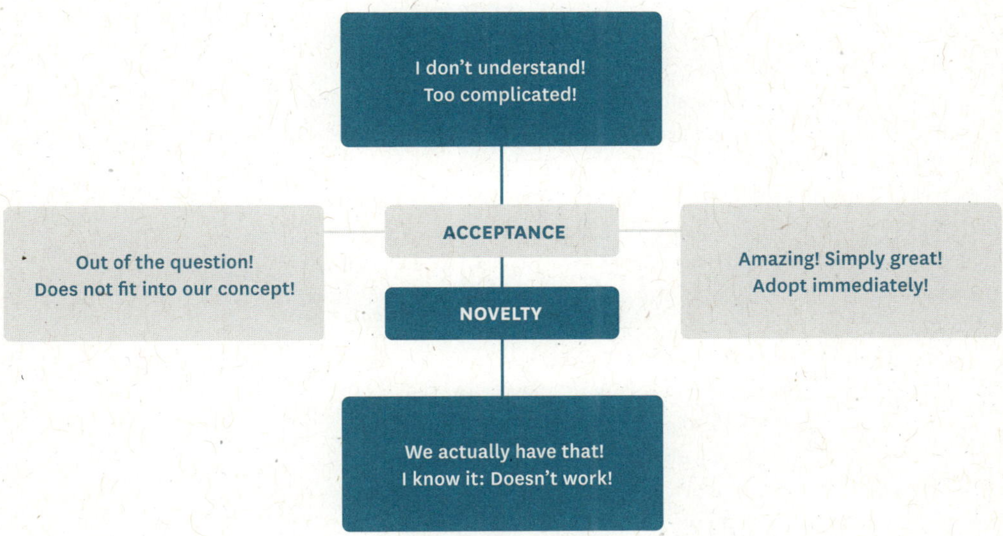

If the school visit is to be used constructively, it must be possible to transform these »visual disturbances« into productive questions. These make it easier to identify the interfaces between the educational concept and the individual architectural solutions of the school visited and to discuss the opportunities and risks of transferring them to one's own planning:

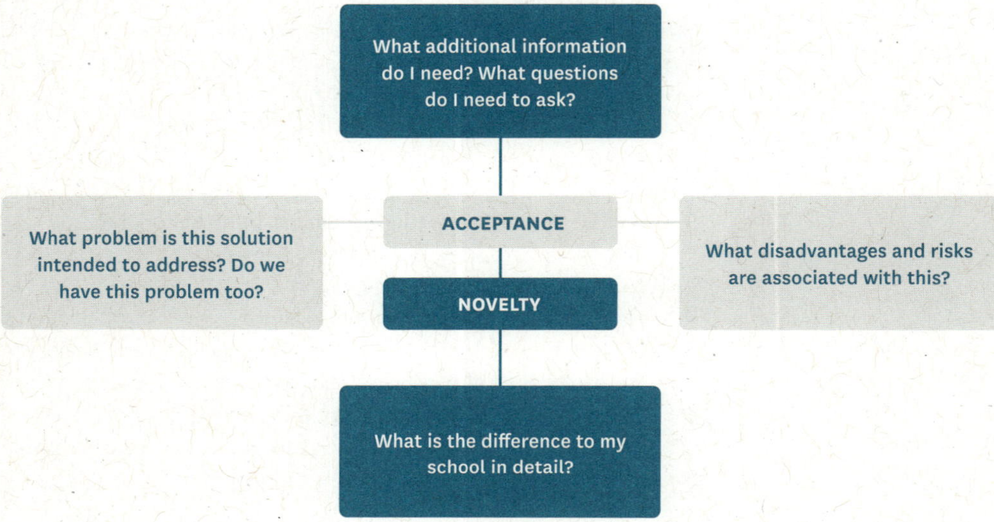

Questions to ask during a visit:

The questions to be developed before the visit must not be too narrow so that unforeseen but perhaps very important features do not fall through the cracks. Every school is different. Therefore, each visit will have its own specific list of questions. These should include conceptual pedagogical questions as well as very specific space-related questions. They can be derived, for example, from the 10 Theses in this handbook. Questions about the pedagogical-architectural interfaces are particularly relevant:

— What learning formats are available at the school?
— How was the school's educational concept developed? How has it changed because of the building design?
— What are the daily routines? How is the all-day program organized?
— What role does inclusion play?
— How is team building carried out?
— How does the visited school address in its everyday pedagogical approach and conceptually in its school program…
 … versatile, multi-purpose areas (workshops, studios) as teaching rooms?
 … classroom clusters?
 … flexibility and adaptability?
 … use of circulation areas?

… activity and recreation areas for the all-day program?
… »old« and new media?
… communication areas and workstations for teaching staff?
… the aesthetic design of the building (materials, colors, spatial relationships, etc.)?
… indoor and outdoor facilities for physical activities?
… sound insulation, lighting, and air; fire safety and fall protection?
… accessibility?
… energy technology?
… meeting places for the entire school community?
… opening up to the district?
… the issue of »expandability« and »adaptability to changing pedagogical concepts«?
… specific furnishing concepts for the rooms?
… etc.

Questions about planning:

— How was the planning process structured?
— What experiences were made during the planning process at the visited school?
— What was important?
— What was difficult?
— What was successful?
— What might work better for us?
— What has changed in everyday teaching and school life because of the new spaces?
— etc.

The more precise the preparation, the greater the chance that the effort will be worthwhile. It therefore makes sense to clarify the following questions in advance:

— Which form of visit is best?
— Who will participate?
— What exactly will be studied?
— Should certain specific questions be assigned to individual participants? (only advisable if the group is large enough)
— What written information should be given to participants in advance?
— What is the schedule of the day (including transportation, meals, etc.)?
— Who will take photos?
— What token of appreciation will the visited school receive?
— Who will be responsible for documenting and summarizing the results?
— How will feedback be given to the school / municipality / city / administration?

Where can schools be found that are suitable for visits?

- Academy of the German School Award (schulpreis.bosch-stiftung.de)
- School network »Blick über den Zaun« (www.blickueberdenzaun.de)
- Award-winning schools in state competitions
- Award-winning schools of the »Jakob Muth Prize for Inclusive Schools« (www.jakobmuthpreis.de)
- List in this book
- Pilot projects »Inklusive Schulen planen und Bauen« and »Schulbau Open Source« of the Montag Stiftung Jugend und Gesellschaft

Chapter 7, *Examples*, pp. 217 ff.

At a glance	
What?	Visit to one or several selected schools
Why?	To develop ideas, broaden horizons, find direction
Who?	Representatives of the teaching staff, the school's »Construction« project group, and the municipal steering group; if possible, additional representatives from all disciplines involved
When?	At the beginning of the process as part of the assessment / survey, before M2.5 (Mission Statement)
How long?	If possible, one day per visited school

Tips for implementation

- There are several ways to organize such visits—from a »flash scan« to a student/teacher exchange to a visit related to the specific building project. The choice depends on the interests of the participants and the current situation.
- It is worth visiting not just one school but several.
- The variety stimulates the imagination needed to develop new, individual requirement profiles for the planning process.
- Ideally, three groups should be sought as discussion partners during or after the site visit: students, teachers, planners.
- External support is particularly helpful when a school's own pedagogical approach needs to be developed in key areas. Consultants who are not involved in the own planning process or the visited school can provide outside information and suggestions.
- It is highly recommended to assemble a mixed group that represents the key stakeholders in the process—from school representatives, planners, and architects to political and administrative decision-makers.
- Experts such as fire safety officers can also make important contributions when visiting other schools. Involving them at an early stage turns those who were previously perceived as »doubters« or »obstructionists« into constructive team members.
- Initial plans and suggestions can be discussed during the trip. This creates a culture of joint constructive action at an early stage, from which everyone benefits later in the process.
- A preparatory meeting should be held in advance. After the visit, a joint evaluation meeting should be scheduled to reach binding agreements for further work.

M2.4: INSPIRATION AND INFORMATION III: INTERNET RESEARCH

In addition to expert presentations, school visits, and other activities, books and the Internet are important sources of inspiration and information. Such research can be distributed among the members of the school's »Construction« project group and then be evaluated together.

At a glance	
What?	Own online research on reference projects
Why?	To collect information, find and share suggestions
Who?	Teaching staff, the school's »Construction« project group, possibly together with municipal project and steering groups
When?	At the start of the process, as part of survey / assessment and halfway through the process, when own topics become clear
How long?	Can vary in the time required depending on the intensity of the search in relevant databases

Tips for implementation

— In addition to the sources and references found on the websites of the Montag Foundations, many architectural firms that have realized school buildings or participated in competitions for school building projects have now published extensive material on their websites. A targeted search for reference projects by architecture and planning firms can therefore provide a wealth of inspiration.

M2.5: REVIEW OF THE MISSION STATEMENT

If a school wants to define its requirements for new construction or renovation in a future-proof and sustainable way, it needs a solid pedagogical foundation. The most effective way to ensure this is through a school mission statement that has been jointly agreed upon by the school's governing bodies. Such a school program typically includes the following elements:

1. The school's starting point / location
2. The school's vision or mission statement, condensed into five to ten concise sentences
3. Concretization of the mission statement, including how it is implemented in the structures of school and teaching organization (e.g., all-day school)...
4. ... as well as in collegial collaboration
5. Short, medium, and long-term development priorities as a basis for school development planning
6. Binding statements on concrete steps for evaluation and future updating of the school program.

Steps 3 and 4 are particularly important for securing the pedagogical foundation of a building project. In our context, therefore, we are not talking about school program work in a broad sense,[81] but specifically about issues at the interface between pedagogy and architecture. The first step in the mission statement is to work out the pedagogical requirements that students and teachers put on the learning environment. Only then can the architectural consequences be determined in dialog with planners and administrators.

81 Cf., e.g., Schratz et al. (2000); Rolff et al. (2000); Brägger / Posse (2007)

In the following, we propose to develop key questions for such a clarification process along the lines of the 10 Theses. They can provide a certain degree of certainty for asking the questions that will be highly relevant in the next step of directly linking the school and the spatial program.

☞ Chapter 2, *10 Theses on Sustainable School Construction*, pp. 20 ff. and Chapter 6, Context, *The 10 Theses in the Pedagogical Discourse*, pp. 178 ff.

THESIS 1

Learning requires many and varied perspectives, approaches, and outcomes.

Key questions:

- How can the diversity of perspectives be increased in all subjects?
- How can the diversity of learning constructive, creative, social, situational, emotional, individual, etc.) be addressed in each subject and in interdisciplinary projects?
- How can methodologically different approaches to learning be created?
- How can the content-related results of all learners be made visible and presentable—also beyond grading?
- What preliminary consequences can be expected for the organization, number, size, design, and equipment of the rooms? What is necessary, what is desirable, what is superfluous?

☞ Detailed discussion of the spatial consequences in M6 *School Program and Space Allocation Planning*, pp. 172ff.

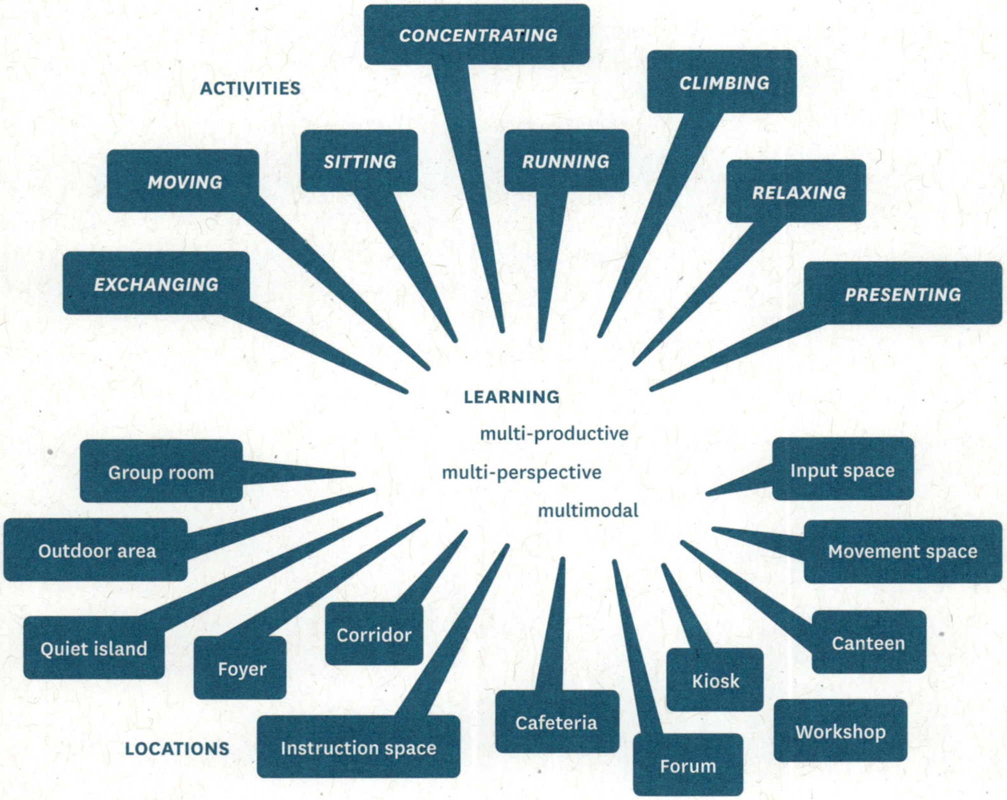

THESIS 2

Students learn alone, in pairs, in small groups, with the entire year group, across age groups, and also as a class.

Key questions:

- How important should the possibility of variation in social learning formations be for teaching (alternation between frontal phases of instruction and individualizing phases of construction or practice; importance of open forms of teaching, internal / external differentiation, etc.)?
- What role does inclusion play in this context?
- How can emotional relationships be developed into a positive school climate (importance of feedback culture; spatial organization, etc.)?
- How can teamwork within the teaching staff be developed (year group teams: yes or no?; importance of subject teams; involvement of teachers, etc.)?
- What differentiated learning environments do students need as a class, as a year group, or across age groups? Which functions should be combined in different room clusters?
- What preliminary consequences can be expected for the organization, number, size, design, and equipment of the rooms? What is necessary, what is desirable, what is superfluous?

☞ Detailed discussion of the spatial consequences in M6 *School Program and Space Allocation Planning*, pp. 172 ff.

OLD SCHOOL

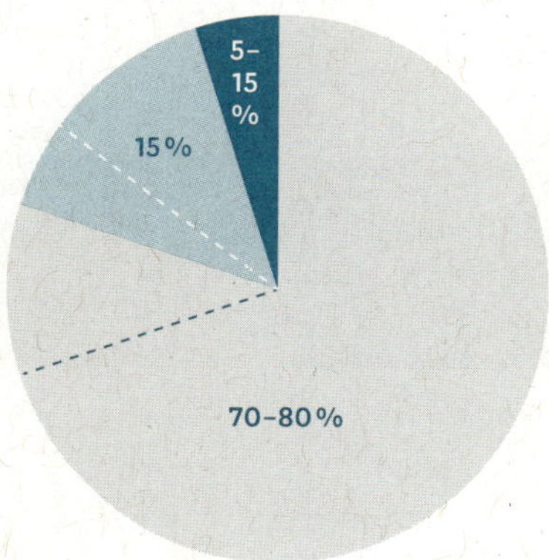

- Frontal learning, mainly teacher lecture or question-based teaching discussion
- Learning during homework periods outside of school or in short practice phases in lessons (students are usually left alone and often receive little supervision)
- Learning in pairs or group work

NEW SCHOOL

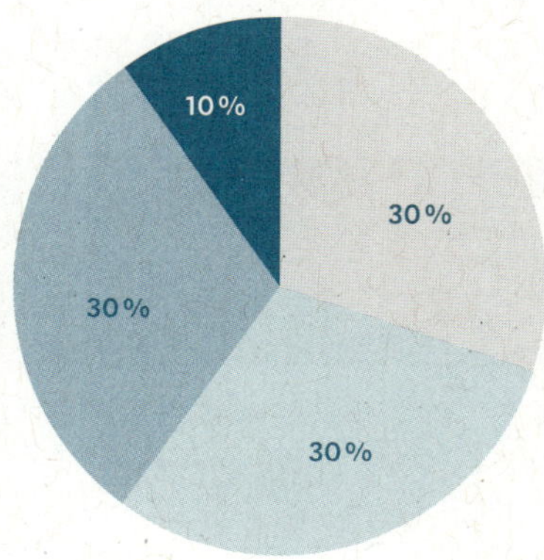

- Frontal learning, teacher / student presentations or question-based class discussion
- Learning alone, each student on their own (but not left alone, instead with clear, binding, verifiable work assignments and a sense of achievement)
- Learning in small groups (between 2–6 students)
- Learning as part of a class / learning group (ideally 15–20 students). Everyone can see everyone else. Everyone talks to each other and can negotiate common issues.

THESIS 3

All-day schooling means learning, moving, playing, romping, lingering, talking, eating, and much more—in a healthy rhythm.

Key questions:

- Which form of all-day schooling is best for students in the long term (integration model or separation model? Open, semi-bound, or fully bound all-day schooling, etc.)? Does it make sense to draw up a long-term development scenario, at the end of which there could be an integrated, fully bound all-day program?
- What kind of classes, differentiation, and specialization should the all-day program offer?
- What do students do additionally or differently in an all-day school than in a conventional half-day school with care services (eating and drinking—meeting other students—moving around—withdrawing, resting, doing nothing —doing homework (individual practicing, reviewing, preparing, elaborating)—trying things out, creating, designing—acting, presenting, performing—celebrating festivals—being able to seek help—meeting teachers, etc.)?
- How can a flexible time structure be achieved? How can a daily rhythm be established that is conducive to learning?
- How can time loss be minimized while still allowing for necessary breaks?
- How can time and space for rest and reflection be guaranteed?
- How is collaboration among teachers, special educators, social workers, and other (educational) staff organized?
- What external partners are involved (music school, sports clubs, etc.)?
- What preliminary consequences can be expected for the organization, number, size, design, and equipment of the rooms? What is necessary, what is desirable, what is superfluous?

☞ Detailed discussion of the spatial consequences in M6 *School Program and Space Allocation Planning*, pp. 172 ff.

Organizing the all-day program	Minimizing time losses	Designing flexible teaching and learning formats with the team	Involving learners as teachers	Managing self-learning
Rules for — daily rhythm and structure — lunch break — breaks — project groups — care/supervision	Rules to avoid — starting too late — ending too early due to substitutions — interruptions	— Projects — Workshops — Self-organized learning — Learning times — Theme-work teaching — Extracurricular activities — Individual development of interests	Students — advise peers — give feedback — prepare learning units or workshops — …	— When? — For whom? — How often? — By whom?

THESIS 4

The culture of digitality changes the culture of textbooks and chalkboards.

Data protection E-portfolio Social media
Samples Cloud services Illustrations Media production
Flip chart Beamer Books Learning apps
Scripts PC Software Models AI
Internet Mindmaps
Chats Senses Laptop
VR / AR Blackboard WLAN
Coding / Programming
Server Digital ethics
Smartphone Robotics
Tablet Video Objects 3D printer
Databases E-book
Document camera Posters Smartboard
Learning platform / learning management system

Key questions:

- What is the media concept?
- How can media be used to support learning?
- What media will be used (PCs, tablets, smart phones)?
- What is the approach to dealing with AI?
- What is the role of media in individualization and differentiation?
- Will a special PC room be needed in the future? Alternatives: (a) Laptop carts allow flexible use in all subjects; (b) personalized tablets
- What media are needed for different forms of presentations, documentation, exhibitions, performances (whiteboard or screen/ blackboard combination)?
- What software / AI will be used?
- Should there be a media lab and what functions should it serve (e.g., a small studio for student and teacher productions)?
- Does teaching provide not only secondary experiences through media, but above all primary experiences, direct personal experiences—taking a closer look, discovering the unknown in the supposedly familiar, allowing a second look?
- Are there »media-free« areas?
- What preliminary consequences can be expected for the organization, number, size, design, and equipment of the rooms? What is necessary, what is desirable, what is superfluous?

☞ Detailed discussion of the spatial consequences in M6 *School Program and Space Allocation Planning*, pp. 172 ff.

THESIS 5

Support in an inclusive school takes place in heterogeneous groups.

Key questions:

- How are heterogeneous learning groups organized (internal / external differentiation; synchronization / individualization)?
- How are school-leaving qualifications at different levels be ensured while maintaining internal differentiation?
- What individual support measures should be in place, and what staffing requirements are necessary? (Special challenges for both high and low achievers?)
- Are there specific types of impairments that require targeted support (such as integration assistants, team teaching, technical aids, etc.)?
- How can students be involved as teachers?
- What preliminary consequences can be expected for the organization, number, size, design, and equipment of the rooms? What is necessary, what is desirable, what is superfluous?

☞ Detailed discussion of the spatial consequences in M6 *School Program and Space Allocation Planning*, pp. 172 ff.

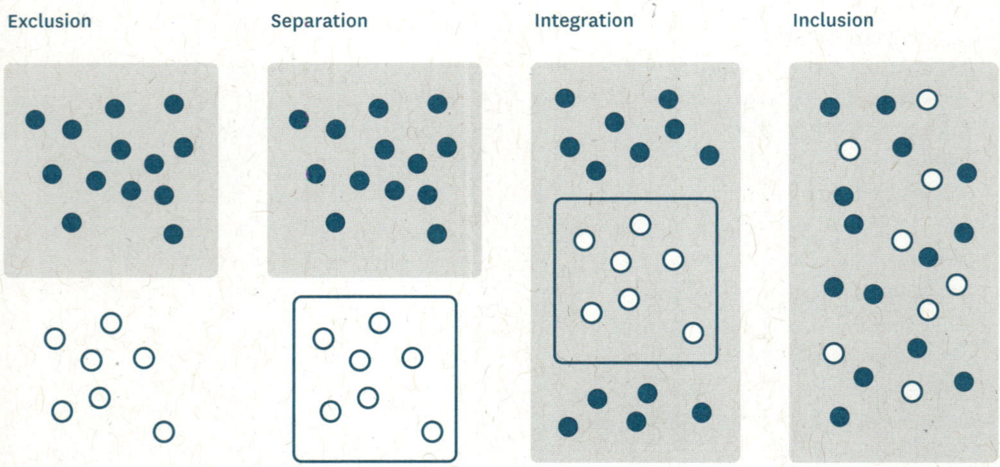

THESIS 6

Cultural and aesthetic education must be conveyed through pedagogy and architecture.

Key questions:

— On which area of cultural learning should the school place a particular emphasis in order to offer professionalism in this area and to provide students with opportunities for active participation and extensive creative freedom?

— What are the criteria for fields and areas that challenge the user's desire to design?

— Which workshop or studio concepts beyond the usual specialist room concepts need to be planned when creating a school profile in this area?

— How can the content-related results of all learners be made visible and presentable?

— What preliminary consequences can be expected for the organization, number, size, design, and equipment of the rooms? What is necessary, what is desirable, what is superfluous?

☞ Detailed discussion of the spatial consequences in M6 *School Program and Space Allocation Planning*, pp. 172 ff.

Drawing
Literature
Stop motion
Animation
Musical
Illustration
Jazz
Circus
Blowing class
Video
Design
Dance
Painting
Graphic
Choir
String class
Movie
Improvization
Comic
Podcast
Architecture and building culture
Orchestra
Percussion
Ballet
3D modeling
Writing
Hip-hop
Pantomime
Photography
Games
Theater
Bands
Puppet theater
Audio and video editing
Music production

THESIS 7

Learning with a focus on health and movement takes place in stimulating environments.

Key questions:

- What kind of indoor and outdoor learning environments and spaces does a healthy school need to support successful learning and promote health?
- How important are light, air, temperature, and acoustics?
- What indoor and outdoor physical activity opportunities should a healthy school offer? How should break areas be designed? What seating, sports, and play equipment should be provided? How much outdoor space should be covered?
- What are the requirements for indoor and outdoor recreation areas?
- What additional special movement incentives can be provided (climbing walls, streetball hoops, swings, fitness area, etc.)?
- What kind of cafeteria concept should be implemented (mixed kitchen, shift system; for younger students: lunch in the cafeteria or in their own classrooms)?
- Should other functions be attached to the cafeteria (coffee bar, kiosk, school social work office, games circulation desk, internet café, teachers' meeting place, etc.)?
- How can the cafeteria / school restaurant be linked to other functions (e.g., the forum)?
- What preliminary consequences can be expected for the organization, number, size, design, and equipment of the rooms? What is necessary, what is desirable, what is superfluous?

☞ Detailed discussion of the spatial consequences in M6 *School Program and Space Allocation Planning*, pp. 172 ff.

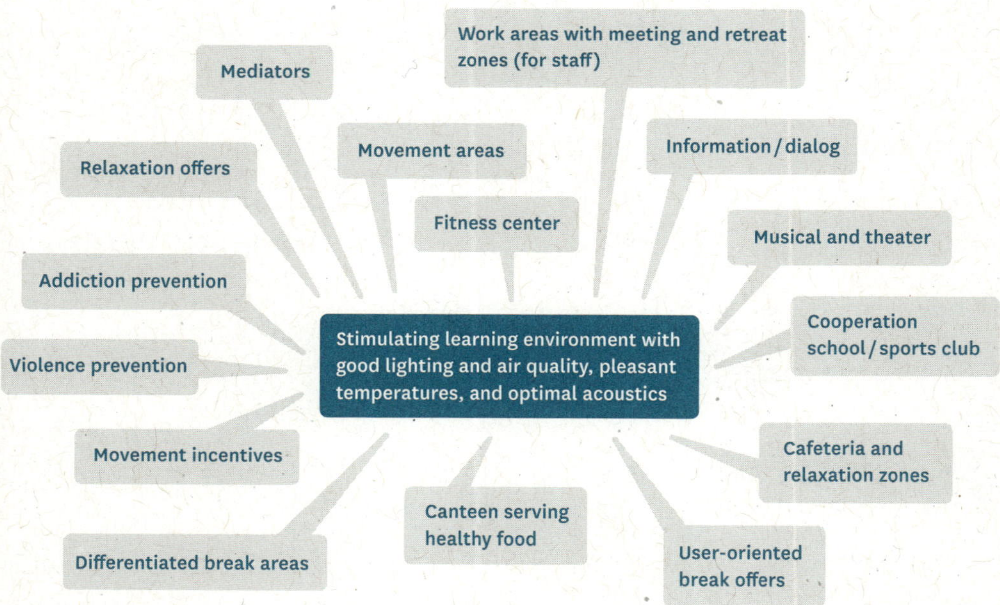

THESIS 8

Democratic learning requires a democratic school.

Key questions:

- How important are school community or grade level meetings (starting or ending the week together, etc.)?
- How important are student committees (student representatives, mediators, school medical service, mentors, etc.)?
- How should the common mission statement with common rules for living together be designed?
- How can social learning, mutual solidarity and support be positively shaped with the involvement of all stakeholders, especially the municipality?
- How can participation be optimized in the balance between co-determination and co-responsibility?
- How are conflicts resolved and how can learners be actively involved in this?
- How can everyone involved in the school play a constructive role in the building project?
- What preliminary consequences can be expected for the organization, number, size, design, and equipment of the rooms? What is necessary, what is desirable, what is superfluous?

☞ Detailed discussion of the spatial consequences in M6 *School Program and Space Allocation Planning*, pp. 172 ff.

Social communication	Solidarity	Participation	Dealing with conflicts
— Mission statement for all — Jointly developed rules — Social community — Joint parties, celebrations, activities, with the school opening to the neighborhood	— Involvement of all — Helpfulness	— Co-determination — Shared responsibility — Class council — School parliament	— Observing the rules — Learning from a model — Involving students
Support through architecture and design			

THESIS 9

School is a role model in dealing with the environment, materials, and technology.

Key questions:

- Which sustainability, resource conservation, and climate adaptation issues should be incorporated into the design of the indoor and outdoor learning environment?
- What does this mean for subject teaching?
- Which building functions that can be addressed in class should be considered in this context? How can they be made tangible, given the fact that many technical processes created and controlled by humans are now virtually invisible?
- How can all stakeholders be meaningfully and actively involved in the sustainable use of resources?
- What preliminary consequences can be expected for the organization, number, size, design, and equipment of the rooms? What is necessary, what is desirable, what is superfluous?

☞ Detailed discussion of the spatial consequences in *M6 School Program and Space Allocation Planning*, pp. 172 ff.

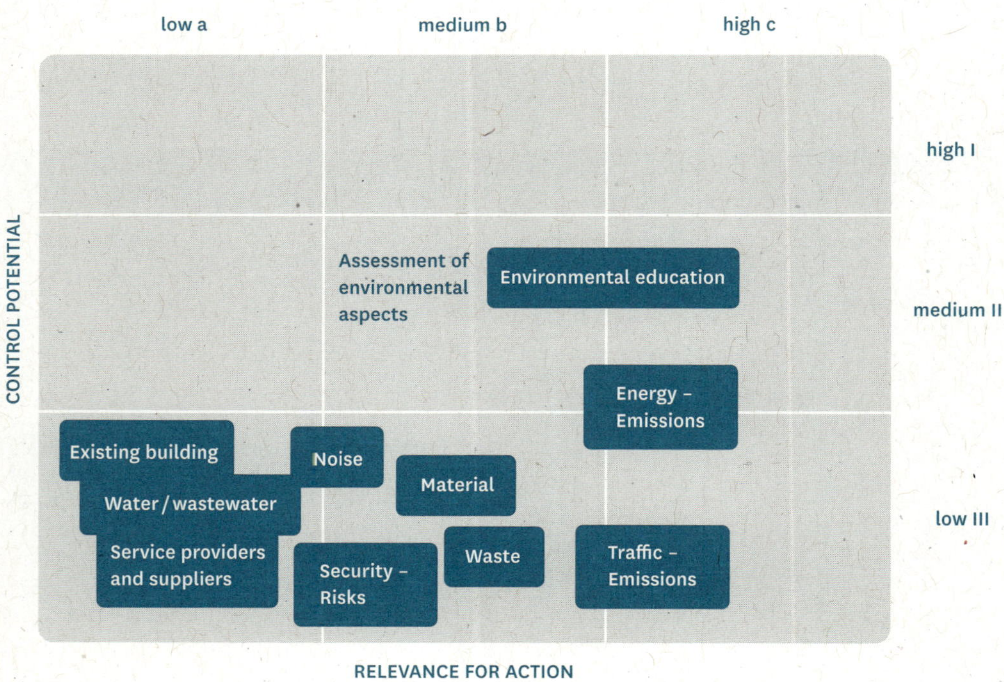

An evaluation matrix can be used for assessment and for clarifying priorities
Source: Matrix for the evaluation of environmental aspects at the Berufskolleg Neuss Weingartstraße, www.umweltschulen.de/audit/umweltaspekte.html

THESIS 10

The school opens up to the city—the city opens up to the school.

Key questions:

- How should the school open up to the neighborhood or the local community? Which areas can be made accessible to the community and which should remain closed?
- What fields of learning outside of school can be opened up and incorporate into the curriculum (theater, museum, city forest, craft businesses, sports clubs, etc.)?
- What measures can the school take to ensure that it is attractive to the neighborhood or the local community and contribute to the positive development of the entire environment through outward-oriented offers?
- What requirements does the public have for the use of the school?
- How can the school grounds be used outside of school hours?
- What preliminary consequences can be expected for the organization, number, size, design, and equipment of the rooms? What is necessary, what is desirable, what is superfluous?

☞ Detailed discussion of the spatial consequences in M6 *School Program and Space Allocation Planning*, pp. 172 ff.

SCHOOL …

… OPENS UP TO THE CITY

- Learning fields outside of the school
- Student-run companies
- Projects
- Events

… INVITES THE DISTRICT

- Inviting experts
- Offering rooms
- Cafeteria
- Educational offers
- Parental work
- Social projects

… AS PART OF THE LOCAL COMMUNITY

- Municipal mission statement
- Partnerships
- Library
- Playground
- Sports facilities
- Social work and youth welfare

At a glance

What?	Development of components for a pedagogical mission statement based on the 10 Theses of this handbook
Why?	To define and concretize pedagogical requirements and goals and discuss them in the context of spatial requirements; to create a reliable basis for planning tasks
Who?	The school's »Construction« project group together with the school development steering group, parent representatives, students, users
When?	After M2.2–M2.4 (Inspiration and Information), before M6 (School Program and Space Allocation Planning)
How long?	If the school already has an elaborated school program, the questions from this module can be dealt with in a one-day workshop (based on a division of labor); otherwise, an internal school process lasting several months must be expected.

Tips for implementation

- The discussion of the theses usually triggers a process within the school, during which far-reaching fundamental decisions about the school structure (e.g., formation of year-level teams, integrated all-day schooling, etc.) must be discussed and agreed upon by all school bodies. It is usually helpful to discuss the open questions during one or more pedagogical days either before or between the Phase 0 workshops, and then present them to the school conference for decision-making. To avoid significant delays in the planning process, it is useful to have this clarification process externally facilitated during Phase 0.
- If necessary, it should be checked where the planning guidelines can still be interpreted in a structurally open manner so that the planning process can begin immediately, or whether it is appropriate to give the school another limited time window for the necessary clarification process.
- For the workshop, it is important that the participants already have a rough idea of the planning processes and steps involved in a building project—where necessary, this can be provided through the other activities described in M2, such as school visits, expert lectures, etc.
- A structured walk through one's own school, prepared with questions, can also be useful for developing a sense of space and becoming aware of potential. This walk can be done within the school or with the involvement of representatives from the municipal project group. It should not be confused with the building assessment (M5).
- The educational stakeholders involved—students, teachers, caretakers, parents—can work on the key questions in a meeting that can be facilitated externally.
- These key questions need to be adapted or expanded in the light of specific issues. The graphic summaries—presented as either slides or posters—can help structure the discussion process.
- The results of the internal school consultation process must be presented at the end and documented in a protocol to be available for the further work of the steering group.

M3
DIALOG

The dialog between educators and planners is key to a successful school construction project. The necessary convergence in seeing and thinking, finding a common language, can be explored with the following module. The section below illustrates how such a dialog can be initiated, and which questions help reach a common understanding of categories and concepts at the interface between pedagogy and architecture:

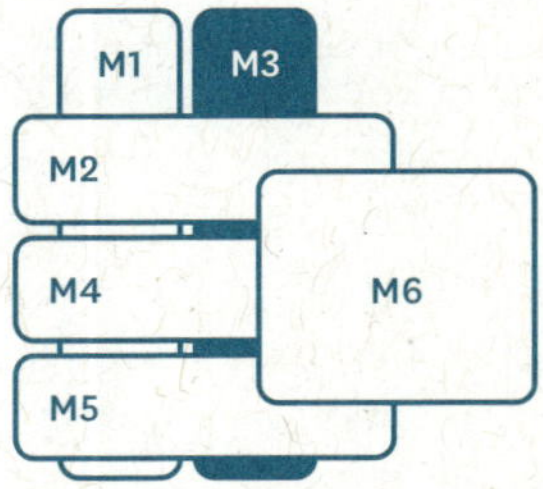

EXAMPLE: OPEN AND CLOSED

— What exactly do the individual stakeholders understand by »open,« what by »closed« …
  … in the pedagogical context?
  … in the spatial context?
— How »open« and how »closed« should the school and the outdoor areas be after the (re)construction measures?
— How can the built environment support the pedagogical idea of »open« or »closed«?
— etc.

Students should be able to work independently in open learning situations (open-ended in terms of objectives, methods, materials, etc.).

At the same time, students need guidance and control not to get »lost« in the complexity of the world.

These concepts are also reflected in architecture, for example at the interface between classroom and corridor: whereas in the past, sending a student out of the classroom was an act of exclusion and disciplining, the area in front of the door is now an optional work and communication space. The challenge is how to gradually calibrate openness from one area to the next. How much transparency is necessary to ensure a visual connection, how much separation (in the sense of privacy, freedom from disruption) does a space need? And likewise: How much acoustic separation is absolutely necessary?

The spectrum of openness ranges from open doors to glass partitions, which can also be closed with curtains or blinds, to open-plan rooms where only the furniture defines the transition. On the one hand, the room defines and creates zoning, but on the other hand, it also offers possibilities for change. Users can decide for themselves how much openness is appropriate at any given moment, when seclusion is required, when a student is encouraged to work independently, when a teacher needs to intervene and offer guidance, and so on. Such solutions allow for a variable degree of »open« or »closed,« adjustable by the users depending on the situation.

Changeability and flexibility here do not mean »anything goes« or simply using furniture on castors or folding walls, but rather the provision of a wide range of options. A differentiated and precise range of spaces should encourage users to make choices and stimulates their creativity in combining spaces. Both students and teachers need to learn to make consistent use of the interplay between closed and open spaces—sometimes by deliberately reinterpreting the original intended use of a space.

Further pairs of term:

flexible and fixed

continuous and discontinuous

familiar and unfamiliar

inside and outside

calm and dynamic

near and far

robust and fragile

diverse and uniform

finished and unfinished

Possible procedure

STEP 1: Selection / definition of pairs of terms
STEP 2: Creative phase: brainstorming on pairs of terms
STEP 3: Reviewing, organizing, and prioritizing identified qualities / issues / implementation ideas
STEP 4: Collecting open questions
STEP 5: Summarizing the results / defining next steps if necessary

At a glance

What?	Exchange between educators, architects / planners, and administration
Why?	To build a common understanding of spatial and pedagogical requirements and their interrelationships
Who?	All involved
When?	Possibly in conjunction with M2.5 (Mission Statement), but can also be carried out independently or at the beginning of work on the space allocation plan in the narrower sense (M6)
How long?	One workshop or several rounds of talks

Tips for implementation

— The module can be used in a variety of contexts in the early stages of the planning process, when creative ideas are still being sought.

— Any form of exchange is possible: for example, moderated or unmoderated teams, project groups, steering groups, or one-on-one discussions.

— The process can vary depending on the group.

— It is worth finding your own pairs of terms—depending on the time available and the overarching question of the specific project.

— Appropriate brainstorming methods can help stimulate associations: placemat method, silent writing (written conversation), image associations using a given collection of motifs on the topic, word associations, mindmap, etc. (for suggestions, see, among others, www.teachsam.de).

— Facilitation tools such as flip charts, sticky dots, etc. can help collect and prioritize questions.

— To encourage dialog between the disciplines, participants should be carefully seated in the workshop: first, by disciplines, then mixed; or deliberately mixed from the beginning (placemat method).

M4
MUNICIPAL BASELINE ASSESSMENT

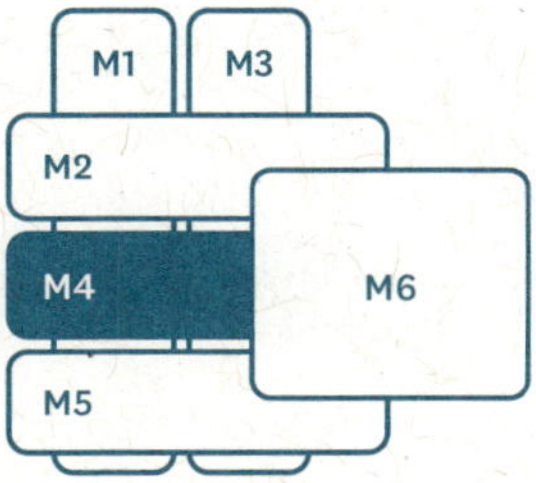

Despite limited resources and a massive investment backlog, municipalities as school authorities must ensure ever-higher quality levels at their schools. How can this be achieved? Individual measures must always be considered within the broader municipal context. To do this, school development planning must evolve into integrated, educational master planning. Beyond the isolated consideration of individual schools, questions of synergy come to the fore: the municipal educational landscape as a networked, mutually complementary system.

This requires a solid understanding of existing needs, the derivation of appropriate educational offerings, and—despite strained public budgets in many areas—the physical implementation of those offerings. It is not enough to distribute the predicted number of students among the known types of schools and to convert them into space and classroom requirements using standard values. What is needed is a qualitative discussion of current and future educational goals: the strategic design of the entire spectrum of educational opportunities available.

Municipal baseline assessment is the basis for such integrated planning. It involves a complex analysis of the overall situation, including the following aspects:
— needs
— legal framework
— financial capacity
— political goals
— priorities for municipal educational and urban development

The latter in particular reveal an increasing need for clarification and a growing scope for action, but also pose a challenging task. This applies equally to the concept of education and urban development.

COMPONENTS OF AN INTEGRATED MUNICIPAL BASELINE ASSESSMENT

1. Forecast of student numbers and their spatial distribution

— Even though local provision remains important, movements between catchment areas will increase due to the freedom to choose a school location and the growing specialization of individual secondary schools. These shifts will be directly linked to demand, resulting in disproportionate shortages or surpluses in school capacity. The analysis should therefore be extended beyond the narrow boundaries of the old school district.

— Particularly in small and medium-sized towns, school choice at the secondary level will be increasingly influenced by political decisions in neighboring municipalities (e.g., decisions to establish community, secondary, or even comprehensive schools in towns without a grammar school). Here, coordination is needed. Timely agreements on student forecasts can help develop realistic scenarios at a very early stage of school development planning. These, in turn, lay the groundwork for more suitable solutions later on.

— Official statistical forecasts on population development and the corresponding number of students—broken down to the district level—are available at www.regionalstatistik.de/genesis/online (German only).

2. Analysis of existing school concepts

These figures need to be assessed in the context of local school profiles and educational concepts.

— What educational concepts exist? What goals are the different types of schools pursuing locally? Which concepts should be supported from an education policy perspective? Do the number of parallel classes and their projected development align with a sustainable municipal school concept?

— These content-related questions are central to defining educational policy objectives and must be discussed in a second step with representatives from schools, school authorities, and the school supervisory authority.

3. Expectations for the future educational landscape[82]

— What expectations should a further developed municipal educational landscape meet from the perspective of political representatives of the school authorities, the school leaderships, but also of parents and students?

— This step requires the involvement of all stakeholders using appropriate methods such as key stakeholder interviews, workshops, etc.

82
In our context, »educational landscape« means the content-related and spatial connection of facilities in the catchment area of a school that contribute to education, i.e., combining the different types of schools and their transitions, local cultural offerings, youth welfare facilities, etc. in an overall offer.

4. Discussion and formulation of future educational provision

- In the fourth step, the contours of future educational provision are to be shaped in dialog with the stakeholders based on the first three phases of school development planning.
- Local politicians must be involved in the discussion at an early stage. This step involves categorizing expectations, long-term development goals, and medium- to short-term implementation steps, considering economic viability.
- Ideally, a sustainable educational concept is developed and jointly endorsed by all stakeholders through broad consensus.

5. Recommendations and resolution on implementation

- In this step, the jointly developed recommendations should be brought to the point where they are ready for resolution. This can be challenging. Responsibilities need to be clearly assigned, and a cost and action plan drawn up in order to establish a binding, politically approved strategic plan for the medium- to long-term development of municipal educational infrastructure.
- Through this step, political representatives take a position on the future of individual schools in the municipality. School closures must be considered, as well as mergers or the construction of new buildings in one location while demolishing existing ones in another.

Concrete and tangible future scenarios can be developed by thoroughly working through the planning steps of a contemporary school development plan outlined above. This can help make discussions more objective and enable decision-makers in politics and administrations to move from an often reactive to a proactive role as shapers of municipal school development.

A new type of school development plan also outlines the contribution of networked structures and municipal educational landscapes to sustainable district and urban development.

Only in rare cases is the outlined planning process for a comprehensive school development plan available before the start of a local building project at a school. In most cases, quantitative capacity issues rather than qualitative profiling criteria are the reason for revising a school development plan. To ensure that school development planning and Phase 0 processes complement each other, a step-by-step planning approach is useful.

At a glance

What?	Integrated analysis of municipal educational provision
Why?	To unlock the potential and synergies of existing educational offerings, and to define goals and strategies for future educational development. This is especially important when the existing school development plan is clearly outdated (due to changes in demographics, government policy requirements, current educational concepts, or changes in school choice patterns). The sooner action is taken, the sooner malinvestments of any kind can be avoided (refurbishment of school buildings or extensions at the wrong location).
Who?	Municipal steering group for school construction, comprising representatives from the education authority, youth welfare office, property management, treasury, urban development, etc.; external consultants or facilitators; school representatives and political decision-makers must be involved at an early stage
When?	As early as possible, at the beginning of the process
How long?	9–12 months

Tips for implementation

- Integrated planning is time-consuming but helps save resources. Detailed knowledge of the framework conditions avoids malinvestments and sharpens the focus on the overall concept and the ongoing development of the educational infrastructure.
- It is advisable to set up a dedicated, cross-administrative organizational unit responsible for school development and for fulfilling the school authority's statutory duties. This unit coordinates the involvement of individual administrative departments such as school development planning and youth welfare, urban development, and location marketing.
- Instead of focusing solely on »external« factors—such as demographic data or spatial/building conditions—integrated educational planning must also increasingly address »internal« factors, including educational policy objectives and pedagogical concepts in schools and educational institutions.
- Every municipality is different, has its own needs, financial resources, or political frameworks. The size of the municipality and its catchment area can also vary greatly. There is therefore no one-size-fits-all model. However, it is worth consulting successful integrated approaches in other municipalities for inspiration.
- A comprehensive analysis of the local educational infrastructure, especially when the process involves decisions on the closure of individual school sites, should be preceded by a survey of existing sites and buildings (M5).
- Planning offices that have already accompanied school development processes can help with planning and coordination.

M5
SITE AND BUILDING ASSESSMENT

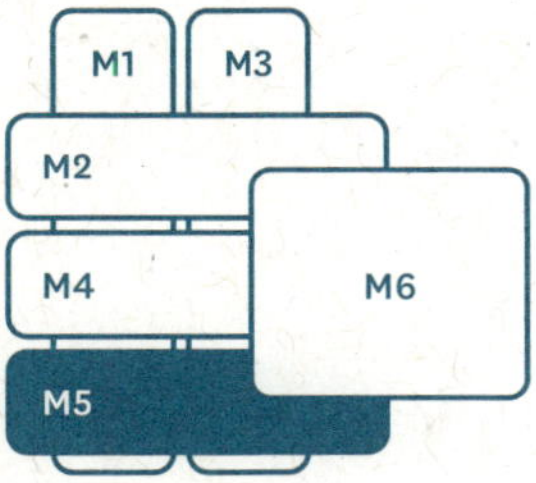

SITE EVALUATION

It is not only in the light of changing student numbers and the fact that many buildings are in need of renovation that municipal authorities are faced with the task of reassessing existing school sites. Fundamental changes in educational concepts also require a fresh assessment of school locations. Possible measures can range from new (replacement) construction to partial renovation of existing buildings, through to the complete decommissioning of a site.

With reference to the school development and educational policy objectives defined at the municipal level (M4), the following aspects need to be evaluated for each individual site:

Location within the city / municipality

— Location and accessibility
— Integration / environmental qualities: social, open space, built environment, etc.
— Synergies: opportunities for collaboration with other educational, cultural, and recreational facilities in the district / neighborhood
— Acceptance of the school use in the adjacent neighborhood

Property

— Accessibility: convenient and safe access, etc.
— Visibility: recognizability and presence within the urban fabric
— Connectivity: public transport (bus and train), bicycle lanes / footpaths, bicycle storage and parking facilities, etc.
— Immission: noise pollution and exhaust fumes, etc.
— Outdoor areas: size in relation to projected number of students, rest and activity areas, sports facilities, possibility for school garden / small animal husbandry, greenery and proximity to nature, etc.
— Development potential: extensibility, expandability of existing buildings, etc.

Buildings (rough assessment)

- Location on the site and accessibility
- Adaptability to user needs: potential for reconstruction or extension, etc.
- Building fabric / condition: assessment whether / where there is a need for structural, energy-related, or design-related renovation (e.g., pollutants, acoustics, lighting, ventilation)
- Spatial capacities: size and distribution, flexibility, adaptability, etc.
- Relationships between interior and exterior areas
- Site selection is particularly important for new construction projects

Building analysis

School construction often means school reconstruction or replacement construction. Converting and adapting or expanding the functions of existing schools will be at the forefront of planning considerations in the coming years. Overall, all-day schooling and the new demands on learning (see Chapter II, 10 Theses) will require additional space.

Chapter 2, *10 Theses*, pp. 20 ff.

»Hard« and »soft« criteria

A detailed survey forms the basis for an assessment of the existing building regarding necessary structural adjustments. Experience has shown that in the past, so-called »hard« criteria—such as the provision of the legally required space by school authorities, ensuring structural integrity, complying with fire safety regulations, improving energy efficiency, traffic safety, etc.—have often been more decisive than »soft« evaluation criteria such as usability, functionality, adaptability, or appearance. In many cases, these two levels of assessment were treated independently.

Seemingly unavoidable constraints resulting from the need for technical renewal—for example, dealing with fire safety requirements—frequently have direct impact on everyday school life. Unfortunately, such changes often result in limitations rather than improvements for educational use. Therefore, particular attention must be paid to the »soft,« use-related aspects of the building assessment.

Before entering Phase 0, the constructional framework must be clarified.

Quantitative and qualitative criteria

Just as on the municipal level, building-level assessments must also integrate both quantitative and qualitative criteria. In the past, renovation needs for school buildings were based primarily on quantitative assessments. A basic question is: Do the existing spaces fall short of or exceed applicable or customary standards? Square footage is the supposedly objective and »appropriate« metric for assessing spatial needs. In some federal states, this is linked to project-related funding opportunities. Model space allocation plans and funding guidelines are often interpreted as binding implementation plans, even though municipalities have more leeway. Recommendations and guidelines can provide general quantitative reference points for school construction planning. However, such

»guard rails« require project-specific qualification and adaptation to user needs.

Components of a spatial assessment

To identify the need for renovation and expansion of a school building, an overview of the spatial conditions is essential. This is best achieved through an on-site inspection and evaluation of existing building plans. This capacity assessment is complemented by a description of the school's teaching culture, activities, and patterns of use. Planning and investment considerations can only be advanced through the interplay between space and activity analysis, between architectural »hardware« and pedagogical »software.« The demand for »more space,« which has been made for decades in the face of cramped spatial conditions, is no longer sufficient; new spatial organization models are needed that reflect contemporary educational concepts.

On-site inspection

— A detailed building assessment should include the following information:
  ... room number
  ... building section
  ... floor level
  ... condition
  ... potential for reconstruction
  ... connectivity
  ... assessment of structural refurbishment needs
  ... accessibility and circulation within the building

— Quantitative and technical data on floor area and room use should be gathered in advance by planning and construction departments; if not yet available, existing plans should be digitized.

— The inspection should be conducted jointly by the administration and the school leadership, if necessary together with external school building consultants. Each room should be inspected and assessed—an initial assessment of the spatial quality and its suitability for everyday educational use should be made (e.g. by categorizing into A, B, C, and D may prove useful).

— All information and assessments should be documented using a customized checklist. The first step is to determine the function and use of each room.

— All relevant room categories should be included in the overview, as defined in standardized space allocation plans and funding guidelines. Ancillary areas should also be included as appropriate.

— When assessing rooms, it is important to note that the functional classifications still in use in many schools often no longer meet contemporary requirements. For this reason, the inspection should also identify spaces where particular conflicts of use arise that contradict the intended educational concepts.

— In subsequent planning phases, it is crucial to first mentally detach from the current state of the building. A useful principle is: school refurbishment should initially be conceived as if planning a new building. As the project progresses, the focus should shift from rooms toward activities and functions. This is the only way to achieve truly sustainable solutions.

Space requirement calculation / quantitative overview

— Based on the on-site assessment and the planning documentation, a detailed floor area summary must be compiled, covering both programmed and ancillary spaces: Which spaces exist, at what size and where? While most municipalities already have such data available, in the vast majority of cases it is not up to date.

— Experience shows that a tabular list alone is not an adequate basis for planning assessment. It is therefore advisable to visualize the floor area summary, for example by representing each room to scale (1:200 or 1:100) in proportion to its actual size. This makes proportions and spatial relationships tangible. Moving away from what is often perceived as immovable structural realities allows for new perspectives to open up and rethinking spatial allocations and room constellations.

Activity diagrams

— Floor area summaries and checklists should be supplemented by activity diagrams that describe the school's daily routines and pedagogical concepts: What happens where and when? This kind of »choreography of everyday life« reveals the direct interrelationship between everyday school activities and spaces.

— »Room notation models,« which record the activities and movement patterns of several user groups—students, teachers, administrative staff—in the building over one or more days, have proven useful. Among the aspects that can be identified are:

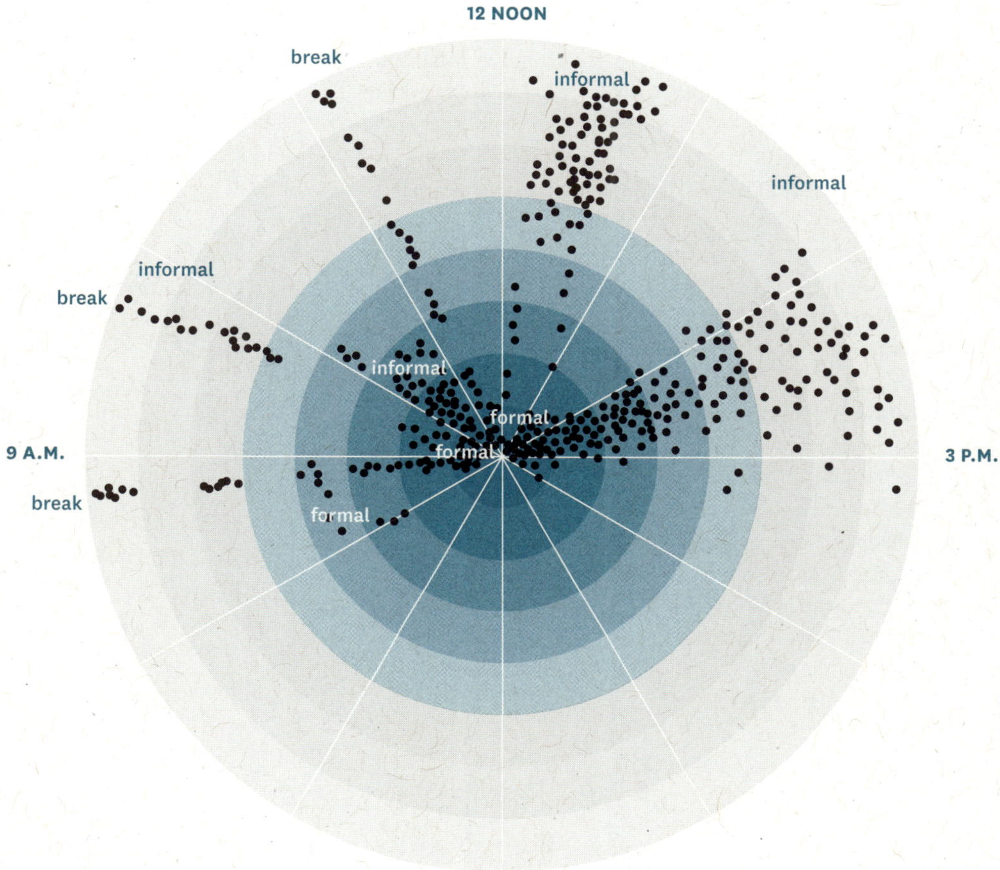

School grounds
Canteen
Foyer
Library
»Performing and Designing« specialist room
Differentiation room
Course room in front of the classroom
Classroom

Source: Based on Hausmann / Pfaff (2004), p.16

... What is the weighting of instruction, teamwork, and individual work?
... What types of activities can be identified—from reading to acting, from sports to sitting final exams?
... Is there a discernible rhythm, and how does it influence the use of space?
... How can a typical day be described—from arrival to departure (or evening use)?
... What activities are specific to certain groups and individuals?
... Who is where and when during the day, week, and year?
... What activities are particularly important in everyday school life?
... Can focal points / usage »magnets« be located?

Atmospheres

- The fourth component of a building assessment is an atmospheric description of the most important school areas in the existing building—supplemented by corresponding photos: What are the spatial atmospheres?
- Unsatisfactory spatial situations should be documented just as thoroughly as positive ones.
- A survey of students and teachers (questionnaire or interviews/marking points on a floor plan) can be useful for identifying atmospheres: Where do I most enjoy spending time? Where do I feel least comfortable (my »non-place«)?

Technical assessment

The assessment in the as-built survey during Phase 0 is based on the findings of a technical assessment. The conventional building assessment (regarding hazardous materials, condition of the technical infrastructure, building fabric, structural integrity, etc.) is not part of the actual Phase 0 process. Depending on the initial situation, such investigations should be conducted in advance or at an early stage, in parallel with, but separate from, the Phase 0 process.

- The results of the expert opinions for the following areas (list is not exhaustive) must be considered.
  - ... fire safety
  - ... structural condition of the building fabric (reconstruction / extension options)
  - ... assessment of energy performance
  - ... testing for hazardous substances (e.g., asbestos)
  - ... acoustics / air quality / lighting in existing buildings
  - ... access and mobility, transport links (school routes and local mobility)
  - ... etc.
- Many municipalities have defined quality standards for energy and sustainability for their new or converted buildings. These must be considered, too.

At a glance	
What?	Analysis and assessment of a school's existing buildings (usually due to upcoming changes such as improvements in fire safety, energy performance, etc.)
Why?	To provide a basis for decisions on necessary/possible construction measures and site development
Who?	Municipal project group, external experts if necessary
When?	Before the development of the educational and spatial programs
How long?	4 to 6 weeks per school

Tips for implementation

— A significant part of the assessment can be carried out by the experts within the local administration.

— External specialist engineers will usually need to be involved for the structural survey; adequate time should be allowed; the sooner expert reports are available, the better.

— A project-specific checklist can provide a solid basis for the assessment. Equipment needs requirements vary depending on the level of the school type—primary, lower secondary, or upper secondary.

— The assessment is an ideal starting point for a collaborative planning process: findings from the on-site inspection and analysis should be presented as part of the first workshop. This ensures an early and transparent—but also binding—planning basis for all stakeholders. Future planning developments should be evaluated on this basis. The results of the assessment should always be thoroughly documented.

— Good solutions are often the result of an intensive discussion of everyday school life and a mutual reflection of pedagogical objectives and spatial capacities. The educational program of the school and the implications for the spatial layout should therefore be addressed right at the start of the assessment.

— For future-oriented planning, a precise assessment of needs and requirements based on pedagogical guidelines is just as essential as the compilation of quantitative data for each school unit.

M6
SCHOOL PROGRAM AND SPACE ALLOCATION PLANNING

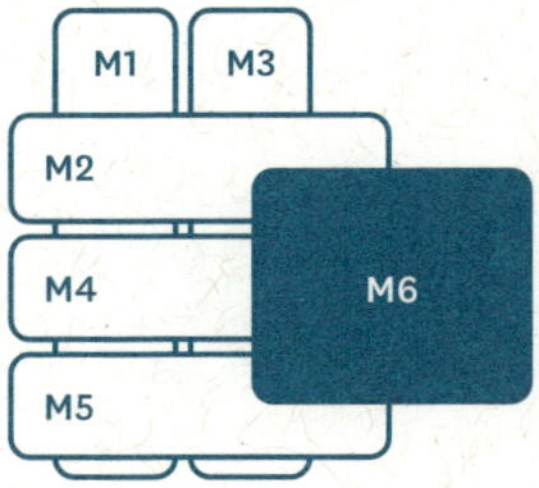

The pedagogical, municipal, and building-related assessment is the basis for determining future usage requirements:

— Which spatial organization / structure is future-oriented?
— How can content-related relationships between the various spaces be represented?
— How can existing spaces be reorganized?
— How important are transparency and flexibility?
— What kinds of spatial atmosphere should be created where?
— What are the potential options for reconstruction?
— What development opportunities does the site offer?
— What forms of cooperation with external partners should be considered?

Workshops have proven to be an effective tool to work with schools in an integrated planning process to address fundamental questions about the (re)construction of a school building. In the first workshop, the findings from the assessment are discussed and development goals are defined; in the second workshop, spatial scenarios (preferably three) are developed, which can be further elaborated in specific areas. For the third workshop, a synthesis plan is developed—including a usage and spatial program—which is then adopted as a recommendation for the construction resolution. Coordination with the steering group takes place between the workshops.

Given the wide range of issues to be addressed, it is advisable to involve external school construction consultants (peagogue and architect) specializing in school development.

Between the workshops (usually between the second and third sessions), excursions to relevant examples of school buildings have often proved helpful, as have pedagogical days presenting the pedagogical concept. In nearly all cases, the upcoming space-related decisions served as a catalyst for an intensive internal school development process and an adjustment of the school's pedagogical program.

INITIAL SITUATION (WORKSHOP 1)

In the first workshop, the findings from the pedagogical, municipal school development, and building/site assessments are presented in a systematic way. The focus is on sharing information and agreeing on a common planning basis.

Spatial usage components

Following the first workshop, it is important to develop spatial organizational models. It has proven useful to start with modular components rather than attempting to formulate a »complete solutions« right away.

For example, the closely related questions regarding the future design of the school's various learning environments should be answered. This includes questions such as: What is their basic structure—Classroom-plus, Cluster, or (partially) Open Learning Landscapes? What usage concept is associated with a particular location? What equipment and furnishing options need to be considered? What level of transparency and what proportions of space are desired? How should science and technology rooms be organized? What will be the »heart« of the school? What is the role of outdoor spaces? How does the »outdoor learning space« relate to other learning environments? What level of connectivity to the surroundings is desired? Interrelationships between pedagogical and spatial concepts can be directly represented in different themes, and the effects of pedagogical and architectural decisions can be illustrated.

Needs for decisions must be defined: Which pedagogical decisions still need to be made (M2) to develop spatial solutions? Where does the building survey need to be deepened? The aim is to establish a common evaluation standard that defines direct dependencies, for example: »If a rhythmically structured all-day program is integrated into the regular school day, then the following areas will be required for general teaching, the following in the communal areas, etc.« The »if-then« principle builds a bridge between usage and spatial organization, but also between the ideas of users, planners, and the city/municipality as the commissioning body.

SCENARIO DEVELOPMENT (WORKSHOP 2)

In the next phase, the usage modules are assembled into concrete spatial development models for the entire building (Workshop 2). Since pedagogical usage requirements inevitably involve contradictions and ambiguities, the various alternatives should also make conflicts and competing demands transparent to then set priorities—as comprehensibly as possible for everyone in terms of plausibility, acceptance, and consistency.

Typical decision-making questions in this phase include:

Organization of the learning environment

- Weighing of instruction, teamwork, and individual work—need for differentiation rooms—importance of the classroom within the cluster (dominance of one or equivalence of many different rooms)
- Integration of the all-day program into the learning environment
- Possibilities of clustering

Organization of specialist classrooms

- Equipment standards (from makerspace to special laboratory, from low-tech to high-tech)
- Flexible and moveable solutions
- Connections and synergies between specialist and everyday rooms

Team structures

- Central teachers' room with different areas of use or decentralized team bases with central communication area, or a combination of both
- Workspaces for educational specialists —integrated or separate (depending on the organization of the all-day program)
- Importance of individual workstations

Common areas

- Organization of library, forum, cafeteria, and possibly clusters composed of specialist subject rooms
- Arrangement and function of all-day recreation areas (degree of integration vs. separation)
- Connection, layout, and function of outdoor and sports areas

Fundamental architectural and design issues must be addressed, such as

- Openness and closedness: at the transition between learning space and circulation area, at the boundary of the cluster, at the interface between building and outdoor areas, at the transition from the school premises and the neighborhood
- Multifunctionality or mono-functionality: what can be achieved by rearranging with flexible furniture, where are fixed settings necessary, what options arise when combining different rooms?
- What kinds of atmosphere should be created where?

Finally, equipment and design principles are to be discussed

- Built-in or flexible furniture
- Color scheme and material requirements
- Digital infrastructure

The development options should not be seen as architectural designs, but rather as spatial organization models. Nonetheless, based on the spatial organization models and the square footage, it is already possible at this stage to provide rough initial estimates of the cost framework (high, medium, low investment requirements) and a structural plausibility check (e.g., fire safety and structural integrity).

The evaluation of alternative organizational models reveals the interdependence between pedagogy and space. Different spatial constellations must be tested for their suitability for everyday use. This process often leads to a refinement of the functional requirements or even a shift in the pedagogical focus.

It is not uncommon for windows of opportunity to open at this point in school reconstruction projects, as the school's perspective in the narrower sense often does not consider such far-reaching interventions that may be necessary—for example, for structural reasons. Conversely, planners and architects gain valuable insights into everyday school life and teaching through the users. The administration, in turn, obtains a reliable basis of arguments for making recommendations to political decision-makers and for preparing funding applications.

Experience has shown that it is helpful to compare three development scenarios. These are created by the school development planner or school construction consultants. The scenarios are presented and discussed in a second workshop. Individual components can then be explored in greater depth in working groups—from the learning environments to subject-specific teaching and team areas, to the organization of the library, forum, and canteen.

SYNTHESIS PLANNING (WORKSHOP 3)

Following an in-depth discussion of the various scenarios, project-specific priorities invariably begin to emerge. Planning decisions are closely linked to the group discussion. The final synthesis plan typically incorporates components from several scenarios. It is presented to all stakeholders for discussion in a final workshop and documented in detail.

The synthesis plan establishes a binding and coordinated foundation for further planning work. It defines the specific room allocation plan, forms the basis for political decision-making, and allows for an initial, more precise cost estimate. It also highlights areas where further refinement of the pedagogical concept may be necessary. The synthesis planning should result in a clear recommendation for resolution by the municipal authorities. The usage program then serves as a binding basis for the subsequent planning process.

FEASIBILITY 1.0

For large and complex building projects involving several schools or construction measures with extensive interventions in existing buildings, it may be advisable to examine the spatial organization model developed during synthesis planning in greater depth in the course of a feasibility study and to support the rough statements on the cost framework with more concrete cost estimates.

Depending on the specific construction project and the level of detail, a feasibility study may be based on different requirements—depending on the type of intervention:

a. reconstruction of existing buildings, minor upgrades to meet educational needs;
b. reconstruction of existing buildings, general renovation, or comprehensive refurbishment;
c. addition / extension to an existing building (possibly including general renovation or comprehensive refurbishment);
d. new construction

In any case, the following planning aspects must be considered:

— compilation of fundamental structural constraints (load-bearing walls, immovable internal service systems, access routes, fire safety requirements, acoustic and lighting conditions, accessibility and inclusive interior design, etc.);
— mapping of new spatial and functional program and new requirements onto the (existing) floor plan; conflicts with constraints must be mapped and either weighed with all parties involved or addressed through the development of alternative solutions scenarios;
— in the case of extensions or new construction: compilation of contextual conditions (any registered building encumbrances, setback requirements, heritage protection in the immediate surroundings, utility networks, parking situation, etc.);
— preparation of cost estimates and coordination with administration and politics;
— additional coordination with neighbors and the local community;
— if necessary, development of a (3D) model for communication purposes;
— documentation of the basis for subsequent architectural design;
— suggestion of a procedure for construction measures;
— detailed scheduling and action planning.

At a glance

What?	Development of a coordinated requirements profile, usage program, and spatial organization model
Why?	To prepare the project brief as a basis for a resolution on construction and measures
Who?	Municipal steering group, school's »Construction« project group, school development planner or school construction consultants, extended user group, politicians
When?	Following the assessment
How long?	4 to 6 months

Tips for implementation

- Developing the school program and space allocation plan—comprising the components of assessment, analysis, scenario development, and synthesis planning—requires considerable work capacities. Therefore, at the beginning of the planning process, the requirements and time capacities of the administration and schools should be clarified and the need for external support should be assessed.
- Personnel continuity must be ensured throughout the planning process to support a consistent decision-making process.
- The decision-making process should be clearly visualized.
- At the beginning, a sufficient but manageable timeframe should be defined for Phase 0.
- Politicians must be informed about the planning process—for example, by attending the workshops as guests; care must be taken to ensure that the discussion process is not determined and instrumentalized by party politics, since the politicians ultimately have the sole decision-making power by virtue of the building resolution.
- A clear distinction must be made between the work process and the participatory process. Between workshops, binding task must be assigned and completed.
- Interdisciplinary collaboration should be ensured from the outset.
- Pedagogical issues must be clarified as early as possible—the clearer the pedagogical statements, the clearer the spatial options can be defined and construction decisions made. Such discussion processes are frequently intertwined because the pedagogical specifications are reflected in spatial solutions.
- The thinking and planning process should be characterized by openness.
- The scenarios should also include an estimate of the required investment.

6

CONTEXT

The 10 Theses in the Pedagogical Discourse

The theses presented in Chapter 2 highlight central aspects of a »sustainable« school, which have far-reaching implications for school construction. They paint a picture of schools in a state of flux: developments at all levels of society are reshaping both the demands on learning and the architectural and spatial design of schools within urban environments. In the following, the 10 Theses are placed in a broader context and their origins in the pedagogical discourse are explained in more detail. The chapter has been expanded and adapted in key areas for the updated 2025 edition, but not completely revised.

Each of the 10 Theses has the potential to be used to derive a comprehensive profile of a school. Indeed, numerous examples of such profiles already exist in the German educational landscape—schools with a strong team-teaching approach, democratic schools, schools with a music focus, or schools that prioritize education for sustainable development (ESD). In these cases, one thesis may take precedence over the others while still incorporating and referencing them.

Occasionally, the »new« and »old« schools are contrasted below. Of course, there is much that is already new in the old schools—and vice versa. Many aspects of what might be considered visionary or representative of the »school of the future,« are already a reality elsewhere. This is demonstrated, for example, by the recipients of the German School Award of recent years—a prize awarded exclusively for excellent educational practice. These schools—and many other schools in Germany—are already implementing numerous elements of alternative approaches to learning, often in spite of the limitations imposed by outdated buildings and facilities.

THESIS 1

Learning requires many and varied perspectives, approaches, and outcomes.

In recent decades, scientific and technological development has seen a shift from the reproduction of knowledge to a focus on skills. From a general perspective, this involves four dimensions:

- *Responsibility:* What do I need to be able to do in order to act responsibly?
- *Application:* How can I do this?
- *Understanding:* Why does it work?
- *(Conceptual) knowledge:* How do you express exactly what is happening in a way that others can understand?

In view of the constant expansion of knowledge and the increasing complexity and differentiation of human activity and work, the pace of change has accelerated in recent years. The OECD sees »a growing need to rethink the goals of education and the future skills of learners,«[83] mainly due to the major drivers of change: digitalization, artificial intelligence, and climate change.

83
OECD, *Lernkompass 2030*, p. 24

Today, learning must be more than just »memorizing« knowledge. There have long been other solutions for finding and storing information available at the click of a mouse. The intelligent search for and linking of new information, as well as the recognition and construction of patterns and rules, is where the human brain excels. It is therefore important to acquire skills that enhance the acquisition, critical evaluation, and application of information and that are as broadly based as possible.

Knowledge, competencies, skills

It is now common to summarize the so-called 4C competencies: collaboration, creativity, critical thinking, and communication.[84] These are considered key skills for the 21st century,[85] and in 2014, Michael Fullan and Geoff Scott added »character« (including personal competence, empathy) and »citizenship« (education for democracy) to the list in their Whitepaper Education PLUS.[86] The 4C / 6Cs are thus a response to the way knowledge is handled in the digital age: Content is no longer simply stored and taught by teachers to learners. Rather, it »flows« in constant communication and collaboration.

84
The idea of the 4C goes back to the US non-profit organization *P21 (Partnership for 21st century skills)* and was coined in German-speaking countries by Andreas Schleicher (OECD, Director of the Directorate for Education).

85
Further information on *skills for the 21st century* can be found in the OECD *Learning Compass 2030*; see also *Spiegel* et al. (2021)

86
Fullan / Scott (2014), pp. 6–7

☞ Chapter 2, *Thesis 1, 2, and 4*, pp. 22ff.

In this context, students must learn to ask the right questions rather than memorizing predetermined answers without reflecting. They must learn how to solve problems themselves, rather than simply imitate ready-made solutions. They must learn to recognize that each solution creates new problems. They need to learn how to access and process information skillfully, and how to evaluate the results for relevance. To do this, they need basic skills of understanding and reflection that can cope with the diversity and complexity of the information world around them.

The ability to access and process information is not simply a »formal« skill. A basic knowledge of elementary facts from nature and technology, society and cultural traditions is still necessary. In addition, the meaning of knowledge in all subjects is shifting. Traditional disciplinary boundaries are becoming less important in professional life and in modern research. The answers to life's crucial questions cannot be sorted according to subject but require—in the sense of the concept of competence formulated above—an overview of complex interrelationships.

In its strategy paper »Teaching and Learning for the Digital World,« the Conference of the Ministers of Education and Cultural Affairs (KMK) also defines overarching competencies that it considers important for »learning, living, and working in an increasingly digitalized world«: »the ability to communicate successfully, find creative solutions, act competently, think critically, and collaborate.«[87]

The OECD *Learning Compass 2030*[88] combines key skills, knowledge, attitudes, and values for 21st century action into a holistic »learning framework.« The goal is to develop action and design skills (»student agency«) as well as transformation skills. The three pillars include »cognitive foundations, including literacy and numeracy, on which digital and data literacy are built; health foundations, including physical and mental health and well-being; and social and emotional foundations, including morality and ethics« (p. 51). The metaphor of a compass is adopted to »emphasise the need for students to learn to navigate by themselves through unfamiliar contexts« (p. 20). Learning here is explicitly not limited to school.

In times of uncertainty, tension, and crisis, the »well-being« factor and the learning of emotional and social skills play a crucial role in the OECD framework. This is also because we are more dependent than ever on (co-)creative solutions and the joint development of new solutions to overcome major social challenges and to promote the cohesion of a global community. Different perspectives and backgrounds of experience are essential for this, and a heterogeneous learning community is a prerequisite.

87
KMK (2021b), p. 8. Similar demands have long been voiced by the business world. At the 2018 World Economic Forum in Davos, Jack Ma, founder of the Alibaba Group, was quoted as saying that the »knowledge-based approach of 200 years ago« is no longer viable. Children will never be able to compete with machines. What matters now, he argued, are soft skills such as »independent thinking, values, and teamwork.« See World Economic Forum (2018)

88
The OECD Learning Compass 2030 was developed as part of the OECD project »Future of Education and Skills 2030« and published in the original English edition in 2019. A German translation was published in 2020.

☞ See also Chapter 6, *Thesis 2*, pp. 183 ff., *Thesis 5*, pp. 195 ff. and *Thesis 7*, pp. 203 ff., on the well-being factor

The results of learning research are clear:

Diverse learning is a prerequisite for learning success. The school systems of the successful PISA countries make use of these findings. They confirm that

- learning is a multifaceted process that combines activities, emotions, cognitions, and situations. The process itself influences what we retain as knowledge and develop as skills. It is not only the rational aspects of cognitive skill acquisition that play a central role, but also the inner forces and expectations that set learning in motion and drive it.
- learning—in the sense of remembering, retaining, changing behavior, inventing—is particularly effective when inner desire, reflection in others (recognition), a high degree of self-activity (»learning by doing«), and self-determination (realizing one's own needs) are intertwined.

— learning is a lifelong process and that, depending on age, different abilities are available as already acquired skills and can be activated to support the learning process.[89]

— interdisciplinary, problem-oriented learning helps transfer what has been learned to new contexts. This support of transfer processes does not exclude further subject-based learning; however, subjects must also fulfill interdisciplinary tasks and be supplemented by remedial and special-interest courses as well as independent and group learning phases. This requires open learning and time concepts.[90]

— different learners always influence each other's learning processes. Learners become more aware of their learning and the improvement of their learning opportunities when they are able to change perspectives—for example, in cross-grade teaching: learners here, teachers there, listeners here, speakers there, observers here, observers there, etc. Above all, mutual learning allows for feedback loops, and both self- and peer-reflection on learning processes.

— all aspects are prerequisites for an effective learning culture.[91] From this point of view, the principle of diversity implemented in an inclusive school system takes on additional weight. The demand for inclusion is therefore not only justified by the goal of giving all learners fair opportunities.[92] Above all, it also brings a completely new quality to this shift of perspective that is essential to learning.

— learning as a reconstruction of already obtained knowledge is not a process of mere imitation or reproduction but must be an active process of appropriation in which the acquired knowledge is always modified, disrupted, or changed from the learner's perspective. To this end, teachers must adopt methodological approaches that allow for action-oriented learning in a comprehensive way: Learning is most effective when it is active and results-oriented. The dominance of lectures or question-based teaching methods in conventional lessons should therefore be viewed critically. Educational research has clearly shown that the monoculture of these methods is ineffective for most learners in terms of problem solving and creative learning.

To promote this kind of learning at school, students must be offered an appropriate time and spatial concept that includes sufficiently long learning phases with self-organized parts and at the same time meets high social, emotional, and aesthetic demands in addition to subject-specific ones.[93] And it needs sufficiently large and well-organized spaces, because the two square meters per student that are still found in some general learning and teaching areas are not enough to achieve this.

The pedagogical concepts of the OECD and UNESCO, as well as the international school performance tests according to PISA, follow these findings in their assessments of the quality of education systems. In summary, from the perspective of international educational research, successful acquisition of skills is essentially based on three criteria that must be met:[94]

89
In its writings, the OECD repeatedly emphasizes that education systems should make full use of the heterogeneity of learners and the diversity of cultural backgrounds in teaching practice. This takes up the classic idea of John Dewey, who emphasized as early as 1916 in his standard work *Democracy and Education* that in a democracy, the school on a small scale is a model for democracy on a large scale.

90
In her book *Critical Lessons - What our Schools Should Teach*, Nel Noddings draws attention to the fact that these skills always include critical thinking, which cannot be nurtured from just one subject area.

91
See e.g., Reich (2008b)

92
Cf. in particular UNESCO (2009)

☞ Chapter 6, *Thesis 5*, p. 195

93
See, for example, the research conducted at the Harvard Graduate School of Education in *Project Zero*: pz.harvard.edu. This educational practice, which was largely inspired by Howard Gardner, is a model school that consistently moves in the direction of a competence-oriented, constructivist-based pedagogy. See also, among others, Reich (2010) for an introduction to this in German-speaking countries.

94
Cf. in particular Reich (2008b). A good derivation of the rationale can be found in Kalantzis / Cope (2008).

1. Learning must offer different perspectives to provide learners with a variety of resources and solutions. These perspectives help develop competencies that include the ability to change perspectives, to learn from insights, to develop democratic attitudes, and especially to reject dogmatic perspectives.
2. Learning must allow for diverse, active, and largely self-determined approaches to learning that reflect the diversity of learning styles and provide opportunities for all learners to improve their individual learning pathways.
3. Learning must lead to results that are verifiable and recognized beyond school grades. In view of today's technical possibilities, these »products« can take very different forms: from a theatrical performance to a presentation on the Internet, from an exhibition at a parents' day to a submission to a youth science contest. Findings from learning research, brain research, and the cultural and social sciences, from their very different research perspectives, have confirmed that this diversity of learning perspectives, approaches, and outcomes is an essential prerequisite for successful learning.[95]

95
In addition to learning research, to which reference has been made so far, this aspect is particularly emphasized by brain research. Cf., e.g., Bauer (2007); Hüther (2010)

THESIS 2

Students learn alone, in pairs, in small groups, with the entire year group, across age groups, and also as a class.

Good relationships between learners and teachers/learning guides within and between their groups are now seen as essential, if not critical, to successful, positive learning environments and learning outcomes. Positive mutual relationships are crucial to learning because learners never learn just for themselves or just the educational material, but always in a social and emotional situation in which they are connected to their learning guide, whom they like, as well as to their classmates.[96] Such relational learning is all the easier when the school is a home, a place of social and emotional security and familiarity, where people treat each other in a humane, understandable and sympathetic, fair and helpful way.

96
Socio-psychological studies in particular have empirically demonstrated the importance of successful communication conditions and emotional factors. For an introduction, see, for example, Aronson et al. (2008). Communication theories have proven the necessity of successful communication in all areas of life, including school.

Student teamwork

Learning requires not only individual initiative but also, equally, recognition, dialogue, and engagement with others. The traditional standard setting—frontal instruction in the classroom—cannot achieve this. Instead, learners need both individual learning experiences in individualized learning environments and teamwork experiences from small to large groups. To achieve this, schools need a concept and a structural framework that combines learning in instructive parts with learners' own actions, interests, and preferences. The social and spatial environment of the school must enable a quick and flexible switch between social forms (instruction, individual work, group work, presentations, performances in front of all), but also larger learning formats such as a self-learning center with individualized materials, project work, and workshops based on interests and preferences.[97]

97
Cf. the learning formats in Reich (2014). The learning environment can also be extended in larger formats to include the neighborhood (see Thesis 10) or the digital space (Thesis 4).

☞ Chapter 6, *Thesis 4*, p. 190 and *Thesis 10*, p. 213

Learning in heterogeneous groups

The expanded concept of education that we advocate corresponds to a concept of education as practiced in high-performing international school systems that embrace the heterogeneity of learning groups. It is based on a variety of learning methods that require varied learning settings in terms of time and space. These always include contexts in which social learning takes precedence over learning as a whole, because this is where the communicative and behavioral conditions for successful cooperation develop despite heterogeneity. No learner should be left behind or excluded in this system. Learners should be supported in such a way that they are encouraged to learn through their own motivation and commitment. To this end, they must be provided with the broadest and most comprehensive educational opportunities and support possible. Those who are mainly confronted with situations that end in failure will learn little. To achieve this for a broad spectrum of the population is crucial to the success of our scientific and technological society.

Teamwork of the learning guides

Good relationships between teachers and other participants are demonstrated above all by good teamwork.[98] In schools, teamwork is not an end in itself. It has four important effects:

1. Teamwork primarily serves to improve teaching and learning as a whole and to support individual students. As a basis of educational work, it enables binding agreements between colleagues teaching a class, the integration of subject knowledge, coordination of annual planning, active exchange of experiences, sharing of tried and tested teaching materials, and the joint search for solutions for students in critical situations.
2. Teamwork creates manageable structures in large schools. When the size of a social unit exceeds 120 to 150 members, the likelihood that everyone really knows everyone else and can get together for joint activities decreases rapidly, as empirical school studies show.[99] A sense of community can increasingly only be conveyed symbolically. The process of anonymization, diffusion of responsibilities, and the uncontrollable destruction and neglect of school buildings is intensifying. The recognition of the relationship between the number of people and the quality of the social and working climate has considerable consequences for schools. However, this does not mean a return to the »one-room schoolhouse.« The solution lies in the formation of semi-autonomous sub-units (e.g., clusters), each organized by empowered (multi-professional) teams.
3. Teamwork greatly reduces strain on teaching staff. Studies on teacher health show a clear correlation between cooperative atmosphere / effective team structures among the teaching staff and a reduction in burn-out symptoms and sick leave.[100]
4. Teamwork serves as a model for individual and social action for students. Only what is specifically role-modelled can be expected in the behavior of learners. The cooperation of all people involved in the school—from students to the janitor, from teachers to parents, from administrative staff to school social worker, school doctor, or school psychologist—serves as a model for the students.

However, in successful schools, learning support teams and collegial cooperation that are effective and resilient in the long term do not emerge from moral appeals or group dynamics exercises, but rather through concrete and methodical structural development. Depending on the number and age of students and the type of school, these structures vary from tandems (e.g., in elementary schools between teachers and social workers), to year-level teams for three to six learning groups, to subject-specific teams. There are also observation teams, long-term planning groups, and temporary project groups.[101] In addition to appropriate

98
In his empirical follow-up study *Visible Learning*, Hattie considers teamwork and team teaching to be one of the most effective factors for greater learning success.

☞ See also Chapter 3, *1. Activities*, p. 53

99
Group sizes and their effects are primarily the subject of socio-psychological research. The larger groups become, the greater the anonymity, even if there are effective pedagogical measures to counter this. Smaller groups are more effective; in school classes, up to 20 learners appear to be favorable. The larger a class is, the more groups are formed, which can make teaching and learning processes more difficult because teachers can no longer respond to learners individually. For an introduction, see, for example, Blatchford et al. (2001)

100
Cf., e.g., Schaarschmidt (2003); also Kliebisch / Meloefski (Eds.) (2009); Schaarschmidt / Kieschke (Eds.) (2007)

☞ Cf., The 4 Cs / 6 Cs in Chapter 6, *Thesis 1*, p. 179

101
Team teaching is an ideal that can be achieved when, above all, several learning groups are combined. Cf. Kricke / Reich (2016)

personnel planning, binding agreements, and schedules, the necessary structure includes a spatial concept that corresponds to the social »logic« of the work processes.

Relationships thrive on direct contact, but they also require protected spaces for communication. This is the foundation of an effective communication culture. Forms of contact close to the learning process are needed, in which learning guides and learners can meet undisturbed to communicate openly, agree on rules, set personal goals, and receive critical feedback. These protected settings are equally important for discussions with parents or team meetings.

An open and communicative attitude, which is now taken for granted in many fields of work, is a prerequisite for being suited to the teachers / learning profession. Reservations about such a redefinition of a professional role previously characterized by »lone wolf« status are still widespread among many teaching staff:[102]

— »Relationship-building requires communication and allows little room for withdrawal. But I need my space.«
— »The extra workload from teamwork is too much.«
— »If the chemistry isn't right, even the best team space is useless.«
— »You can't force people to work together.«
— »Year-level teams don't work because colleagues have to switch between different year groups.«
— »Teachers end up alone in front of the class anyway.«
— »Students don't bond with a team, but with *their* teacher.«

These views are often shaped by negative experiences with unsuccessful collaboration. However, collaboration that meets the standards described above is generally successful if

— it is not introduced half-heartedly by the school leadership, but consistently and with clear priorities;
— it is managed professionally (team size, time frame, task, leadership, documentation, feedback loops, etc.);
— expectations are kept realistic (a team is not a circle of friends);
— and it proves successful in practice in terms of improved learning outcomes.

In summary, successful school systems in the future will be characterized by strong relationship-building and communication. These must first be developed within the teacher and school leadership teams to serve as a role model for the entire school.[103] The quality of the school as a social place is crucial: If it is possible to establish fair and opportunity-enhancing relationships and appreciative communication, the investments made and the willingness to act as a social role model will pay off. Clear studies already exist that examine the long-term economic impacts for society associated with this.[104]

102
Cf., e.g., Reich (2007) on the changing patterns in teacher training resulting from this development.

103
See Reich (2012) on the requirements profile here

104
Cf. Wilkinson / Pickett (2010). From the perspective of the OECD regarding the ineffectiveness of a school system with weak role models that fails to improve opportunities: OECD (2010e)

THESIS 3

All-day schooling means learning, moving, playing, romping, lingering, talking, eating, and much more—in a healthy rhythm.

The expansion of all-day schooling and childcare facilities has been underway for decades. This is also reflected in the increasing use of these facilities—all-day schools are becoming a reality for more and more children and young people. For elementary schools alone, the statistics for child and youth welfare for the 2021/2022 school year report about 1.7 million children in all-day school programs (including about 500,000 in after-school programs).[105] This corresponds to an all-day elementary school participation rate of about 55 percent across Germany[106]—although there are significant differences between both the federal states and between Eastern Germany (participation rate 84 percent) and Western Germany (participation rate 47 percent). In the 2022/2023 school year, a total of 3,832,653 students nationwide participated in all-day schooling at all types of general education schools, which corresponds to 48.9 percent.[107]

105 Autor:innengruppe Bildungsberichterstattung (2024)

106 Stöbe-Blossey (2023)

107 KMK (2023)

Various goals are associated with the expansion of all-day schools. In addition to improving the compatibility of family and work life, the reduction of disparities related to students' socio-economic backgrounds and providing individual support are important here.[108] At the beginning of the expansion, there was no empirical evidence that all-day schools contributed to greater equality of opportunity.[109] Even after many years of development and expansion, there is still no evidence that comprehensive compensation for performance deficits and an associated reduction in educational disadvantage has been achieved.[110] However, studies show that voluntary participation in programs designed to reflect the interests of children and youth has a positive impact,[111] and a positive effect on children's social learning has also been demonstrated.[112] It can therefore be concluded that the opportunities offered by all-day education and care have not yet been fully exploited and that the focus should continue to be on improving the quality of the offerings, not on merely expanding the quantity.

108 BMFSFJ (2021)

109 Steinmann / Strietholt (2019)

110 Sauerwein / Heer (2020)

111 StEG (2015)

112 Fischer (2020)

As the phased implementation of the legal entitlement to all-day education and care for elementary school children begins in the 2026/2027 school year, a growing demand for care services is expected, partly due to demographic changes in society.[113] This will necessitate staffing and structural changes in schools. According to the Standing Conference of the Ministers of Education and Cultural Affairs (KMK) definition, the number of all-day elementary schools nationwide has increased from 11,018 in the 2021/2022 school year to 11,136 in 2022/2023, meaning that 73 percent of all elementary schools are now organized as all-day schools.[114]

113 Prognos / ITES (2023)

114 KMK (2023)

To meet parental demand by the time all children in grades 1 to 4 are legally entitled to attend all-day school, about 300,000 additional places will have to be created nationwide by the 2029/2030 school year in the status quo scenario, in addition to those already available in 2022/2023; about 481,000 new places are needed in the dynamic scenario.[115] On average, 390,000 new places are needed by 2029/2030. About 342,000 additional places are needed to meet the projected demand from parents in 2026/2027—the first year the legal entitlement comes into effect.[116] Forecasts for the coming decade vary considerably in terms of anticipated demand growth on the parents' side. It is undisputed, however, that there is a very large backlog and that it will take years to meet the acute demand.

115 Prognos / ITES (2024)

116 Prognos / ITES (2024)

In addition to changing societal demands on schools, there is a second driving force behind this structural transformation: the »new« teaching and learning concept described in Theses 1 and 2 is currently also transforming half-day schools into all-day facilities. In modern school systems, learning is organized with a different rhythm and greater differentiation than in the past. When learning is structured around the development of competencies, both time requirements and spatial concepts change.

Learning—understood as active learning—requires more time and more space. Time and space for movement, play, and lingering in stimulating environments are just as important as time and space for cognitive, social, or aesthetic work in a narrower sense. The former are a prerequisite for the latter. For this reason, several companies across various industries—particularly those that depend on creativity and communication skills among their employees—are already incorporating elements from the fields of wellness, sport, and experience into their working environments. These emerging work scenarios offer a glimpse into the kinds of requirements schools of the future will be expected to fulfill.

New time rhythms

Against this backdrop, the structure of the school day is changing considerably:[117] Many successful pilot schools no longer organize the school day in 45-minute units. Instead, they seek solutions that reflect the time needed for learning processes, rather than relying on predefined, narrow templates. The details of how time concepts will develop remains open. In Germany, for example, there is currently a trend toward double-period lesson concepts or 60-minute blocks, which allow for a greater variety of teaching methods than the traditional 45-minute format. There are also emerging profiles in which the day is divided into longer units, which vary depending on each school's specific approach. Going forward, greater attention will likely be paid to the biological and learning rhythms of learners as they are unable to absorb content from many subjects throughout the day. Studies are also providing growing evidence of the benefits of variable school start times, and demands for more flexible scheduling are becoming more insistent.[118] Some schools are responding by offering variable starting times.[119]

117 Cf. Höhmann / Holtappels (2006); Rabenstein (2020)

118 Oster / Behlau (2024)

119 See Spiegel Online (2010); (2015)

Expanded spatial requirements

The all-day school should be designed as a living and working space that offers students and teachers not only classrooms, but also an appealing learning environment with different activity and retreat areas where very different needs can be met. The space must support the rhythmic structure of the school day. Different forms of learning and places for working and lingering must be considered: arrival areas, lounge areas for individual, quiet work and study, study areas for joint, intensive group learning, indoor and outdoor recreation areas, sports and play areas, school gardens and green spaces, if possible including outdoor water features, areas that are kept clean as well as places for »messy« work, niches for doing nothing, a cafeteria, a theater stage, a library, etc. are just as important as learning and working areas in the narrower sense. It must be possible to divide a large school into smaller areas that give students and teachers the feeling of a manageable and inviting living environment that stimulates activity without making it anonymous.

Many all-day schools are now entering into productive collaborations with youth music schools, sports clubs, and other cultural institutions.[120] The schools benefit by gaining reliable partners who contribute additional staff to the all-day context.[121] The partners, on the other hand, benefit because children and young people now have time for their offerings as they spend more of their day at school. Most importantly, children and young people benefit from these partnerships because formal and non-formal education is integrated into the all-day school system, allowing them to alternate between different learning opportunities throughout the day. The main advantage of integrating child and youth work into all-day schools is that all children can be reached. Since school attendance is compulsory, every child can be reached, whereas child and youth work offers are informal and selective and do not always reach the desired target group.[122]

120 StEG (2019); Coelen (2014)

121 Deinet / Icking (2020)

122 Coelen et al. (2017)

Increasing acceptance

Growing equality in education has a positive effect on society as a whole: the higher the level of education in a society, the better its economic and social starting position. With all-day education, all children and young people can access educational offerings that would otherwise depend on the social status of their parents. In Germany, the correlation between a child's educational success and their family's social background is still very high.[123] All-day schools offer an ideal opportunity to counteract this imbalance. This view is increasingly shared by the public: In 2003, according to an Allensbach study, only 49 percent of the German population supported the concept of all-day schools, while 29 percent opposed it; by 2011, the number of supporters had risen to 61 percent, with only 19 percent opposed.[124] In a 2014 Jako-O education study, a survey of parents found that 70 percent of parents in Germany with school-age children up to 16 years were looking for an all-day school for their child.[125]

123 Autor:innengruppe Bildungsberichterstattung (2024)

124 Vodafone Stiftung (2011)

125 Killius / Tillmann, quoted from Alt / Hüsken (2016). See also Klemm / Zorn (2016)

From teacher to all-day learning guide

All-day schooling is also changing the role of teachers. Traditionally, teachers define themselves as representatives of their subject and see educational and social responsibilities at school primarily as the domain of the social pedagogical staff.[126] However, the transformation of schools requires a change in attitude on the part of all staff:[127] schools and teaching are becoming more child-centered, and teachers are now also taking on social pedagogical responsibilities. Their relationships with students are increasingly characterized by greater closeness.

The communicative and supportive potential of schools will play an important role in the future. This means that the daily school routine will also become more varied for teachers working in all-day programs. Aspects such as longer on-site presence or changing job requirements are more likely to be accepted if the school provides appropriate working conditions and a supportive environment. This includes the necessary spatial conditions: individual workspaces and common meeting and break areas for learning guides.

126
Cf. Breuer (2015)

127
Cf. Reh et al. (2015)

THESIS 4

The culture of digitality changes the culture of textbooks and chalkboards.

Digital media, tools, and technologies now have a natural place in the lives of children and young people. They are transforming everyday life and community life as well as daily learning and teaching in schools. Access to knowledge has changed radically, and teachers and students can and must live and work with a veritable flood of information. It is no longer (only) the teacher who corrects mistakes. AI creates new content, spellcheckers correct texts, and there are few questions for which a student with Internet access still seems to depend on a teacher. What does this mean for schools?

Learning in the digital world

Schools have the task of preparing students for the world of tomorrow. That world will be different from the one that today's education system was designed for. New work, artificial intelligence, dealing with fake news or global interconnectedness are aspects of this transformation. There are several models that try to describe the characteristics of this world: The VUCA model stands for volatility, uncertainty, complexity, and ambiguity. The BANI model stands for brittle, anxious, non-linear, and incomprehensible. Both models try to capture how today's world and its changes are perceived.

Digitality plays an important role here. The changes it brings are not only technical in nature. They lead to »a broad cultural and societal transformation that has an impact on teaching and learning in schools as well as on how children, adolescents, and young adults manage and shape their life and work processes.«[128] This is how the Standing Conference of the Ministers of Education and Cultural Affairs (KMK) describes it in its recommendation *Lehren und Lernen in der digitalen Welt (Learning and Teaching in the Digital World)*. This recommendation complements the strategy *Bildung in der digitalen Welt (Education in the Digital World)* published by the KMK in 2016/2017, which calls for significant action in »pedagogical, didactical, and technical-infrastructural« areas.[129]

128 KMK (2021b), p. 3

129 KMK (2017), p. 59

Culture of digitality—culture of digitality in schools

The process of digitalization has created a new reality, which Felix Stalder describes as the *culture of digitality*. Today, digitality has the scope of a »cultural constellation« that not only involves the diffusion of technology but also leads to changes in all areas of life.[130] The observed change is not caused by digital technology alone, but by the way digital technology is used and how people are changing their actions through and with it. Culture is understood here as a lived practice that emerges through people's actions and interaction with technology.[131]

130 Stalder (2016), p. 11

131 Ibid.

132 Knauf (2024), p. 56; Cf. also Allert/Asmussen (2017)

133 Knauf (2024), p. 57

134 Stalder/Kuttner (2022)

It thus becomes an »inevitable basic condition of everyday actions«[132] that shapes all areas of social life, including education and schools. Based on this approach, Knauf argues that »digitality in schools« is not limited to changes brought about by »the use of digital technology in the classroom,« but rather transforms »the school as a whole.«[133] It is therefore about a »transformation of school culture(s) as a whole.«[134]

The use of digital tools by all and a critical approach to digital technologies are core competencies.

In this sense, schools must teach their students how to use »artificial intelligence« intelligently. This task is particularly important for those who do not have access to devices at home or do not receive guidance on how to use them responsibly and effectively. Students without digital literacy will remain excluded from almost all active processes of economic and cultural life, as is already the case in many areas. For all learners to be able to participate on an equal footing, this means—in addition to the universal provision of equipment—usability and accessibility.[135]

135 Cf. KMK (2017), p. 59

The critical use of digital technologies and content is a key aspect of media literacy. The mechanisms of social media and other services also plays an important role. The phenomenon of »algorithmicity« is omnipresent in today's offerings. It refers not only to technical aspects, but also to the »pre-structuring« of cultural processes by machines.[136] Fake news and AI are key topics here. As the *Shell Youth Study 2024* shows, young people themselves are very concerned about these issues: According to this study, 90 percent of young people, regardless of age group, gender, or social background, think it is »(very) important that dealing with digital media and recognizing fake news are taught as compulsory subjects at school.«[137]

136 Stalder (2016), p. 144

137 *Shell Youth Study* (2024), Summary, p. 23

A critical and at the same time creative engagement with media is best learned through hands-on production—learning by doing. Through active learning, the mechanisms, techniques, modes of operation, opportunities, and risks can be questioned and understood together in concrete applications. To make this possible, schools need to be equipped with components of a multimedia studio, including technology for photo, video, and sound production, so that learners can create their own media productions locally and edit them centrally.[138] Digital presentation walls, document cameras, and interactive boards can be used for both centralized and decentralized presentations. Schools need to be built to accommodate the rapid changes in the digital and media sectors.

138 See, for example, the offer from »TUMO—Center for Creative Technologies,« where young people can learn modern technologies outside of school.

Opportunities of digital technology: interactive, multi-channel, self-correcting

To support equitable education with the help of digital technologies, the Conference of the Ministers of Education and Cultural Affairs (KMK) emphasizes that »all those involved in the design of the respective educational process, i.e., teachers, trainers in vocational training, and other educational professionals in schools, must be qualified to provide the necessary support for children, adolescents, and young adults and to work together.«[139] This means that schools must also teach learning guides to use digital technology as naturally as they used blackboards and books in the past.

Digital tools and media have fundamentally new qualities that, when used correctly, can effectively support learning, for example through multiple interactive learning channels (auditory and visual) and the possibility of self-correction. Students' independence and self-activity can be expanded, and fundamentally new qualities of learning and teaching can be created. Increasingly, adaptive learning applications will be able to identify learners' needs and provide them with a learning experience that is optimally tailored to them, or even take on feedback functions, thus increasingly enabling digital learning support that simplifies personal advice from learning guides.

139
KMK (2021b), p. 5

Cf. the lernlog web app, the digital learning guide that enables independent learning at schools and a gradual transition to digital collaboration. lernlog is an initiative of the Montag Stiftung Jugend und Gesellschaft.

The medial role of the learning guides

According to learning research, learning guides should establish a good relationship and open communication with their students, but then talk a step back: Learners must acquire learning content themselves and develop the differentiated competencies as responsibly and autonomously as possible—in various social forms. This cannot succeed if they are accompanied, guided, and monitored at every step, only to be suddenly left alone during performance tests. The use of media can support learning guides in encouraging students to work independently and in allowing themselves to take a step back. The content and methods of teaching—especially in areas focused on measurable knowledge acquisition—will change when a student using a smartphone or AI »knows« more than the teacher. The rapid development, especially in adaptive learning technologies that correct students' mistakes in solving problems and give them individually tailored learning tips, are radically individualizing the process of knowledge acquisition. This can help relieve teachers. Massive Open Online Courses (MOOCS) will also replace traditional instruction in many areas.

Chapter 2, *Thesis 2*, pp. 25ff.

Delocalization of education?

Do we still need school buildings in their current form if, one day, digital tools and technologies enable a new level of delocalized educational processes? The vision that the ubiquitous electronic availability of information and the use of increasingly powerful mobile devices might render schools as physical locations completely obsolete has not yet materialized—not even in the technologically advanced elite universities. Learning processes remain largely dependent on interaction and role models. Digitalization and mediatization do not render learning guides obsolete. On the contrary, in the world of digital technologies—including in schools—learning guides are becoming increasingly important: they are essential in helping learners navigate, select, and make sense of digital environments. Digital tools and techniques should be designed to enhance learners' own strengths and reflective capacities, not to diminish them.

Precisely because of the virtual appeal of modern technologies—which are often used in superficial ways—learners need not only media-based but also direct and immediate access to all learning content. The aim of schooling is not merely to reproduce a diverse world in small pieces, but to explore it through inquiry-based learning and to develop skills in the process. Virtual secondary experiences cannot replace direct primary experiences. What's more, school is not only about individuation (i.e., the development of one's own personality), but also about socialization. And it is only through community, through living, experiencing, and exploring together that one becomes capable of participating in community.

☞ Cf. Explanations of future skills in Chapter 6, *Thesis 1*, p. 179

Integrated learning—blended learning

The mix of digital and in-person formats, as well as remote formats and working from home, have become well established in the world of work—not least due to the coronavirus pandemic. Such concepts have also emerged for learning, informed by findings from learning psychology, and are discussed under the terms »blended learning« or »integrated learning.« The idea is to combine face-to-face learning and online-supported learning.

Such concepts are not just a matter of technical implementation. They require clear pedagogical rationale and design. It is essential to manage the transition from analog to digital and back to analog in a way that benefits learners.[140] Technological progress can take over many tasks from the learning guides, but it cannot replace them, because personal exchange, role models, encouragement, and praise cannot be replaced by a machine.

140 Reich / Reich (2025)

In terms of spatial requirements, this means the introduction of learning formats in schools that provide a learning environment for larger groups that enable a smooth and quick switch between self-study at individual workstations with high-quality technical equipment, project work in small groups, short teaching phases for groups, large group meetings for presentations, and more.

Deceleration—as quickly as possible

Against the backdrop of comprehensive digitalization, which is shaping all areas of society in terms of work, leisure, and social life, schools have an important compensatory role to play. In support of this role, they can confidently let go of certain »content.« The acceleration that the media reinforce with fast images and abrupt cuts must be decelerated. In addition to the contemporary use of digital tools and technologies, schools must also give sufficient space to the slowness that deep and reflective learning requires. For example, someone who reads a text slowly, takes notes, and follows the thread of thought will be better able to recall and reflect on the content than someone who watches fast-moving images. Videos or films can make reflection more difficult and are therefore not suitable for all learning situations or age groups. When in-depth reflection on a particular learning topic is to be encouraged, »quiet« media such as a book or a picture are more appropriate. To counter attention issues, some federal states have also adopted the strategy of banning mobile phones in schools, at least for certain age groups. In Germany, there is still no uniform nationwide regulation.

In the analog-digital transformation, it is essential to offer different learning phases: periods of digital Internet research, working with AI, digital creation of presentations, analyses, and documentation should alternate with phases in which students' own direct experience, active creation with all their senses, and discussions have priority. However, these shifts can only succeed if curricula are radically streamlined and restructured. To safeguard primary experiences and enable learners to shape their own access to knowledge actively, the overwhelming and often excessive content load of current curricula must not stand in the way.

THESIS 5

Support in an inclusive school takes place in heterogeneous groups.

The international organizations UNESCO and OECD, of which Germany is a member, have shown that school systems worldwide must deal with the issue of »heterogeneity and diversity« in a comprehensive way. Germany has a legal obligation to introduce an inclusive school system that does not exclude any child by prematurely assigning them to special education. This obligation has been binding for Germany since 2009, following the ratification of the UN Convention on the Rights of Persons with Disabilities.[141] However, the »Concluding Observations« of the UN Committee on the Rights of Persons with Disabilities in the context of the *2023 State Review* are still extremely critical: *»The Committee is concerned about the lack of full implementation of inclusive education throughout the education system«* (p. 12, observation 53), *»the lack of a clear mechanism to promote inclusive education in the Länder and at the municipal level« (53a), and even »misconceptions about and negative perceptions of inclusive education on the part of some executive entities«* (53b).[142]

141
This means that the UN CRPD »has the status of an ordinary federal law and must (…) be implemented by all state authorities.« Kroworsch (2023), p. 14

142
In section IV. Follow-up, the Committee emphasizes the importance of all the recommendations and once again draws attention to the urgent measures to be taken in the field of education (Art. 24, para. 54). CRPD/C/DEU/CO/2-3, pp. 16f.

The issues of »heterogeneity,« »individualization,« and »inclusive school«—i.e., a school that includes all children and young people—are sometimes more and sometimes less at the center of educational policy and pedagogical discourse. However, both social and learning psychology impulses are leading to a necessary, increased focus.[143]

143
Cf. Reich (2014)

Lifelong learning

☞ Chapter 2, *Thesis 1*, pp. 22ff. *and Thesis 4*, pp. 31ff.

Our complex present in the age of digital transformation is evident in social life as well as in the world of work. This has a fundamental impact on attitudes towards learning. The early and one-sided segregation of children and young people into predetermined educational pathways (Hauptschule, Realschule, or Gymnasium) is no longer appropriate. More than ever, all talent is needed at a high level. No future-oriented society can afford to prematurely sort out children, depriving them of genuine opportunities for development—and this is based on a far too narrow understanding of human intelligence, which often focuses solely on mathematical and linguistic skills. Added to this is an aging society.[144] The shortage of skilled workers in Germany threatens to take on dramatic proportions. Lifelong learning is important for all professions. The traditional rules of professional conduct no longer fit the highly dynamic world of work, in which everyone involved must continue to learn. This is also emphasized by the OECD in its thematic focus »Adult Skills and Work« (2023).[145] In this context, Andreas Schleicher stressed in 2018: »Achieving greater equity in education is not only a social-justice imperative, it is also a way to use resources more efficiently, and to increase the supply of knowledge and skills that fuel economic growth and promote social cohesion. Not least, how we treat the most vulnerable students shows who we are as a society.«[146]

144
Cf. El-Mafaalani et al. (2025), p. 11: »In 2024, more than twice as many people celebrated their 60th birthday as children were born… The mid-2020s mark the beginning of a fragile demographic phase that will last for decades.«

145
Cf. in detail: oecd.org/en/topics/adult-skills-and-work.html

146
From the foreword to the study OECD (2018), p. 4

The global consensus on the new, universal education goal was made possible by UNESCO through a broad international consultation process with the active participation of Germany: to ensure quality education and lifelong learning opportunities for all by 2030. With its focus on inclusion, equity, quality, and lifelong learning, the global community has for the first time adopted an ambitious education agenda that addresses all member states—developed and developing countries alike.[147] The universal »Education 2030« agenda requires a change of perspective in Germany: Like all industrialized countries, Germany must not see itself solely as a donor country within the framework of international development cooperation. Rather, German education policy must live up to its responsibility as an architect of the national education landscape and thus assume responsibility as a key player in the implementation of educational goals in Germany.[148]

147
The OECD had already announced in 2016 that it would comprehensively assess its own data in the context of this fourth goal: »Education at a Glance has always focused on data collection and reporting; but now, in the service of Goal 4, our indicators can contribute to improving well-being and economic outcomes across many more countries, for many more people.« Cf. OECD (2016), p. 14; in OECD (2024) (focus on equity in education), a dedicated chapter is devoted to the educational objective of the 2030 Agenda – SDG 4.

148
Cf. Deutsche UNESCO-Kommission (2016), pp. 29 f. and UNESCO (2016; www.bne-portal.de; sustainabledevelopment.un.org/sdgs. In 2019, the KMK (Conference of the Ministers of Education and Cultural Affairs) reaffirmed its commitment to the goals of the Education 2030 Agenda and emphasized »the strong alignment between the education policy of the federal states and the goals of the Education 2030 Agenda, whose core goals—participation, equal opportunities, quality of education, and lifelong learning—are the focus of intensive educational policy efforts by the federal states.« (KMK (2019)). In 2024, the KMK renewed and reaffirmed its recommendation on education for sustainable development in schools.

Homogeneity is an illusion

Each class or learning group is fundamentally heterogeneous: differences in students' current performance potential have always been the norm. It has proven to be an illusion to assume that a learning group, put together using elaborate testing procedures based on the principle of equality, could really be homogeneous. On closer inspection, the norms and values, inclinations and interests, innate abilities, and social backgrounds of individual learners are too different in each class or learning group.[149] The idea of heterogeneity is reinforced by the social development of »superdiversity«: Germany is an immigration country. One in five people was born in another country. Immigrants come from more and more countries and regions of the world. Immigration-related diversity is most pronounced among children and young people. Aladin El-Mafaalani speaks of »super-diverse childhoods«: »The concept ... is both a tangible finding and a new perspective on childhood and the transformation of society as a whole ... and it focuses on the real complexity. At the same time, it can be assumed that all children have very similar needs and interests, but very different origins and starting conditions.«[150]

149
Impressive evidence of developmental psychology research on this can be found in the Zurich Longitudinal Studies. See Largo (2009)

150
El-Mafaalani et al. (2025), p. 66

Human educational potential cannot be developed along the lines of soccer: in that sport, various leagues aim for relative competitive homogeneity in district, state, and national leagues through exciting relegation and promotion battles, because in the end, only one will win. This is fundamentally different in education: here, everyone wins when diverse learners enrich the learning environment with their respective abilities.

Heterogeneity is not the exception but the norm in schools and society.[151] Far from being a disadvantage for learning in a group, diversity is a great opportunity: an increase in experience and knowledge through mutual stimulation and support. Especially in times when we are dependent on new solutions and approaches, new things can emerge from these co-creation encounters.

151
See also Hattie (2023)

☞ Chapter 2, *Thesis 2*, pp. 25 ff.

Heterogeneity offers mutual stimulation potential

»When a community succeeds in recognizing, appreciating, and using the forms of diversity that exist within it, it becomes more experienced and competent. Security and quality of life are enhanced because inclusive cultures reduce threats and exclusion. Heterogeneity is also economically interesting for our society: if everyone recognizes each other in their diversity and becomes accustomed to negotiating and productively engaging with differences, completely new structures, offerings, and ways of using these emerge in a community. The less exclusion there is, the more the support for a few can be shared among all. The burden on society decreases, while the identification and commitment of all increase.«[152]

The most successful school systems in the world are those that teach heterogeneous groups in a common school over a long period of time, i.e., groups in which the students help, stimulate, motivate, and push each other. The aim is not only to prevent slow learners from being segregated at an early stage, but also to ensure that the higher-achieving students develop the competence to apply their knowledge effectively: In a heterogeneous group, they can learn precisely by helping classmates who learn at a slower pace. The usual justification in Germany for the early selection of grammar school students, mostly after the fourth grade, is refuted by the significantly better performance results in countries with a school system that separate educational tracks only after nine or ten years of school. The fewer school types there are and the later young people are distributed among them, the smaller the social achievement gap between schools and young people in OECD countries. At the same time, the later the transition and the fewer the types of schools, the lower the percentage of students in the at-risk group and the higher the percentage of young people performing at a high level.[153]

Commenting on the 2009 PISA results, former OECD Secretary-General Angel Gurria said: »In the most successful education systems, the political and social leaders have persuaded their citizens to make the choices needed to show that they value education more than other things. But placing a high value on education will get a country only so far if the teachers, parents and citizens of that country believe that only some subset of the nation's children can or need to achieve world class standards. This report shows clearly that education systems built around the belief that students have different pre-ordained professional destinies to be met with different expectations in different school types tend to be fraught with large social disparities. In contrast, the best-performing education systems embrace the diversity of students' capacities, interests and social backgrounds with individualized approaches to learning.«[154] In particular, as a study by the National Institute for Quality Development in Education (IQB) shows, the advantage of smaller class sizes in special schools combined with smaller learning steps is not a model for success. On the contrary, the study shows that comparable students with special educational needs consistently achieve better results in language and mathematical skills when placed in mainstream classes.[155] Aurélien Sallin also

152
Pact for Inclusive Education, unpublished concept paper, 2025. Empirical educational research shows that inclusive education promotes social integration and has a positive influence on the well-being of children and young people and also leads to greater job satisfaction (see in detail Lütje-Klose et al. (Eds.) (2017); Rathmann / Hurrelmann (2018); Kocaj (2018); Hascher et al. (2018)

153
Cf. OECD (2018), p. 14: »An analysis of data (…) finds that disparities in performance related to socio-economic status develop early – even among pupils as young as 10 – and widen throughout students' lives.« For more information on the German school system, see Matthewes (2020): »There is therefore much to suggest that a later division into different types of school that applies to everyone—as already practised in the three federal states of Berlin, Brandenburg, and Mecklenburg-Western Pomerania—is an effective educational policy instrument for combating the lack of skills in our schools, from which everyone benefits.« (pp. 6 f.)

154
OECD (2010c), p. 4

155
Cf. Kocaj et al. (2014)

unveils that in inclusive schools, the entire student population generally performs better in terms of academic achievement and integration into the labor market.[156]

156
Cf. Sallin (2022)

Education without discrimination

An inclusive school does not only include students (and teachers) with disabilities. It seeks to prevent disadvantages for all people as comprehensively as possible.[157] Such disadvantages arise from social structures as well as from individual characteristics, which are associated with attributions of various kinds: attributions related to skin color, culture, and subculture, ethnic and linguistic origin, disabilities, diseases, socioeconomic status, age, social status at birth, nationality and place of origin, belief, religion, biological sex and gender identity, sexual orientation, family status, marital status, and other factors. According to the OECD and UNESCO, the actual and necessary goal of an inclusive school system is to address all of these causes of disadvantage—not just the »classic« assignment to special needs schools.[158] The Toronto District School Board in Canada, which has successfully implemented inclusion, summarizes this task in its mission statement as follows: »to enable all students to reach high levels of achievement and to acquire the knowledge, skills and values they need to become responsible members of a democratic society.«[159]

157
Cf. Reich / Asselhoven / Kargl (Eds.) (2015)

158
See Reich (2012); Reich (2023). In its »Concluding Observations« of the second and third state review by the United Nations, the Committee on the Rights of Persons with Disabilities recommended that Germany »adopt the legal and other measures necessary to provide for explicit protection from multiple and intersectional forms of discrimination« (B, 12. c), CRPD/C/DEU/CO/2–3, p. 4; see also the recommendations for action developed by Mark Rackles (2021) in order to counter the »inertial forces of exclusion« with »necessary transformation impulses.«

159
Cf. TDSB, Toronto District School Board, »Accountability for Student Achievement,« p. 1

A new understanding of learning

The call for a fully inclusive school system is not only justified in terms of educational equity or the goal of securing as many high-quality qualifications as possible. It is based on a fundamentally different understanding of what »learning« means and how it can be organized most effectively. An inclusive school strives to provide optimal support for all learners, including both joint and differentiated instruction.[160] The ability to learn is not limited to a narrow preference for certain constant patterns. Learning processes are always open to change, readjustment, and disruption—like the composition of any class or learning group, they are always different.

160
For an introduction, see, e.g., Ainscow / Booth / Dyson (2006)

Learning is no longer primarily about memorizing concepts, cramming »content« that is tested and then quickly forgotten. Learning is no longer a special offer only for select groups. Learning means: discovering structures and patterns, regularities and deviations, relationships, causes and effects, reasons and outcomes, with the diversity of learners making the learning process lively and eventful.[161]

161
Cf. Schönig / Schmidtlein-Mauderer (2015)

Learning can mean experimenting, trying things out, exploring new ways of doing things—often together with other learners. Learning can also mean trial and error, learning from mistakes, imagining new things, but also implementing whatever proves feasible, expressing ideas through performance, images, or text, transforming things, inventing, etc. Students can take on this active role when the teacher no longer acts primarily as a communicator of content in front of the class, but as a designer of a prepared learning environment that enables individual and group learning. To this end, multiple perspectives, approaches, and outcomes must always be allowed for.

Paradigm shift

In the past, it was assumed that a good teacher could, through skillful instruction, teach everything to all students in a class at the same time, according to their abilities. The core of this idea of schooling dates back to the early 20th century. Although alternatives to this paradigm had already been proposed 100 years ago by various educational reform movements, it is only in the past 30 years—particularly through internationally successful school development in the PISA top-performing countries—that this model has been fundamentally challenged:[162]

— learning takes place in different spaces with different groups, the »lockstep« approach has been overcome in favor of individualized learning independently and in small groups;
— individualized learning is differentiated and gives learners space and time necessary for their own development;
— a large proportion of the entire cohort can be guided all the way to the Abitur (German university entrance qualification);
— high-quality vocational preparation can also be provided for those who do not pursue the Abitur;[163]
— the role of the teacher shifts from being an instructor leading a class in lockstep to that of a learning guide supporting individuals at their own pace.

162
UNESCO's inclusion model is particularly forward-looking here: *Policy Guidelines on Inclusion in Education* (2009). In 2017, the Deutsche UNESCO-Kommission adopted the resolution »For inclusive education in Germany.« In it, the commission calls for the systematic implementation of inclusive education in the German education system, throughout life and in formal and non-formal contexts—which also speaks in favor of inclusive all-day educational facilities, among other things.

163
Cf. the annual OECD reports, *Education at a Glance*

☞ Chapter 2, *Thesis 2*, pp. 25 ff.

Germany's special path

Even if the results of international school performance tests are the subject of controversial debate in Germany, researchers at least agree that learning must be seen as a complex process that requires precise diagnostic support and differentiated support measures. When comparing Germany with international top performers, it becomes clear that in Germany

— the classes are too large;[164]
— teacher training and the selection of teaching staff are in urgent need of improvement;[165]
— too much content is taught, while still too little emphasis is placed on acquiring practical and future-oriented skills;
— selection takes place not only too early, but also means that the correlation between social background and educational success in Germany is one of the strongest in the world.[166]

Unlike in Germany, the heterogeneity of learning groups is preferred worldwide today, because in almost all countries around the world there is no fundamental selection of students before the ninth or tenth grade. Germany (and likewise Austria)[167] has yet to provide evidence that its selective school system, which separates students after the fourth grade, is more successful than those of other countries (see above). Long-term comparisons by the OECD and UNESCO consistently show unfavorable

164
According to the 2018 OECD report, class sizes in Germany are larger than in many other industrialized countries. This makes individual support more difficult. See The OECD *Teaching and Learning International Survey (TALIS)* (Ainley / Carstens (2018))

165
In Germany, admission to teacher training programs in many places is based on a numerus clausus (NC). In other successful countries, such as Finland, candidates undergo a multi-stage selection process that places particular emphasis on future-oriented skills such as communication and cooperation, as well as on applicants' motivation for entering a profession that enjoys high social recognition. See Kricke (2016)

166
Cf. OECD (2010d); Bertelsmann Stiftung (2010)

167
Austria has a two-tier school system, which is also not among the top performers. Switzerland also still has a two-tier school system but invests significantly more in education.

results for Germany: more unqualified individuals, more students leaving school without qualifications, fewer students completing higher secondary education (Abitur), and weaker PISA results compared to other similar countries.

The observation that Germany has made too little progress toward achieving the goals of the UN Convention is the result of an analysis of average national data. A look at the federal states reveals a more differentiated picture: In some states, the proportion of students educated in special schools—and thus in exclusive settings—has increased since 2008, meaning that these states have therefore move away from the goal formulated in the UN Convention since 2008/09. On the other hand, there are 12 states where the exclusion rate has decreased, in some cases significantly, over the same period: Bremen, Schleswig-Holstein, and Berlin, with exclusion rates of 0.76 percent (Bremen), 2.28 percent (Schleswig-Holstein), and 2.37 percent (Berlin).[168] There are also major differences and outstanding developments in individual municipalities. The city of Jena, for example, achieved an exclusion rate of 0.5 percent in 2020 after 10 years of municipal school development.[169] Conversely, the »persistence of exclusion« is also evident in the fact that several states »can report improved inclusion rates, but continue to expand exclusive structures contrary to the UN CRPD.«[170]

168
Cf. Klemm (2013b); (2015)

169
Stadt Jena (2021)

170
Rackles (2021), p. 67

At the same time, municipalities expect investment to focus on building accessible facilities and providing additional space. »Looking ahead, half of the municipalities surveyed expect spending on measures to support school integration to increase, while 47 percent expect spending to remain the same. Municipalities see an increasing need for funding, especially for the necessary hiring of additional staff (57 percent), the provision of inclusive all-day programs and additional rooms (50 percent each), and the procurement of additional teaching and learning materials.«[171]

171
See the *KfW-Kommunalpanel 2016* with the focus topic: Education, schools, and inclusion, p. 32

And it is repeatedly confirmed that Germany still has too many early school leavers and too few high school graduates compared to the rest of Europe.[172] Moreover, spending on education as a percentage of gross domestic product has fallen slightly instead of rising.

172
OECD (2011c)

German companies are increasingly warning of the high follow-up costs of our school system, which is no longer competitive in the long term.[173]

173
Cf., e.g., Wössmann (2007); Wössmann/Piopiunik (2009)

THESIS 6

Cultural and aesthetic education must be conveyed through pedagogy and architecture.

The expansion of learning in the direction of musical, kinesthetic, emotional, and spatially creative learning has long been recognized in research on teaching and learning.[174] Cultural learning fields from the areas of music, dance, art, and movement create the basis for creativity—and have an unsurpassable intrinsic value beyond all considerations of usefulness: They open up possibilities for personal expression and creative development that cannot be achieved through language alone. Cultural practice creates individual access to cultural traditions that remains closed off when presented only through theory-based »instruction.«

German schools are dominated by languages and STEM subjects: German, English, and mathematics (which, upon closer inspection, can be seen as a highly formalized »language«), engineering, science, and technology are currently the favored subjects in terms of school resources. These subjects receive the highest proportion of instructional time, have the most differentiated curricula, and are decisive for promotion to the next grade.[175] PISA and other comparative tests have long focused almost exclusively on this sector, partly because it seems easier to measure than, say, the arts.[176] At first glance, this priority seems plausible, since language skills in the broadest sense are indeed a crucial key to the modern world of work and participation in social life. However, this priority must not lead to a narrowing of education in the broader sense at school, when it marginalizes stimuli from other areas, especially with regard to the demands of our digital world.

Skills acquired through learning are always future-oriented. They cannot be based solely on the example of a school that focuses primarily on linguistic and mathematical-operational performance while neglecting other cultural subjects. It is also a problem that several cultural subjects appear to be of secondary importance because they are not considered particularly attractive as a profession in society (due to uncertain career paths, lower income, difficult career planning). Skills, however, do not emerge from a single subject or can be limited to specific subject content. They need to be awakened, interconnected, and activated across subjects. The experience of experimental schools and schools that have won the German School Award shows that drama and dance, singing and design, movement and physical challenges in many different forms produce strong outcomes in these areas—and that achievement in these areas also have a positive impact on school performance overall. For instance, a series of musical performances can have a positive impact throughout the entire school. Whether this effect is due to direct cognitive stimulation—which is

174
The research findings of Howard Gardner, for example, who practically studies his theses of »multiple intelligence« in »Project Zero« at Harvard, are decisive here. For an introduction, see, for example, Gardner (1991); (1993); (1997)

175
Unless, as in Hamburg and Berlin, promotion regulations are generally abolished.

176
Two trends are emerging: In response to the demands on competencies in the 21st century, skills such as the 4C / 6C, the aspect of »well-being,« or transformation skills (»student agency,« see OECD (2019)) are moving into focus. At the same time, the nationwide »Startchancen-Programm« (2024–2034), for example, is particularly aimed at strengthening basic skills such as reading, writing, and arithmetic; www.bmbf.de/startchancen-programm

☞ Chapter 1, *Education as a Human Right*, p. 13

difficult to measure—or to a change in attitude toward the school, which has an indirect effect on motivation, does not necessarily need to be determined.

Cultural offerings are often found in minor subjects, which are always struggling to survive in schools as the subject load in core subjects increases. Nevertheless, successful school systems are increasingly recognizing the value of the active and creative learning process of these subjects. There is enormous potential here for the development of future-oriented skills such as creativity, but also for promoting the well-being of students through active experiences of self-efficacy. However, these subjects can't just be taught in theory. They have to establish their own practice in which what seems culturally desirable is applied. This requires a current and active engagement with cultural practice. Schools have been particularly successful in this regard when they have, for example, been able to integrate an artist for a long-term project, or visited places of learning in the neighborhood and their local actors. This approach is particularly advantageous when schools avoid a common pitfall: trying to »teach« as much as possible and thus conveying too little of anything. Instead, the focus should lie on the consistent implementation of one or a few specific projects.[177]

☛ Chapter 2, *Thesis 10*, pp. 49 ff.

177
See the »*Rhythm is it!*« project by Royston Maldoom and the Berlin Philharmonic Orchestra, an exceptional project, but one that impressively demonstrates the impact of artistic / aesthetic learning and can therefore serve as an inspiring example. Internationally, there are numerous different approaches to implementing cultural education in schools through collaboration with artists. These programs often vary greatly in terms of their goals, content, and working methods, illustrating how diverse the possibilities for school practice can be. Cf. Bamford (2006); Eger (2014)

Finally, the school buildings themselves and their surroundings also contribute to the students' »building culture awareness.« This focus is explicitly addressed in the federal government's 2024 Guidelines for Baukultur: *Co-designing spaces for the common good.* In Guideline 3, the federal states are encouraged »on the basis of their cultural sovereignty, to advocate the compulsory teaching of Baukultur at kindergartens, schools, vocational schools, universities and colleges...« (p. 49). One example of this is the »B wie Baukultur« project in North Rhine-Westphalia, which focuses on engaging with our living environments. By raising awareness in this area, children and young people are empowered to actively participate in improving their surroundings. This, in turn, can have a positive impact on the well-being and thus the personal development of learners.[178]

178
See bwiebaukultur.nrw; Bundesstiftung Baukultur (2024b)

☛ Chapter 6, *Thesis 4*, pp. 190 ff.

THESIS 7

Learning with a focus on health and movement takes place in stimulating environments.

Research on learning, the brain, and health has demonstrated in a variety of ways that learning is not just a matter of the mind. It involves the whole body.[179] Meeting basic physiological needs such as light and air, rest and exercise is essential for successful learning and healthy living and working.

179
See, for example, Hunger/Zimmer (2024); Andrä/Macedonia (Eds.) (2020); Lueg (2024); BMG (2022)

This requires an appropriate learning environment that appeals to all senses and is optimally designed in terms of work psychology and ergonomics, with bright natural light, regular air exchange, appropriate temperature control, good room acoustics, and avoidance of reverberation. Adequate breaks, a healthy diet that includes plenty of fresh and uncooked vegetarian food, and, finally, clean and atmospherically appropriate sanitary facilities that are accepted and used by the students are also particularly important.[180]

180
Cf. Brägger/Posse (2007)

Exercise and nutrition

The ratio of group size to room size is essential for the necessary freedom of movement in the learning/teaching area. The more space available, the better the variety of activity needs can be met in a differentiated learning setting. The current standard of two square meters per student in the general learning and teaching area—especially in all-day schools—is far from sufficient to integrate a variety of movement phases into everyday learning routines. For this reason, the guidelines for efficient school buildings in Germany recommend a standard of 4.5–5.5 square meters per pupil for general learning and teaching areas (including differentiation rooms and pedagogically usable circulation areas, e.g., in a cluster). Equally important, however, is the outdoor space: areas protected from rain/sun as well as outdoor areas with a wide range of challenging movement opportunities, not limited to the specific situation of »physical education.«

A balanced diet and sufficient physical activity are even more important given the overall alarming state of student health in Germany. In 2013, the Robert Koch Institute (KiGGS study) published the results of a first wave of surveys involving more than 12,000 children and adolescents aged 0 and 17—overweight and obesity among adolescents had »stabilized at a high level,« as confirmed by the second KiGGS wave (2014–2017).[181] Children from low-income or immigrant families are particularly affected.[182] Schools must take proactive steps to counter this problem. In an increasingly sedentary culture, physical activity not only improves health and supports learning but also helps establish behavioral patterns that remain effective in adulthood. Just as knowledge must be acquired to

181
Robert Koch Institut (2003–2017)

182
Cf. Bilz et al. (Eds.) (2016)

navigate a culture, movement must be learned to sustainably strengthen health and fitness while being tailored to individual motivations: Preserving a child's natural desire to move is far more important than achieving technical perfection in any athletic discipline.

The topic of movement also involves the important issue of safety. There is often the problem that (illusory) efforts to eliminate all residual risks can lead to massive restrictions on physical activity—without actually being able to avoid the unavoidable residual risks. Everyday experience also shows that overprotected young people will eventually seek out risk in their own way to test their limits—sometimes with far riskier consequences.

Well-being

The concept of well-being in education, which goes beyond health, now has a broader approach, also in an international context. It is both a goal and a quality. Well-being has been recognized and studied as a relevant factor for learning success for many years.[183] The OECD *Learning Compass 2030* places particular emphasis on this concept. It emphasizes the connection between physical and mental health, and between the well-being of individuals and that of society. Well-being is described as a guiding concept and a common goal of learning. It is a holistic concept that links different aspects of personal quality of life with material conditions and the overall context. The concept includes health, work-life balance, quality education, community spirit, civic engagement, the environment, personal security, and subjective life satisfaction on the one hand, employment, income, and housing conditions on the other.[184]

In general, the mental well-being and mental health of children and adolescents have come to the fore, especially during and since the coronavirus pandemic. Today, they also play a key role in the context of an increasingly digital culture and living environment.[185]

183 Hascher/Hagenauer (2011); CODE Consortium (2018); DKJS (2019)

184 OECD (2019), p. 28

185 See also *SINUS Youth Study* (2024), pp. 214 ff.

☞ Chapter 6, *Thesis 4*, pp. 190 ff.

THESIS 8

Democratic learning requires a democratic school.

Democratic action is necessary in a democratic society if people are to live together with successful communication and non-violent conflict resolution. Schools must not limit themselves to teaching such behavior merely as knowledge of rules and institutions. Rather, such behavior must be available to children and young people as a model within the family, at school, and in everyday life, so that it can be understood and practiced. Schools have a special role to play here, as they can create a preferred place and framework for preparing children and young people specifically for democratic participation and for fostering a sense of democratic engagement. In many OECD countries, democracy on a small scale is therefore seen as an essential foundation for democracy on a large scale—a democracy based on the separation of powers, political equality, and unconditional respect for the dignity of all people, as enshrined and legally protected in democratic constitutions.[186]

186 See also the BMFSFJ's federal program »Live Democracy!,« which entered its third funding period in January 2025 (2025–2032). demokratie-leben.de. It is possible to work with children on democracy and their rights from nursery and elementary school level, as shown by the successful »Kinder-Rechte-Schule« project run by the elementary school association. weltinderschule.uni-bremen.de/detail/kinder-rechte-schule.html

Political interest among young people

Democratic learning builds awareness of the existence and nature of democratic structures on both a small and large scale. It also includes awakening an interest in politics among children and young people to give them an insight into the mechanisms and authorities of a democratic state. The *2024 Shell Youth Study* shows that there is still a need for action in this area. Although it confirms that young people's interest in politics is increasing in relative terms, a closer look at the absolute figures is worrying: well over 50 percent of young people still have no interest in getting involved in politics. The latest *SINUS Youth Study* also describes young people's political interest as »limited.« The main reasons cited are a perceived lack of influence and low levels of political knowledge[187]—both of which underscore the urgent need for democratic education in schools.

187 *SINUS Jugendstudie* (2024), p. 304

Interest in politics on the rise

Political interest 2002 to 2024 in comparison

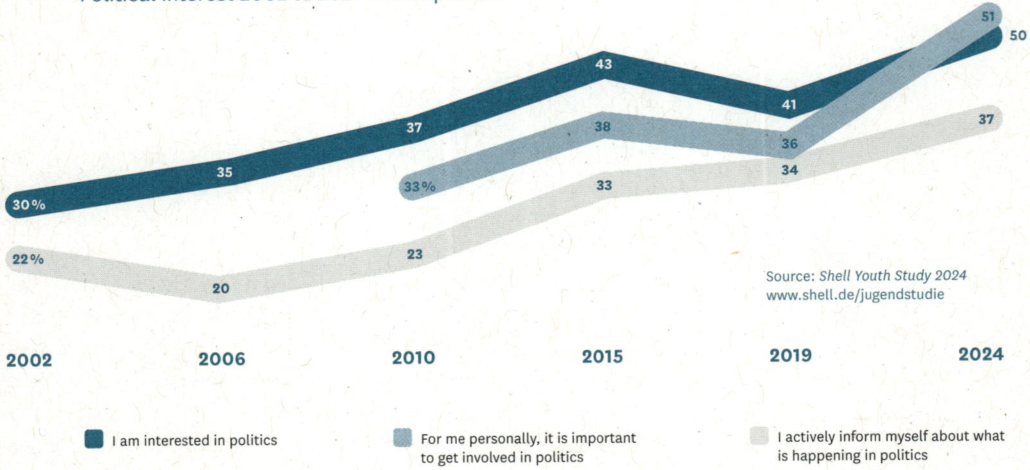

The 2022 ICCS study points to massive differences in average political knowledge between school types. Conclusion: The findings underscore the urgency of discussing how school systems can better fulfill their responsibilities to prepare all students—not just privileged subgroups—equally for their role as citizens in a democracy, and to create conditions in which the necessary skills can be developed.[188]

188 Abs et al. (Eds.) (2024), p. 11

New fears

Young people are afraid of …

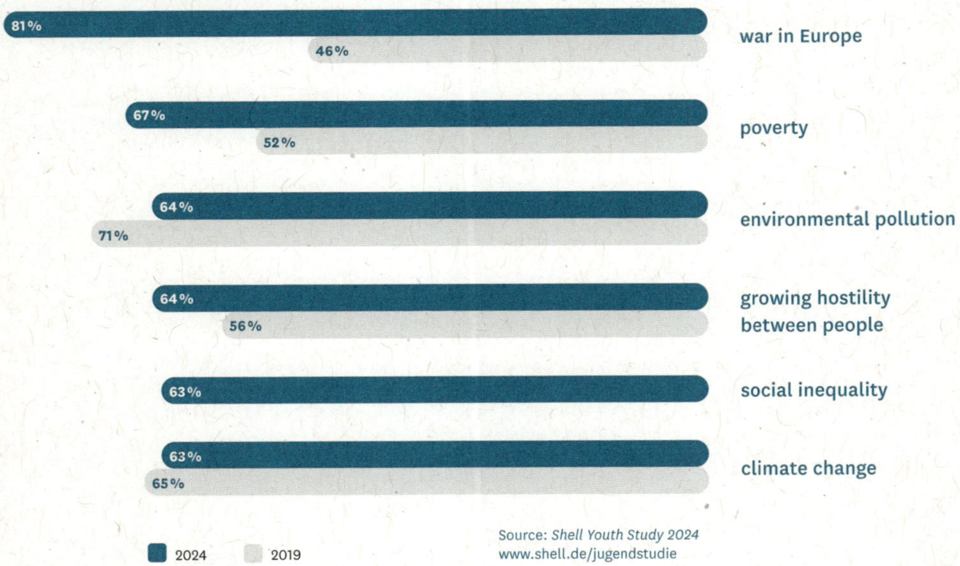

At the same time, fears are increasing. Fears of war in Europe have increased significantly up to 35 percent compared to 2019.[189] Fears of poverty and growing hostility between people have also increased. When it comes to the current issue of immigration, defensive figures predominate. Only 34 percent of young people are afraid of immigration, while more than half are afraid not of foreigners but of xenophobia. The SINUS study *How do young people tick in 2024* lists climate change, war, inflation, artificial intelligence, and surveillance through technology as general »social concerns« of the young people surveyed. It also points out that young people associate hopes with the future, while worries are primarily personal in nature.[190] As a result, there is a growing tendency toward loneliness, especially among young people.[191] This is partly due to the use of social media, where people may be well connected on Instagram or TikTok, for example, but have no or few friendships in real life. The coronavirus pandemic is also known to have worsened the overall mental health of children and adolescents.[192] Even years later, the accompanying COPSY study (2020–2024) found stagnation and worse mental health conditions than before the pandemic: Anxieties, »particularly those related to global conflicts and the climate crisis, are now affecting quality of life and well-being.«[193]

In the context of democracy, digital media are both a curse and a blessing. Global accessibility and open communication channels for everyone have made the world of information more accessible. There is (almost) no one who cannot participate. Ultimately, it is in the nature of things that technologies can (always) be used for different purposes. However, critical views now prevailed, especially regarding children and young people. Instead of enabling an unprecedented diversity of opinions, so-called »social« media are now best known for spreading disinformation, fake news, populism, hate speech, and other phenomena that threaten democracy.[194] The *17th Report on Children and Youth* of the Federal Ministry for Family Affairs, Senior Citizens, Women and Youth devotes a separate section to the topic of »Digitalization and Democracy.«[195] It refers to the spread of »anti-democratic and authoritarian positions« via social media. The underlying mechanisms are described as a »danger to the basic democratic order«: »With the perspective of post-digitality, i.e., the normalization of the digital in social reality, these—sometimes complex—mechanisms and their consequences are increasingly coming to the fore.«[196] In this context, schools have an educational and enlightening function—which, according to the *Shell Youth Study*, young people expect and demand from schools.[197]

The attitude of the learning guides is the basis

The basis of social learning is the opportunity for students to have a real say and to act independently and together in everyday school life. To this end, the willingness of teachers/learning guides to seriously relinquish a considerable amount of their own power and to allow sufficient freedom for genuine participation is of paramount importance. At the same time, patience and consistency are needed to keep encouraging learners to actively participate. This is the only way they can learn to

189 *Shell Youth Study* (2024)

190 *SINUS Jugendstudie* (2024), pp. 150 f.

191 See BBC (2018), The *BBC Loneliness Experiment*. The study surveyed more than 55,000 people aged 16 and over from 237 countries. In the analysis, it was not only surprising that it was predominantly young people who suffered from loneliness, but also that more men than women did so. In the Shell Youth Study (2024), on the other hand, »more than one in four young women (27 percent) and more than one in five young men (21 percent)« stated that they often feel lonely.

192 The COPSY study conducted at the University Medical Center Hamburg-Eppendorf (UKE) has been investigating this since 2020.

193 Press release of the UKE Hamburg, 04.12.2024

194 See, for example, the study by Lorenz-Spreen et al. (2023), Kompetenznetzwerk Gegen Hass (2024)

195 BMFSFJ (2024), pp. 105 f.

196 Ibid., p. 106

197 *Shell Youth Study* (2024), Summary, p. 22

assess how complex democratic processes are and how much effort they require. This works best when both sides can experience such democracy as meaningful and beneficial to their thoughts and actions.

Overall, young people's trust in institutions, willingness to vote, and voter turnout among 16- to 29-year-olds have risen steadily, as has their interest in politics. Three-quarters of young people are fairly or very satisfied with democracy.[198] In practice, however, questions of concrete participation at school often take a different course. The task is to create a framework at school in which students can experience the demands of democratic life at an early age:[199] Acting democratically means accepting the difficulty of negotiating one's own opinions and interests with or against others. This includes the initially disappointing experience that democracy does not mean that one's own interests always »win,« but that it involves compromises that are not always easy to bear. And it includes the experience that every social system defines limits that are not negotiable in the participatory process.

198
Shell Youth Study (2024); however, after a long period of increase, satisfaction with democracy among young people in Eastern Germany is now declining again (currently 60 percent).

199
For further orientation, see also Reich's pool of methods, methodenpool.de; a comprehensive collection of examples and theoretical justifications of democracy can be found at: www.demokratisch-handeln.de

Learning itself as a subject of democratic participation

The seriousness with which a school embraces democratic learning is determined by the sensitive question of whether and to what extent learning itself becomes a subject of participation: Students should be actively involved in the selection and design of their learning content. If self-determination, co-determination, and independent action interact at the heart of the educational process and condition one another, then they can also become the basis for later action after school. This has implications not only for learning democracy, but also for learning itself: just as autonomous activity is the basis for the successful creation of self-determined processes, the opportunity to learn in a self-determined way also serves as a motivating foundation for becoming active, i.e., for advancing a fruitful learning process through independent work. It emphasizes how important it is for learners to take responsibility through »independent action and design competence.« In a changing education system, the role of students »is changing from participants in the classroom learning by listening to directions of teachers with emerging autonomy to active participants with both student agency and co-agency in particular with teacher agency, who also shape the classroom environments.«[200]

200
OECD (2019), p. 13

This focus is also confirmed by the work of the Citizens' Council for Education and Learning: children and young people were involved in all stages of the project, which lasted several years, and in their own workshops.[201] Motivation and willingness to participate were high. The exchange among the children themselves, with the adults in the Citizens' Council, and with politicians made democratic processes tangible (»Oh, that's how democracy works!«). Encouraging and revitalizing one's own creative power and self-efficacy as powerful drivers for active participation is therefore a central task for a democratic school in which everyone feels a sense of belonging.

201
The project was initiated by the Montag Stiftung Denkwerkstatt. The children and young people's recommendations were published in 2023 under the title *»Hört uns zu!« (Listen to us!).*

Rules for co-determination

Schools will never be a place free of power and authority, as envisioned by some utopian school reformers. There can be no equality in the strict sense, simply because of the age-related advantage in experience and the legally prescribed responsibilities of adults. Inequality of power in itself is not a problem. The risk of abuse of power is reduced, for example, when clear rules for dealing with each other are drawn up together and constantly updated, setting out not only demands but also responsibilities and comprehensible checks. Students also want such rules—but they also want to be asked which rules should apply and to what extent they make sense. The goal is to give students as much self-determination as possible. This basic democratic principle always begins on a small scale and develops step by step in line with the students' age and maturity.

Listen, let others finish, be attentive

It is not enough to draw up and write down rules. It is necessary to be aware that learners and their guides are not, as usual, two parties (often working against each other) whose tasks are clearly separated: teachers plan and structure the learning process and set the learning objectives; learners follow this structure and have to achieve the learning objectives if they want to be promoted or rewarded. In a school that seeks to foster democracy, a different attitude must prevail. Learning guides and learners are jointly responsible—albeit in different proportions—for the success of the school year and the pedagogical process. This includes, for example, the culture of conversation that must apply to both students and teachers: listening, letting others finish, being attentive. In this way, discussions and disagreements can be resolved. In these discussions, it is assumed that certain procedural rules are followed that govern this process. It is part of the fundamental democratic experience that rules are developed and established together with the learning group. In such a framework created for the three »Rs« of school life—rules, rituals, realms—learners and teachers can develop self-confidence and self-esteem: »This is our school!«

Democratic institution – democratic culture

The school should form a coherent concept of democratic education, which finds institutional expression in various successive forms—from the class council per class or year level, to the student council, parents' representatives, school parliament, and school assembly. In addition to student participation, the school explicitly provides for parental participation and involvement. The Standing Conference of the Ministers of Education and Cultural Affairs (KMK) also »regularly addresses the strengthening of democratic education and attaches great importance to the expansion of student participation.«[202]

202 BMFSFJ (2015), p. 20

A school mission statement adopted by the school council reflects the school's most important goals and methods. On the one hand, it should provide a conceptual framework that does not have to be constantly questioned but can be lived by mutual agreement. At the same time, it should be constantly evolving to adapt to changing environmental conditions.

There are basic democratic rules that apply to all schools. However, each school must develop its own mission statement process and make its own rules and implementation understandable. Only in this way can the democratic role model effect be achieved through the chosen attitude and conviction of all.

An open flow of information is the basis for the transparency of decisions and their preparation. This flow of information is institutionalized through the intranet and other modern media, but above all through direct personal communication.

A democratic culture also includes continuous evaluation of the school, the results of which are made public within the school community. Strengths and weaknesses should be identified to enter a continuous, collaborative process of improvement. Such a democratic culture develops and manifests itself publicly in the school and in the district or municipality. It exhibits, presents, and celebrates its results.

THESIS 9

School is a role model in dealing with the environment, materials, and technology.

To meet the global environmental, economic, and social challenges we face, everyone must change the way they think and act. A shift in mindset is necessary because the decisions people make about how they consume affect others—both locally and globally, today and in the future. People around the world need not only knowledge, but also skills and values that enable them to act responsibly. This is the goal of Education for Sustainable Development (ESD), which is also enshrined in *Education 2030*.[203]

203
Cf. Deutsche UNESCO-Kommission (2015)

Schools are always part of a larger environment and represent an attitude toward nature and technology, both internally and externally. With regard to environmental education, which has become an essential part of education today, schools should make a positive relationship with the environment tangible.

Overall, public interest in sustainability and environmental issues has declined in recent years. In the latest survey conducted by the German Environment Agency, environmental concerns now rank only fifth among the most important political issues—behind health, education, social justice, and security policy.[204] However, young people between the ages of 14 and 22 see things differently: 74 percent of them rank environmental and climate protection as the most pressing issue facing our country today, followed by the state of the education system.[205] At the same time, there has been a decline in sustainable behavior and political engagement for environmental and climate protection.[206]

204
Umweltbundesamt (2016), p. 21

205
Umweltbundesamt (2023)

206
BMUV/UBA (2024), p. 25

There is still a certain helplessness among young people about how to solve these problems in a meaningful way. As individuals, they often feel unable to change the environment for the better. They place the main responsibility on politicians—calling for, among other things, stricter regulations for industry and greater independence form lobbying interests.

The authors of a study by the Federal Environment Agency, *Einblick in die Jugendkultur – Das Thema Nachhaltigkeit bei der jungen Generation anschlussfähig machen (Insights into Youth Culture—Making Sustainability Accessible to the Young Generation)*,[207] identify the following main reasons based on an in-depth analysis of the attitudes of the various youth scenes in Germany:

207
Thío/Göll (2011)

— the high complexity and limited comprehensibility of environmental and sustainability issues;

— the overshadowing of these topics by concerns that feel more immediate to young people, such as the threat of unemployment and difficulties in finding their way in a complex society;

— the pragmatic discrepancy—which young people themselves are well aware of—between the articulated attitudes or environmental awareness of young people on the one hand, and their everyday world or their everyday behavior on the other;
— shortcomings or inadequacies in environmental and sustainability communication.

The same study provides a detailed account of how ineffectively the topic has so far been anchored in the everyday life of most schools in Germany (ibid., pp. 81 ff.)—and how great the opportunities could be if schools embraced this task with creativity and practical examples of implementation.

Take waste management as an example: Those schools have proven effective that not only provide opportunities for students to separate and recycle their waste, but also involve them directly in cleaning and tidying up using environmentally friendly techniques. Any money saved through these practices should be reinvested directly into learning projects.

Such supervisory and accountability structures need to be jointly developed and clearly defined based on each school's experience, since they rarely emerge on their own in ideal form. The spectrum of topics for hands-on sustainability education is broad, ranging from
— green classroom to school garden (see www.gruen-macht-schule.de);
— student positions like »energy monitors« to whole-school eco-audits;
— student-run businesses selling »fair trade« products to tree-planting project in the city forest;
— »healthy lunchbox« initiatives to regular air quality testing on the way to school, with the results published in the local press;
— »Bike to School« campaigns to municipal policy projects addressing shortcomings in public transport, and so on.

The school building itself serves as a role model: Sustainability criteria for construction, operation, convertibility, and demolition have already reached a high standard under current guidelines. However, it is equally important to make these technical connections visible and actively comprehensible for students—for instance, through appropriate monitoring devices used in student projects.

The outdoor areas of the school should offer a variety of learning and experimental opportunities, which are also linked to fostering an awareness of the use of resources and the maintenance of facilities. Especially in the form of projects, learners can link environmental and technical learning across different subjects—provided that an interdisciplinary approach is jointly developed in the school and transferred to all school subjects.

THESIS 10

The school opens up to the city—the city opens up to the school.

In the most recent Shell Youth Study (2024), 40 percent of young people (across all school types) reported being frequently active for society or simply for others. Compared to 2019, social and civic engagement among young people has increased, but from a long-term perspective, it still remains at the same level as in the past twenty years. To counteract this, a growing number of initiatives are currently being developed in the federal states under the umbrella term »Service Learning« (also known as LdE = »Learning through Engagement«).[208] Opening up schools to the city plays a crucial role in this. In the past, the problem was essentially self-inflicted: The traditional school was a largely »closed system,« aiming to provide all the necessary resources internally. This system was rightly criticized as an artificial learning environment, disconnected from the realities of life and work. If the shift toward competence-based education is to be effective in preparing students for life and work, then schools must consciously open up and depart from the outdated model.

208
E.g., servicelearning.de/; aktive-buergerschaft.de/service-learning/service-learning-mit-sozialgenial/

From an educational point of view, such an opening has an internal and an external dimension. The internal opening involves overcoming excessively narrow, subject-specific perspectives in all disciplines and developing a more holistic view. What is the point of acquiring more and more specialized knowledge in all subjects, if general education suffers as a result? Each subject needs to be reviewed to determine to what extent interdisciplinary skills are conveyed and what specialized knowledge is needed when shifting to competence-based education. All subjects must address relevant real-life applications—and not just offer preparation for specific professions. For instance, mathematics lessons should not primarily benefit future mathematics majors.

The external opening refers to the fact that schools today, more than in the past, are actively seeking connections to the outside world. This includes, but goes beyond, mandatory student internships. From a pedagogical point of view, four types of opening up schools to the community can be distinguished, some with considerable implications for the spatial design of school buildings.[209]

209
See Seydel (2015), pp. 23 ff.; Imhäuser (2016)

	School facilities	Municipal facilities
Low/no institutional integration	Co-use by non-school groups outside of school hours (sports clubs, music schools, adult education centers, etc.)	Co-use by the school during school hours (sports facilities, public library, park, multi-purpose hall, etc.)
Institutional integration	»Brede School« school as a community center)	Educational landscape/»community school« (city as a school)

Double occupancy: School premises are made available outside regular teaching hours to non-school users such as sports clubs, music schools, children's art academies, adult education centers, etc. It is possible for students to participate in such activities. The primary motivation is initially economic synergy through dual usage. Public budgets can be relieved by using school facilities in the evenings, on weekends, and during holidays. The same is true in the reverse case when the school uses the sports field of the nearby football club for physical education in the morning, the municipal multi-purpose hall as an auditorium, etc. What may begin as a side benefit—such as the option for students to take part in music school courses held at the school in the afternoons—can evolve into a specific profile for the school, such as a focus on music education. Moreover, a school can become a real cultural »magnet,« with its energy radiating back into day-to-day teaching and learning, for example, when a foyer, extended into a school hall, serves as a public theater stage, a venue for local political forums, an art exhibition space, and much more.

School as a community center – community center as a school: Several non-school but school-related institutions are not merely »temporary tenants« in the evenings but move permanently into the school with their own spaces, also during school hours. This might include not only the municipal library, but a wide range of social and cultural institutions that are important both for the community as a whole and for the education of children and young people. However, these are not »schools« but independent institutions. Examples of this »concentration model« can be found in the Netherlands (Brede Schools).

External experts from the district as part of the learning process: This variant is spatially neutral. The focus is solely on the direct educational benefit for the students. People from the district (and beyond), from »real life,« are specifically invited to the school for individual learning units or temporary projects: as discussion partners, experts, co-learners, critics. Examples include: a politician for the panel discussion, a beekeeper for the bee project, an actor serving on the jury of a reading competition.[210]

Educational landscape – city as a school: The term »educational landscape« is currently used for the fourth variant, the »dispersion model,« of which the school is just one institution among many. Here, however, the term encompasses more than just an organizational network of various institutions that coordinate their work priorities. By purposefully opening the school to the outside world, the students are actively exposed to other environments and prepared for transitions after leaving school. The Community School concept, which originated in the Anglo-Saxon world, was discussed intensively in the 1980s.[211] At that time, it was often associated with far-reaching political visions suggesting that educational structures could directly compensate for social disadvantages. Today, this »political and moral charge« of the concept has largely receded. Instead, the introduction of all-day schools has increased the importance of extracurricular activities. For all-day schools in particular, it makes sense to actively seek cooperation with various local partners. These could be directly involved

210
See Sliwka / Frank (2004). Helpful suggestions can also be found in Strenger / Fritsche (2006). Cf. also International Academy gGmbH (INA) / Institute for Community Education

211
Zimmer / Niggemeyer (1992); Buhren (1997)

in the school's projects or extracurricular groups or even take them over completely.

At least as valuable—especially for upper secondary students—is to provide »time slots« within the all-day program during which they (are required to) go beyond the boundaries of the school to be active in local non-school organizations. Feedback and reflection loops with the school, which have proven successful for social and work experience internships, can be adapted for these contexts to ensure the school continues to fulfill its duty of supervision and support. Another variant for the consistent shift of educational processes back into »normal« social contexts beyond usual school routines is found in »production schools.« These have recently increasingly focused on students who have lost out in education or refused to attended school—with an ultramodern concept that originated 100 years ago.[212]

The OECD defines four scenarios for the future of education, all of which involve the opening up of schools in a broader sense. In addition to collaboration, outsourcing, and delocalization, schools are becoming »learning hubs« that reach beyond their own boundaries and walls to connect with the neighborhood—thus unlocking new possibilities for learning: »favouring ever-changing forms of learning, civic engagement and social innovation.«[213]

212
Cf. werkstattschule-bremerhaven.de; bv-produktionsschulen.de

213
OECD (2020), p. 7. One example is the city of Vilnius, which sees itself as a holistic place of learning and invites people to learn beyond school (»Vilnius is a school«).

7

ANNEX

Examples
FAQ
Glossary
Bibliography
Index

EXAMPLES

We have cited the following examples in previous editions of this book. There are many other interesting examples, and new ones are constantly emerging—it's worth doing some research!

#CLASSROOM-PLUS

A.P. Moller Skolen (Schleswig, Germany)
Architecture: C.F. Moller Architects, Aarhus

Bildungszentrum Tor zur Welt (Hamburg, Germany)
Architecture: bof architekten, Hamburg; Breimann & Bruun Landschaftsarchitekten, Hamburg

Gesamtschule in der Höh (Volketswil, Switzerland)
Architecture: Gafner + Horisberger Architekten GmbH, Zurich; Landschaftsplaner Guido Hager, Zurich

Grundschule Herringhausen (Herford, Germany)
Architecture: fun architekten + ingenieure, Herford

Grundschule Landsberger Straße (Herford, Germany)
Architecture: Sittig + Voges (Bovenden, architectural office); Dr. Wilfried Buddensiek (Paderborn University, pedagogue); Rainer Schweppe (Head of the School Department); Martina Hoff (Landschafts-architecturebüro Hoff, Essen)

Internationale Friedensschule Köln (Cologne, Germany)
Architecture: plus+ bauplanung GmbH Hübner-Forster-Hübner-Remes Freie Architekten, Neckartenzlingen

Munkegaard Skole (Gentofte, Denmark)
Architecture: Arne Jacobsen (1957), Copenhagen; Dorte Mandrup Arkitekter (2009), Copenhagen

Neues Gymnasium Wilhelmshaven (Wilhelmshaven, Germany)
Architecture: Hausmann Architektur, Aachen

St. Nicolaaslyceum (Amsterdam, the Netherlands)
Architecture: DP6 Architectuurstudio, Delft

#CLUSTER

Bildungscampus Sonnwendviertel (Vienna, Austria)
Architecture: PPAG architects, Vienna

Bildungshaus Westpark (Augsburg, Germany)
Architecture: Hausmann Architektur, Aachen

Bildungslandschaft Altstadt Nord (BAN) (Cologne, Germany)
Architecture: IAA Architecten, Enschede; gernot schulz : architektur, Cologne

Grund- und Mittelschule Welsberg (Welsberg, Italy)
Architecture: Otto Irsara, Bruneck

Grundschule am Ilse-von-Twardowski-Platz (Munich, Germany)
Architecture: balda architekten GmbH, Fürstenfeldbruck

Gymnasium Neubiberg (Neubiberg, Germany)
Architecture: ARGE Venus Architekten, Munich, balda architekten GmbH, Fürstenfeldbruck

Gymnasium Trudering (Munich, Germany)
Architecture: felix schürmann ellen dettinger architekten, Munich

Gymnasium und Integrierte Sekundarschule Allee der Kosmonauten (Berlin, Germany)
Architecture: PPAG architects ZT GmbH

Heisenberg-Gymnasium (Bruchsal, Germany)
Architecture: Hausmann Architektur, Aachen

IJburg College (Amsterdam, the Netherlands)
Architecture: LIAG architekten en bouwadviseurs, The Hague

Integrierte Gesamtschule Alexej von Jawlensky (Wiesbaden, Germany)
Architecture: Zaeske und Partner Architekten BDA, Wiesbaden

Jenaplanschule (Weimar, Germany)
Architecture: gernot schulz : architektur, Cologne, Hausmann Architektur, Aachen

Neue Schule Wolfsburg (Wolfsburg, Germany)
Architecture: Kirstin Bartels, Hamburg; Schneider + Sendelbach Architektengesellschaft mbH, Braunschweig

Ordrup Skole (Gentofte, Denmark)
Architecture: Bosch & Fjord, Copenhagen (reconstruction, interior design); CEBRA arkitekter, Aarhus with Sören Robert Lund arkitekter, Copenhagen (extension)

4 elementary schools in modular design (Munich, Germany)
Architecture: wulf architekten, Stuttgart

#CORRIDORS AS EDUCATIONAL SPACES

Bildungshaus Westpark (Augsburg, Germany)
Architecture: Hausmann Architektur, Aachen

Corlaer College (Nijkerk, the Netherlands)
Architecture: Broekbakema, Rotterdam

Fioretti College (Lisse, the Netherlands)
Architecture: Broekbakema, Rotterdam

Heisenberg-Gymnasium (Bruchsal, Germany)
Architecture: Hausmann Architektur, Aachen

IJburg College (Amsterdam, the Netherlands)
Architecture: LIAG architekten en bouwadviseurs, The Hague

Neues Gymnasium Wilhelmshaven (Wilhelmshaven, Germany)
Architecture: Hausmann Architektur, Aachen

Oulun Normaalikoulu (Oulu, Finland)
Architecture: Heikki Taskinen, Oulu

Ringstabekk Skole (Baerum, Norway)
Architecture: div. A arkitekter, Oslo

St. Nicolaaslyceum (Amsterdam, the Netherlands)
Architecture: DP6 Architectuurstudio, Delft

#FOYERS, AUDITORIUMS, CAFETERIAS

Bildungshaus Westpark (Augsburg, Germany)
Architecture: Hausmann Architektur, Aachen

Bildungszentrum Tor zur Welt (Hamburg, Germany)
Architecture: bof architekten, Hamburg; Breimann & Bruun Landschaftsarchitekten, Hamburg

Corlaer College (Nijkerk, the Netherlands)
Architecture: Broekbakema, Rotterdam

Fioretti College (Lisse, the Netherlands)
Architecture: Broekbakema, Rotterdam

Grevelokka Skole (Hamar, Norway)
Architecture: Otto Ostli, Hamar, with Jacobsen & Reiten Arkitektkontor AS, Gjovik

Gymnasium Kirschgarten (Basel, Switzerland)
Architecture: HHF architekten GmbH, Basel in collaboration with Gido Wiederkehr

Gymnasium Trudering (Munich, Germany)
Architecture: felix schürmann ellen dettinger architekten, Munich

Heisenberg-Gymnasium (Bruchsal, Germany)
Architecture: Hausmann Architektur, Aachen

Kirkkojärvi-Schule (Espoo, Finland)
Architecture: Verstas Arkkitehdit Oy, Helsinki

Neue Schule Wolfsburg (Wolfsburg, Germany)
Architecture: Kirstin Bartels, Hamburg; Schneider + Sendelbach Architektengesellschaft mbH, Braunschweig

Ringstabekk Skole (Baerum, Norway)
Architecture: div. A arkitekter, Oslo

ROC van Twente (Hengelo, the Netherlands)
Architecture: IAA Architecten, Enschede

Schulhaus Im Birch (Zurich, Switzerland)
Architecture: Peter Märkli, Zurich with Gody Kühnis, Trübbach

St. Nicolaaslyceum (Amsterdam, the Netherlands)
Architecture: DP6 Architectuurstudio, Delft

#LIBRARIES AND SELF-STUDY CENTERS

A.P. Moller Skolen (Schleswig, Germany)
Architecture: C.F. Moller Architects, Aarhus

City Library on the Bildungscampus Osterholz-Scharmbeck (Osterholz-Scharmbeck, Germany)
Architecture: kister scheithauer gross architekten und stadtplaner, Cologne; Feldschnieders + Kister, Bremen; Horeis + Blatt, Bremen

Grundschule Welsberg (Welsberg, Italy)
Architecture: Klaus Hellweger, Bolzano

International Salem College (Uberlingen, Germany)
Architecture: Lederer + Ragnarsdóttir + Oei, Stuttgart

LocHal (Tilburg, the Netherlands)
Architecture: Civic Architects, Amsterdam; Braaksma & Roos Architectenbureau, The Hague
Interior design: Mecanoo, Delft

Munkegaard Skole (Gentofte, Denmark)
Architecture: Arne Jacobsen (1957), Copenhagen; Dorte Mandrup Arkitekter (2009), Copenhagen

Oulun Normaalikoulu (Oulu, Finland)
Architecture: Heikki Taskinen, Oulu

SBW Haus des Lernens (Romanshorn, Switzerland)
Overall architectural and interior design: Doris Fratton, Fratton Raumgestaltung, Amriswil

Schulzentrum Schreinesch (Friedrichshafen, Germany)
Architecture: Planungsgemeinschaft Lederer + Ragnarsdóttir + Oei with Staub Architekten, Friedrichshafen

St. Nicolaaslyceum (Amsterdam, the Netherlands)
Architecture: DP6 Architectuurstudio, Delft

#OPEN LEARNING LANDSCAPES

Corlaer College (Nijkerk, the Netherlands)
Architecture: Broekbakema, Rotterdam

Heliosschule – Inklusive Universitätsschule (IUS) (Cologne, Germany)
Architecture: Schilling Architekten, Cologne

IJburg College (Amsterdam, the Netherlands)
Architecture: LIAG architekten en bouwadviseurs, The Hague

Lernhaus im Campus (Osterholz-Scharmbeck, Germany)
Architecture: kister scheithauer gross architekten and stadtplaner GmbH, Cologne; Feldschnieders + Kister, Bremen; Horeis + Blatt, Bremen

Nærheden Learning Center (Høje-Taastrup, Denmark)
Architecture: Christensen & Co, Copenhagen

Orestad College (Copenhagen, Denmark)
Architecture: 3XN, Copenhagen

Ringstabekk Skole (Baerum, Norway)
Architecture: div. A arkitekter, Oslo

SBW Haus des Lernens (Romanshorn, Switzerland)
Overall architectural and interior design: Doris Fratton, Fratton Raumgestaltung, Amriswil

#OTHER COMMUNAL AREAS

Bildungscampus Sonnwendviertel (Vienna, Austria)
Architecture: PAG architects, Vienna

Herzog-Ulrich-Grundschule (Lauffen am Neckar, Germany)
Architecture: Coast Office Architecture, Stuttgart

Hilde-Domin-Schule (Herrenberg, Germany)
Architecture: Behnisch Architekten, Stuttgart

Kirkkojärvi-Schule (Espoo, Finland)
Architecture: Verstas Arkkitehdit Oy, Helsinki
Landscape architecture: LOCI Maisema Arkkitehdit Oy, Helsinki

Ludwig-Hoffmann-Grundschule (Berlin, Germany)
Architecture: AFF architekten GmbH, Berlin

Munkegaard Skole (Gentofte, Denmark)
Architecture: Arne Jacobsen (1957), Copenhagen; Dorte Mandrup Arkitekter (2009), Copenhagen

St. Nicolaaslyceum (Amsterdam, the Netherlands)
Architecture: DP6 Architectuurstudio, Delft

#OUTDOOR SPACES

Amstelmeerschool (Amsterdam, the Netherlands)
Landscape architecture: Carve, Amsterdam

Bildungscampus Sonnwendviertel (Vienna, Austria)
Architecture: PPAG Architects, Vienna

Bildungszentrum Tor zur Welt (Hamburg, Germany)
Architecture: bof architekten, Hamburg
Landscape architecture: Breimann & Bruun Landschaftsarchitekten, Hamburg

Brede scholen Getsewoud Noord & Zuid (Harlemmermeer, the Netherlands)
Landscape architecture: Carve, Amsterdam

Freiherr-vom-Stein-Schule (Neumünster, Germany)
Architecture: KRESINGS Architektur, Münster

Geschwister-Scholl-Gesamtschule (Lünen, Germany)
Architecture: Hans Scharoun, Berlin

Grundschule am Arnulfpark (Munich, Germany)
Architecture: Hess/Talhof/Kusmierz Architekten und Stadtplaner, Munich

Grundschule Helsinkistraße (Munich, Germany)
Architecture: Fink + Jocher Architekten, Munich

Hauptschule Meierfeld (Herford, Germany)
Architecture: Real Estate and Wastewater Management (IAB) of the City of Herford, Andrea Ortmann, in collaboration with Architekturbüro Beckmann, Dirk Beckmann, Herford

Jenaplanschule (Weimar, Germany)
Landscape architecture: arge studio urbane landschaften, Hamburg; Station c23, Leipzig

Quartierscampus Benölkenplatz (Bocholt, Germany)
Landscape architecture: DTP Landschaftsarchitekten, Essen; bueroschneidermeyer, Cologne / Stuttgart

Ringstabekk Skole (Baerum, Norway)
Architecture: div. A arkitekter, Oslo

Rosenmaarschule (Cologne, Germany)
Architecture: Otto Scheib (1957), Cologne
extension: Dipl. Ing. Jörg Ziolkowski, Cologne

Talentencampus Venlo (Venlo, the Netherlands)
Landscape architecture: Carve, Amsterdam

#SPECIALIZED LEARNING AND TEACHING AREAS

Fioretti College (Lisse, the Netherlands)
Architecture: Broekbakema, Rotterdam

Friedrich-Eugens-Gymnasium – Schülerhaus (Stuttgart, Germany)
Architecture: Drei Architekten Haag Haffner Stroheker, Stuttgart

IJburg College (Amsterdam, the Netherlands)
Architecture: LIAG architekten en bouwadviseurs, The Hague

Jenaplanschule (Weimar, Germany)
Architecture: gernot schulz : architektur, Cologne; Hausmann Architektur, Aachen

Mittelschule Welsberg (Welsberg, Italy)
Architecture: Otto Irsara, Bruneck

Munkegaard Skole (Gentofte, Denmark)
Architecture: Arne Jacobsen (1957), Copenhagen; Dorte Mandrup Arkitekter (2009), Copenhagen

St. Nicolaaslyceum (Amsterdam, the Netherlands)
Architecture: DP6 Architectuurstudio, Delft

#WORKPLACES AND TEAM ROOMS

Bildungszentrum Tor zur Welt (Hamburg, Germany)
Architecture: bof architekten, Hamburg; Breimann & Bruun Landschaftsarchitekten, Hamburg

Ener Ungdomsskole (Hamar, Norway)
Architecture: Anderssen + Fremming AS, Hamar

Grevelokka Skole (Hamar, Norway)
Architecture: Otto Ostli, Hamar, with Jacobsen & Reiten Arkitektkontor AS, Gjovik

IJburg College (Amsterdam, the Netherlands)
Architecture: LIAG architekten en bouwadviseurs, The Hague

Lernhaus im Campus (Osterholz-Scharmbeck, Germany)
Architecture: kister scheithauer gross architekten and stadtplaner, Cologne; Feldschnieders + Kister, Bremen; Horeis + Blatt, Bremen

Neues Gymnasium Wilhelmshaven (Wilhelmshaven, Germany)
Architecture: Hausmann Architektur, Aachen

Orestad College (Copenhagen, Denmark)
Architecture: 3XN, Copenhagen

Oulun Normaalikoulu (Oulu, Finland)
Architecture: Heikki Taskinen, Oulu

Ringstabekk Skole (Baerum, Norway)
Architecture: div. A arkitekter, Oslo

The following examples are projects by the Montag Stiftung Jugend und Gesellschaft:

#PILOT PROJECTS BY THE MONTAG STIFTUNG JUGEND UND GESELLSCHAFT

Bildungslandschaft Altstadt Nord (Cologne, Germany)
Architecture: IAA Architecten, Enschede; gernot schulz: architektur, Cologne

Heliosschule – Inklusive Universitätsschule der Stadt Cologne (Cologne, Germany)
Architecture: Schilling Architekten, Cologne

Phase Null (Phase 0)

Carlo-Mierendorff-Schule (Griesheim, Germany)
School design consultants: Andrea Rokuß, confidio, Aachen *(pedagogy)*; Raphaella Burhenne de Cayres, gernot schulz: architektur, Cologne *(architecture)*

Gemeinschaftsschule Neubulach (Neubulach, Germany)
School design consultants: Otto Seydel, Institut für Schulentwicklung, Überlingen *(pedagogy)*; Jochem Schneider, bueroschneidermeyer, Stuttgart / Cologne *(architecture)*

Gesamtschule Rosenhöhe (Bielefeld, Germany)
School design consultants: Thomas Wetzel, Lüneburg *(pedagogy)*; Anke Weber, atelier für raumbildung, Hamburg *(architecture)*

Geschwister-Scholl-Stadtteilschule (Hamburg, Germany)
School design consultants: Otto Seydel, Institut für Schulentwicklung, Überlingen *(pedagogy)*; Jochem Schneider, bueroschneidermeyer, Stuttgart / Cologne *(architecture)*

Glückaufschule Ückendorf (Gelsenkirchen, Germany)
School design consultants: Britta Grotkamp, JAS – Jugend Architektur Stadt e.V., Essen *(pedagogy)*; Päivi Kataikko-Grigoleit, REFLEX architects_urbanists, Essen *(architecture)*

Grundschule am Baumschulenweg (Bremen, Germany)
School design consultants: Otto Seydel, Institut für Schulentwicklung, Überlingen *(pedagogy)*; Jochem Schneider, bueroschneidermeyer, Stuttgart / Cologne *(architecture)*

Grundschule am Opferweg (Leipzig, Germany)
School design consultants: Raimund Patt, Schulhorizonte – Entwicklungsbüro Bildung *(pedagogy)*; Kirstin Bartels, Hamburg *(architecture)*

IGS Süd (Frankfurt am Main, Germany)
School design consultants: Egon Tegge, Hamburg *(pedagogy)*; Kirstin Bartels, Hamburg *(architecture)*

Staatliche Gemeinschaftsschule Weimar (Weimar, Germany)
School design consultants: Walter Heilmann, Cologne *(pedagogy)*; Hausmann Architektur, Aachen *(architecture)*

Wilhelm-Dörpfeld-Gymnasium (Wuppertal, Germany)
School design consultants: Raimund Patt, Schulhorizonte – Entwicklungsbüro Bildung *(pedagogy)*; Kirstin Bartels, Hamburg *(architecture)*

Ganztag und Raum (All-day schooling and space)

Grundschule am Dichterviertel (Mülheim an der Ruhr, Germany)
Process support: Karin Babbe, *(pedagogy)*; Fee Kyriakopoulos, Baupiloten, Berlin *(architecture)*

Grundschule »An der Este« (Jork, Germany)
Process support: Nicole Raabe *(pedagogy)*; Maria Isabettini, nonconform ideenwerkstatt, Berlin *(architecture)*

Grundschule an der Melanchthonstraße (Bremen, Germany)
Process support: Andrea Rokuß, confidio, Aachen *(pedagogy)*; Dorle Zweering, gernot schulz : architektur, Cologne *(architecture)*

Martin-Schaffner-Schule (Ulm, Germany)
Process support: Andrea Rokuß, confidio, Aachen *(pedagogy)*; Christian Schmutz, A-U-R-A – Architecture, Urbanism + Research Agency, Ulm *(architecture)*

Tinsberger Schule (Lüdenscheid, Germany)
Process support: Klaus Grab, Hamburg *(pedagogy)*; Hanne Banduch, Karolin Kaiser, büro luchterhandt & partner, Hamburg *(architecture)*

Schulbau Open Source (School construction Open Source)

Berufsschulen B5 und B14 (Nuremberg, Germany)
Architecture: aff Architekten, Berlin

IGS Süd (Frankfurt am Main, Germany)
Architecture: BUERO BB, Stuttgart

Offene Schule Waldau (Kassel, Germany)
Architecture: C. F. Møller Architects, Copenhagen

Staatliche Gemeinschaftsschule Weimar (Weimar, Germany)
Architecture: Hausmann Architektur, Aachen (Phase 0, building design HOAI service phases 1–2); gernot schulz : architektur, Cologne (»critical friend« HOAI service phases 1–2, building design HOAI service phases 3–9) together with Ernst2 Architekten, Stuttgart (building design HOAI service phases 6–9)

Phase Zehn (Phase 10)

Realschule am Rhein, Cologne
Process support:
nonconform ideenwerkstatt, Berlin
Architecture: gernot schulz : architektur, Cologne

Freinet-Schule, Cologne
Process support:
nonconform ideenwerkstatt, Berlin
Architecture extension/refurbishment:
gernot schulz : architektur, Cologne

#SPACE AND INCLUSION

References from the study »Raum und Inklusion—Neue Konzepte im Schulbau« by Meike Kricke, Kersten Reich, Lea Schanz, Jochem Schneider, Weinheim and Basel 2018, initiated and funded by the Montag Stiftung Jugend und Gesellschaft.

Freiherr-vom-Stein-Schule (Neumünster, Germany)

Gebhardschule (Konstanz, Germany)

Gemeinschaftsschule Campus Hannah Höch (Berlin, Germany)

Georg-Christoph-Lichtenberg-Gesamtschule (Göttingen, Germany)

Grund- und Mittelschule (Thalmässing, Germany)

Grundschule auf dem Süsteresch (Schüttorf, Germany)

Heliosschule – Inklusive Universitätsschule der Stadt Köln (Cologne, Germany)

Meduxnekeag Consolidated School (Woodstock NB, Canada)

Oulun Normaalikoulu (Oulu, Finland)

Paula-Modersohn-Schule (Bremerhaven, Germany)

Primusschule Berg Fidel (Münster, Germany)

Regine-Hildebrandt-Schule (Birkenwerder, Germany)

Rosenmaarschule (Cologne, Germany)

FAQ: PEDAGOGY

1. WHY DOES SCHOOL HAVE TO CHANGE?

Education is the foundation of the knowledge society. This society is under pressure from global changes that affect both economic and social conditions. To provide all children and young people with an education that prepares them for the future, we need schools that offer every individual the best possible opportunity to develop their personal potential—and must do so in a way that responds to the needs and specific conditions of society. These conditions are no longer the same as when today's school structures were established: Technical and economic frameworks have fundamentally changed, as has the entire world of work and life for which students need to be prepared. Schools must respond to these transformations: To enable children and young people to appreciate their present and to prepare them for the challenges of the future, schools must also change their own framework—both in terms of learning and teaching, and in terms of their architectural and spatial structures.

2. WHY SHOULD STUDENTS LEARN DIFFERENTLY TODAY?

In the past, students learned to memorize and reproduce as much knowledge as possible. Today, information is available everywhere. Learning is therefore no longer a question of simply memorizing as much existing knowledge as possible, but above all of knowing how to deal with knowledge and information: Students need to be able to absorb, evaluate, present, and apply a variety of information in both their present and future personal and professional lives. This kind of learning is not about reproducing knowledge, but about understanding contexts, assessing the truth, origin, relevance, and validity of information, and solving problems. In addition, more recent learning research suggests that learning is more effective when it is a constructive process linked to the learner's own active and varied activities. Passive, receptive learning, as common in traditional forms of schooling and teaching, is now considered less effective.

3. WHY DOES A MODERN SCHOOL NEED AN ALL-DAY PROGRAM?

Internationally, all-day schools are standard today. They allow for more equity and justice in education and support widespread family models, in which afternoon childcare is difficult due to both parents working or single parenting. Many parents are unable to provide sufficient educational support for their children on their own. All-day schools ensure that all children and young people have access to quality education and appropriate support. This not only benefits educationally disadvantaged groups—it also opens up new learning opportunities for children from more privileged backgrounds.

4. WHAT IS THE ROLE OF INCLUSION?

Schools will no longer exclude children: Inclusion has been a human right since the 2006 UN Convention. It is also the central educational goal of the international community for the decade 2015–2030. Inclusion brings about a shift in the goals of education: the focus of the content is no longer solely on the curriculum. Instead, goals such as connectedness, belonging, and well-being form the umbrella under which a willingness to learn and perform, curiosity, and a joy of learning can flourish for meaningful learning content. The demand for inclusion applies not only to children and young people with specific disabilities, but to all forms of disadvantage and deviation from a (fictitious) norm. Mainstream schooling for children with disabilities and other children with special needs is thus becoming a reality in Germany.

This will require changes to schools' personnel and spatial structures to enable inclusive learning and teaching for children and educational staff alike.

In the long term, inclusive and supportive schools will lead to significantly lower social and economic costs for society compared to a school system that excludes children.

5. DOES SUPPORT-ORIENTED TEACHING HARM GIFTED LEARNERS?

Learners with lower performance levels are not a threat to the supposedly more gifted. Existing school systems with joint learning up to year 9 or 10 prove the opposite: joint learning helps everyone when students with learning advantages actively help those who are struggling while being given differentiated opportunities for their own development. Students who take on the role of a teacher can benefit greatly from these activities.

6. WHAT IS THE ROLE OF (NEW) MEDIA AND ARTIFICIAL INTELLIGENCE?

Media education means more than just equipping schools with tablets and WLAN. Today's teachers are learning for themselves about the possibilities, limitations, and challenges of new and »old« media, how to use them meaningfully, and when it is better to do without them. With each new generation of teachers in the digital age, digital literacy, the use of pedagogically appropriate software and tools, and the development of media education concepts in schools will continue to grow. New media will always remain a teaching tool: they are designed to strengthen students' skills and must not become an end in themselves. Artificial intelligence is an important factor in schools too. It is transforming learning by enabling personalized educational pathways and responding to individual student needs. It promotes creativity, reduces teachers' workloads by automating routine tasks, improves inclusion, and facilitates access to knowledge. At the same time, dealing with AI-generated content is becoming an important skill and thus part of the learning process itself.

7. HOW IS PERFORMANCE ASSESSED IN HETEROGENEOUS LEARNING ENVIRONMENTS?

An assessment system that supports learning focuses not only on grading but also on giving performance feedback in the form of a description of objectives and individual support. In the world's leading education systems (especially the top-performing PISA countries), grade retention is no longer a factor, as it has proven counterproductive to learning. With consistent support and differentiation, evidence shows it is possible to prevent weaker learners from falling further behind and to avoid holding back stronger students.

FAQ:
ARCHITECTURE

8. HOW CAN SPACES BE DESIGNED FOR DIVERSE LEARNING SITUATIONS?

Cluster-like room sequences and, even more so, open learning landscapes allow for a variety of room combinations for different learning settings through visual connections and acoustic separations. This can be achieved, for example, with different lighting and furnishings or with small, enclosed room boxes and moveable room cells. Movable systems enable room layouts to be designed, built, modified, and dismantled as needed. Loose and fixed furnishings in harmony with the architecture also play an important role here.

An easy-to-implement expansion option that is also suitable for older school buildings is the growing room: partition walls or small doors are equipped with double doors, sliding doors, or folding walls. In this way, small rooms can grow into one large room. In addition to openings, visual connections are essential for the use of extended areas. This allows teachers to fulfill their supervisory duties while remaining accessible to students at all times. Separate rooms can be connected for temporary activities, and obvious added value can be created for existing rooms with little effort. Easily movable or fixed elements that divide a space in different ways can also expand the range of possible uses: for example, variable furniture combinations, moveable seating, or cabinets with surface finishes that also serve acoustic purposes. In order to make full educational use of corridors in particular, a revised fire safety concept is often required.

9. DO NEW SCHOOL TYPOLOGIES NEED MORE SPACE?

New school building typologies do not need more space because they use existing space more effectively. The »classroom-corridor« school is an additive school building typology that adds together self-contained rooms to form a whole. Cluster structures and open learning landscapes are generally characterized by overlapping uses and a high degree of transparency, which have a significant impact on the effectiveness of building use.

This means that more space is temporarily available to users because existing space can be distributed among fewer people. In Phase 0, it is possible to find out, discuss, and decide which uses can be successfully overlapped due to their scheduling and requirements in terms of equipment and room sizes.

10. CAN NEW SPATIAL SOLUTIONS BE IMPLEMENTED IN EXISTING BUILDINGS?

Existing conventional »classroom-corridor« schools offer many opportunities for contemporary reconstruction. With relatively simple structural measures, such as creating visual connections in combination with a change in furnishings (more than just tables and chairs) and a new definition of usage units according to fire safety requirements, major changes can be achieved in the structure and usability of rooms. Corridors become part of the learning landscape, and classrooms can be connected to each other and to the corridor through openings. Such changes are also possible in listed school buildings. For these solutions to be sustainable, they must be developed in accordance with future-oriented pedagogy.

11. WHAT ROLE DO OUTDOOR AREAS PLAY?

Outdoor areas are an integral part of any learning landscape. In a place where children and adults spend most of their day, all classrooms should be connected to outdoor areas that can be used as an extended (and barrier-free) learning environment. These include open and neutral spaces, balconies or terraces, as well as rooms and spaces with a special atmosphere, such as loggias, conservatories, arcades, small amphitheater, small animal pens, or gardens. Indoor-outdoor spaces such as malls or arcades can be used for larger events and presentations. Different uses and educational requirements, as well as the needs of specific user groups, must be considered from the beginning of the design process.

12. HOW CAN THE OPENING OF SCHOOLS TO THE OUTSIDE WORLD BE COMMUNICATED?

The open, expanded school requires—in addition to a diversified mix of uses—appropriate urban and aesthetic coding. On the one hand, this is achieved through everyday uses and activities that make it clear that extracurricular activities are also possible. On the other hand, the connection to the surrounding area should ensure that the school also opens up to the neighborhood. Such coding can refer to specific urban landscape motifs or spatial connections to streets, paths, squares, or parks. It is about the self-image that the school belongs to its surroundings—with all their beautiful and ugly characteristics. In this way, the visible and invisible thresholds of educational institutions are also transformed aesthetically.

13. WHAT FUNCTION DO OPEN SCHOOLS HAVE FOR THE CITY?

Education is, and is increasingly becoming, an integral part of urban culture. This presents schools with the opportunity to become embedded in the urban and public everyday life and, in turn, to become a part of that everyday life themselves. All-day schools in particular will take on this role of enriching the urban fabric. This shift in significance is all the more relevant given the clear trend that all-day schools will, in the foreseeable future, eclipse all other school models, as they are best equipped to anticipate demographic and social developments, as well as changing needs and lifestyles. The traditional separation of education and training, of knowledge production and creative learning, of living and working, of the public and the classroom, of school buildings and the city, will become blurred in the future. There is already a growing tendency—in Switzerland, South Tyrol, the Netherland, Finland, Norway, Canada, and Australia—to no longer view school buildings as functional buildings or distinct building types but as multifunctional structures. The same applies to outdoor spaces, especially in urban contexts where open spaces are scarce.

14. WHAT CAN MODERN SCHOOL DESIGN BE BASED ON?

The starting point for a school construction project can no longer be the question of how many square meters are needed for which functions. The questions are changing: What learning settings can and should be created? Which should coexist, which should be separated? How are they connected? And which spaces and atmospheres are suitable? These questions can only be answered in relation to the urban context and the possibilities of each school. Diversity and complexity can neither be reflected nor fulfilled by conventional space allocation plans. Even if they remain the basis of planning, they should be overlaid and reconsidered with a different planning method—one that is less focused on floor area and building, but also includes descriptions of quality and use.

Phase 0 is not only more realistic than abstract square meter figures and space allocation plans alone, it also makes it easier to decide which learning scenarios are desirable and which are not.

In addition, scenarios must be considered that will only become relevant in the future—such as those arising from new teaching and learning methods that will continually evolve and expand as a result of new technological possibilities.

15. SCHOOLS ARE CONSTANTLY CHANGING. WHAT DOES THIS MEAN FOR SCHOOL CONSTRUCTION?

The planning complexity of school buildings corresponds to objective uncertainties, so that the planning and construction of schools can never truly be considered finished. This is true in two ways: teaching methods are constantly being renewed, requiring spatial adaptations. In addition, the standards for what is considered »beautiful« and »ugly« change over time. Schools should therefore be designed with adaptability in mind and provide the opportunity for ongoing development and extension.

16. CAN EXAMPLES FROM ABROAD BE IMPLEMENTED IN GERMANY?

In Germany, new typologies are neither easier nor more difficult to implement than in other countries. There are several reasons why many good examples can be found abroad. One is that in other countries, the planning of the schools' content *(pedagogy)* and buildings *(architecture)* is much more closely integrated within the administration than is traditionally the case in Germany, due to the separate responsibilities of the communal, federal, and state governments. As a result, these countries have often been planning mixed-use functions more consistently and for a longer time. The many examples in this book show that a lot is also possible in Germany. All the typologies presented have already been realized in Germany.

FAQ: ADMINISTRATION

17. WHAT IS PHASE 0?

Phase 0 is the crucial phase at the beginning of the planning process. It sets the course for the building process. If all parties involved—education, architecture, politics, and administration—work closely together at this early stage and coordinate their respective requirements, a solid foundation for a successful project is laid. Because Phase 0 is not included in the German Fee Schedule for Architects and Engineers (HOAI), it must be budgeted separately. The cost is usually borne by the municipality, which will benefit from significant savings in the subsequent construction and operation of schools.

18. DO REGULATIONS SUCH AS FIRE SAFETY PREVENT THE CONSTRUCTION OF AN OPEN SCHOOL?

Building codes—especially fire and safety regulations—can conflict with school design that seeks to implement pedagogical innovations. This is especially true for the implementation of multi-purpose, adaptable rooms, generous spatial sequences and connections. In order to meet the growing demand for more open-plan layouts in school buildings, however, some federal states and municipalities have adapted their school building guidelines or developed their own fire safety requirements for open-plan structures (such as clusters, open learning landscapes, learning studios, etc.). The Model School Construction Regulations *(Muster-Schulbaurichtlinie)* will be adapted in 2025. However, there is always the possibility of negotiating constructive solutions with fire safety experts in each specific case. The most important prerequisite is a planning process that identifies the relevant conflicts at the outset and puts them up for discussion. The more transparent, comprehensible, and competent this negotiation process is, the more likely it is that potential obstacles will be seen as opportunities.

19. ARE SMALL SCHOOLS BETTER AND LARGE SCHOOLS CHEAPER?

In addition to construction and maintenance costs that are cited as arguments in favor of large schools, there are also many indirect costs associated with satisfaction, operational capacity utilization, transportation demands, and the day-to-day and urban planning role of a school. On balance, large schools are not necessarily more cost-effective. Conversely, large schools, especially for older students, can be planned and realized with the advantages of small schools—for example through clusters or the model of several »schools within a school.« Up to lower secondary level, priority should be given to integration into the local community close to home.

20. CAN SUSTAINABILITY BE ACHIEVED COST-EFFECTIVELY?

There is now a consensus among experts that ecological building materials should be used, that materials should be recycled, that alternative heating systems with effective technology should be used, that a reduction in CO_2 emissions and, in the long term, climate neutrality should be aimed for, and that, ultimately, education on sustainability should be improved. Nevertheless, it is still common practice—both in new construction and reconstruction projects, for individual elements to be cut from an otherwise sustainable overall concept, with the result that the entire design collapses. It is important to keep the big picture in mind. The true cost of a project must always be assessed based on the overall balance, which includes not only follow-up costs—such as maintenance, rental income, amortization, the energy required to produce solar panels, interest charges, and demolition costs—but also intangible values, such as social integration and equal educational opportunities.

21. HOW DEMOCRATIC SHOULD THE PLANNING PROCESS BE?

Planning a school is a decision-making process that is influenced by many factors. The challenge is to incorporate as much knowledge and expertise as possible into the process and to ensure that decisions are made on as broad a basis as possible, so that they are supported and accounted for by those involved in the long term. A structured, collaborative planning process with competent and accountable leadership is recommended. During this planning phase, additional new knowledge can also be gained through field trips, for example. This makes it less likely that old ways of thinking will determine future planning decisions. The decision-making body should be large enough to bring together relevant knowledge and expertise and to coordinate decisions democratically. At the same time, it should not be so large that it becomes difficult to make decisions, because too many interests—be they political, ideological, or financial—complicate the actual planning task. The basis for such a process is the willingness to reach a balanced consensus with majority support and to find constructive solutions and compromises. The result of Phase 0 is ultimately a pedagogically qualified and well-founded space allocation plan, the implementation of which must be decided by the school authority, i.e., the municipal or city council.

22. WHAT EXTRACURRICULAR USES ARE CONCEIVABLE IN AN OPEN SCHOOL?

The available space should serve as many purposes as possible, so that uses can alternate between school and extracurricular activities, either temporarily or for longer periods of time. Which extracurricular activities create synergies that are also a permanent gain or can compensate for a shrinking or growing need for learning spaces in the short or medium term depends on the specific case. For this reason, existing deficits in supply, services, and recreational facilities in a district or residential area should be analyzed at an early planning stage. For example, it is possible to link the development of all-day schools and youth services with urban development.

In addition, a cafeteria, which is essential for all-day schooling, can often be used as a neighborhood café if it is designed with local stakeholders from the outset. A cafeteria with a flexible layout can also serve as a meeting place for community members and clubs. Locating the cafeteria toward the public space makes it more accessible to the public than a cafeteria in the middle of a closed off school complex.

23. HOW CAN THE SECURITY OF AN OPEN SCHOOL BE MAINTAINED?

In the face of school shootings or night-time vandalism, there is a growing desire to (once again) hermetically »seal off« schools from the outside world. However, this is a problematic development: walls and fences do not solve the dangerous situation, they only move it outside the school. Such an enclosure has significant design consequences, changes the users' attitude to life (locked in instead of safe), and signals to the outside world: »Guests are not welcome«—the opposite of an open school. Rather, the goal must be to anchor the school in its surroundings in such a way that a sense of vitality and shared responsibility strengthen the security on both sides. In this respect, the integration of everyday public life into the school's operation also serves security—far more than technically highly complex security systems. Nevertheless, neither an open nor a closed school can offer absolute security.

24. HOW IMPORTANT ARE EDUCATION AND SCHOOLS FOR THE CITY?

The availability of educational facilities is already a top priority for companies when choosing a location. In particular, it is a key factor for recruiting qualified employees and for potential cooperation with other companies or universities. The availability of educational opportunities and the proximity of schools also play an increasingly important role in people's choice of where to live.

GLOSSARY

Accessibility
Barrier-free access to places and, in a broader sense, to content, media, information, etc.; allows all people unrestricted access to all areas of public or school life.

All-day school
Educational offerings that covers the entire (school) day and, from a pedagogical perspective, include formal, non-formal, and informal educational activities. The all-day staff comprises a multi-professional team that supports children and young people throughout the day (teachers, educational staff, physical therapists, speech therapists, psychologists, school assistants, housekeeping staff, etc.).

Architectural competition
Designing a building project within the framework of a competitive, usually anonymous design process for architects on the basis of a call for entries; in Germany, such competitions are conducted according to the RPW 2013—Guidelines for Design Competitions; an independent jury is appointed to evaluate the submissions; the aim of the competition is to obtain the best possible solution through alternative design proposals; the final selection of the architect is usually made in a subsequent VgV procedure (according to the German Regulation on the Award of Public Contracts) involving the prize-winners.

Assessment (baseline assessment)
Clarification of the prerequisites for a construction project and an important part of Phase 0; in addition to the municipal situation, the site, and the building, it is also essential to assess the school's »pedagogical assets«—that is, the existence and potential need for adjustment of the school's educational concept—as a basis for planning.

Basic evaluation
Determination of the initial parameters for a planning process; increasingly important planning service due to the complexity of school construction projects; in the past, it was only carried out to a limited extent during HOAI service phase 1, mainly as a quantitative comparison between the status quo and model space allocation plans; today, it is absolutely necessary for the development of a reliable planning basis, especially for reconstruction and conversion projects.

Building administration
Administrative department at the municipal level that deals with planning and building issues, including school construction.

Building regulations
General legal regulations in the construction sector; it serves to protect public safety and order in the field of public building law by preventing potential hazards.

Building supervision
Building control departments supervise compliance with public law regulations and ordinances during the construction, alteration, conversion, use, maintenance, and demolition of a building; relevant measures are enforced through building permit and building code procedures.

Child-friendly rhythm
A daily schedule that flexibly adapts educational activities to the different needs of children and young people. Formal, non-formal, and informal educational activities alternate throughout the day, offering opportunities for learning and recreation in a sensible balance. In addition to the educational concept, the spatial design of the building supports a child-friendly rhythm by providing

areas for retreat, movement, focused work, community gatherings, and other learning activities.

Classroom-plus
One of three prototypical organization models for the general learning and teaching areas of a school: the classroom is extended by making it significantly larger and/or adding an adjacent group room; circulation areas are activated wherever possible. See Cluster and Open Learning Landscape.

Classroom-corridor school
Outdated, but still prevalent in many schools, the classroom-corridor school is no longer appropriate for today's ways of learning, teaching, and living. There are new spatial solutions for schools—just as they are for offices, homes, etc.—that respond to the rapidly changing needs of users.

Client / Commissioning entity
In the case of public schools, this is usually the local authority; in an integrated planning process, schools also assume responsibility as competent client representatives in close cooperation with the municipal authority.

Cluster
A group of rooms that combines learning and teaching rooms with areas for differentiation, recreation, and relaxation and, if necessary, decentralized work areas for teachers, sanitary facilities, and other ancillary rooms to form units; facilitates synergy effects and flexible use of areas and rooms. Along with the Open Learning Landscape and Classroom-plus, the Cluster is one of three prototypical organizational models for modern learning environments.

Digitality
Digitality shapes our working and living environments. In schools, it has a wide range of effects on how, where, and what is learned. Critically using and understanding the possibilities and challenges of digital media and a digital world are among the skills taught in future-oriented schools. At the same time, learning in schools also provides a counterbalance to a digitally dominated reality.

Differentiation
Targeted individual support for learners with different abilities may also require spatial differentiation to allow flexible division into different learning groups. »External differentiation« means dividing a class into different groups (usually in different rooms), »internal differentiation« means offering different levels/topics, etc. to individual learners in a class (requires additional space in the classroom).

Educational equity
Unrestricted access to education for all—regardless of socio-economic or ethnic background, family situation, etc.; goal of all-day schooling and inclusion, among others.

Educational landscape
The integration of various educational offerings within a city or region into a jointly organized, interconnected framework; part of future-oriented neighborhood and urban development. Different models exist and should be selected based on the specific context of each location.

ESD

ESD stands for Education for Sustainable Development, an educational approach that raises learners' awareness for sustainable development and empowers them to actively participate in shaping a sustainable future. In light of global challenges such as climate change, poverty, and social inequality, curriculum proposals have been developed based on the 17 Sustainable Development Goals to integrate ESD as a cross-cutting principle into everyday learning at daycare centers, schools, and universities.

Existing buildings

Existing buildings or parts thereof that must be incorporated into the new or reconstructed building; existing structures imply specifications or restrictions (e.g., historic preservation, structural condition, etc.), but can also be used and interpreted creatively to create future-orientated learning environments.

Feasibility study

Assesses whether the proposed solutions are feasible within the given municipal, spatial, and financial parameters; provides a recommendation for the planning process.

Fire safety

The sum of all measures and regulations designed to prevent the spread of fire and smoke as best as possible; the current legal situation often sets narrow limits on possible uses. The fire safety requirements for school construction are laid down in the respective state building regulations and in the model school construction guidelines, which the states adopt or adapt. North Rhine-Westphalia has already adapted the school building guidelines to clusters and open learning landscapes.

Flexibility

Possibility of implementing different usage constellations in or between rooms without great effort; the equipment must be adapted to the variance of offers and settings that contemporary learning requires today.

Follow-up costs

The operating costs, the costs for care and maintenance, as well as the costs for dismantling and disposal are summarized in the follow-up costs, which make up around 80 percent of life cycle costs. Well-founded planning of school buildings in line with their location and requirements can prevent high follow-up costs being incurred over the building's entire life cycle.

Furnishings

Flexible furnishings are an important component of new spatial concepts for schools in order to enable different forms of activity and social interaction. Moveable elements are strategically supplemented by precisely positioned, permanently installed furniture that provides a clear structure, is multifunctional, and can be used for educational purposes. A good furnishing strategy is essential to ensure that a »well-designed« space can unfold its potential in use.

Groups with steering functions

At the school and municipal levels, there are various groups with a steering function in school development. The names of these groups vary. The following terms are used in this book: *The school's internal pedagogical steering group* is concerned with the development of the respective school, i.e., the concept of the school as a whole, beyond the current building project. The *school project group »construction«* is established within the school specifically for an upcoming building project. It represents the school throughout the process and is the interface to the other stakeholders involved in the building process. The *municipal steering group* brings together the various stakeholders in a specific school building project at the municipal level. The *municipal school planning group* acts across individual schools and deals with the overall structure of school development within the municipality.

Heterogeneity
Diversity among learners in a group or class; heterogeneous learning enables individual support for all learners—both those who excel and those who need additional assistance.

HOAI (Fee schedule for architects and engineers)
Federal ordinance regulating the fees for architectural and engineering services; defines planning phases, services, and fees for architects and engineers; serves as orientation for all planning steps; does not cover the important early phase of project development, Phase 0.

Inclusion
A UN-recognized human right since 2006; implies the fundamental right of all children to be educated together; ultimately leads to the abolition of special schools and the tiered school system; marks a paradigm shift in both pedagogy and school architecture; requires concrete assessments of spatial resources and organization models based on qualitative criteria for the spatial arrangement of collaborative teaching and their translation into concrete spatial and area concepts.

Learning guide / support
Learning support staff are individuals who assist students during their learning process, provide feedback, motivate them, listen to them, and act as a point of contact for questions. In contrast to traditional classroom teaching, this approach involves a change in learning culture: students work largely independently and learning support is provided on an individual basis. Learning guides can be teachers, educational staff, educators, or social workers.

Learning House concept
Classes are not grouped by year level (as in the year-group team model), but as a »cohort«—for example, grades 1 to 4 of an elementary school or grades 5 to 10 of a secondary school. Since 2015, the Learning House concept has been the standard for all new school buildings in Munich.

Life-cycle costs
Includes not only the design and construction costs but also follow-up costs such as maintenance and operating costs.

Mission statement
Fundamental pedagogical concept of a school; prerequisite and basis for the planning of construction measures, among other things.

Model space allocation plan / model area program
Exemplary, but often binding, specifications for the function and size of school spaces at the federal state level; part of school construction and funding guidelines; simplifies planning through standardized calculation formulas, but often prevents good solutions when quantitative specifications do not meet actual needs. In contrast, a model area program allows for more flexibility in how space is allocated across different rooms.

Multi-age group / peer learning
Learning groups composed of students of different ages in which older students can take on the role of teachers; stronger and weaker students learn from each other; supported by flexible spatial concepts.

Multi-professional teams
Inclusive and all-day schools require a wide range of different skills: teachers, social workers, and/or social pedagogues, educators, school support staff, school psychologists, musicians and artists, craftspeople, etc. All these professions work together in the school to meet the needs of all students. All these professions work based on common pedagogical approaches and didactic (teaching and learning) concepts for dealing productively with diversity in cooperative teams.

Open Learning Landscape
One of three prototypical organizational models for modern learning environments: A large (partially) open learning area is available to a group of classes. It is combined with structured and delimitated zones for group work, individual learning, and input phases. The degree of »openness« can vary. See also Cluster and Classroom-plus.

Phase 0
First project development phase of the planning process; not a regular service component of the HOAI, but crucial for the construction process because all important decisions are made in this phase; well-coordinated decisions in Phase 0 save costs and resources in the subsequent construction process.

Phase 10
Like Phase 0, not part of the HOAI; describes the process of provide commissioning and, in a broader sense, the ongoing monitoring of appropriation, interpretation, and further development by the users to enable successful use in the long term.

Polyvalence
Versatile usability of spaces and areas through the option to choose between different rooms and atmospheres; functions are no longer rigidly assigned to specific spaces, allowing for a variety of usage scenarios.

Quantity structure
Overview of the various space requirements and existing areas in a school; to be supplemented by a spatial organization concept.

School authorities
The school authority for public schools is typically the city or municipality, or (for vocational schools) the (urban) district. The school authority—supported by state funds—covers the premises and material costs of running the school (but not the personnel costs of teaching staff). The school board usually owns the building, but it may also be rented or leased. The school authority is not responsible for the educational quality of the school (see school supervision).

School building guidelines
Due to the cultural sovereignty of the German federal states, school construction is one of their core responsibilities. To ensure quality and provide a basis for the financing of construction projects, school building guidelines have been issued. In recent years, however, some federal states have

increasingly treated these guidelines as recommendations, shifted responsibility to the local level, reduced them to fire safety regulations, or even abolished them entirely. Current guidelines define quality standards that meet the changed requirements for school buildings and support contemporary learning and working.

School construction consultants

Interdisciplinary team of—usually two—external school construction consultants and planners with both educational and architectural/urban planning expertise. The more complex a project, the more advisable it is to involve this team in project management and facilitation.

School development plan

Long-term municipal planning of the school landscape within a catchment area, primarily from a quantitative point of view; depends on the development of the population structure, student numbers, and the local school structure; ideally covers the catchment area beyond municipal boundaries to enable synergies with the surrounding area. Not to be confused with the internal pedagogical development of an individual school based on a school program.

School supervision

A responsibility of the state education authorities aimed at ensuring the implementation of educational policy, pedagogical standards, legal regulations, personnel management, disciplinary procedures, and health-related standards in school practice. A distinction is made between academic, administrative, and legal supervision. The federal states hire the teachers and monitor them in accordance with employment and school laws.

Space and requirements planning

Supplementary component of HOAI service phase 1; usually involves purely quantitative calculation of space and room requirements; reliable requirements planning, however, also calls for the inclusion of qualitative criteria.

Space requirements

Quantitative per-capita reference value that is defined in model space allocation plans; contemporary flexible use of space does not reduce the per-capita requirement but allows for more usage options.

Special Infrastructure Fund (Sondervermögen Infrastruktur)

Special fund of the German Government amounting to 500 billion euros, which is intended for public investment in transport routes, digitalization, and education, among others. The Montag Stiftung Jugend und Gesellschaft, the Association of German Architects (BDA), and the Association for Education and Training (VBE) are committed to ensuring that these funds for school construction are allocated according to criteria that ensure the future viability of education in Germany and thus the sustainability of investments.

Specialist subject room principle

Teaching rooms in a school are assigned to specific subjects or teachers. As a result, it is the subject or the teacher that gives the room its distinctive »face« or »identity«; in contrast to the classroom principle, where teachers come to the students, here the students go to the teachers.

Startchancen-Programm

A federal support program in Germany aimed at disadvantaged schools to reduce social inequality and promote equality of opportunity. The program is scheduled to run for ten years (2024–2034), with the federal and state governments planning to provide a total of €20 billion in funding to approximately 4,000 schools facing particularly challenging circumstances across Germany. The funding is divided into three pillars: school infrastructure (pillar I), school and teaching development (pillar II), and financial resources for additional staffing for multi-professional teams (pillar III). To ensure the program's long-term impact, it is essential to consider all three program pillars in conjunction: Measures to create supportive learning environments (pillar I) can only be meaningfully planned following a school development process (pillar II) involving the full multi-professional team (pillar III), from which specific infrastructure needs for pillar I can be derived.

SAI

Statutory accident insurance: in addition to providing benefits, it advises on occupational safety, health protection, and accident prevention. Among other things, it provides information and regulations on the structural design and equipment of schools from a preventive and health-promoting perspective.

Teacher's workstation

A teacher's personal workstation at the school; a prerequisite for ensuring that teachers have the opportunity to complete writing and other individual tasks in the school at all times.

Teachers' room principle

Decentralized rooms where teachers (alone or in pairs) each have their »own« dedicated space that they can shape and personalize; in contrast to the traditional classroom principle, where teachers come to the students, here the students go to the teachers.

Team room / station

With the expansion of all-day operations, rest and exchange areas are needed, as well as workspaces for the multi-professional team. These can be arranged centrally as team stations or decentralized in team rooms. They can be personalized or designed as flexible workspaces that are not assigned to specific individuals. The team room is available to all employees during the school day. It provides workstations where multi-professional teams can hold discussions. Individual workstations are also available for individual preparation or follow-up work. It is recommended to separate areas for focused and quiet work from those for discussions and breaks.

Typology

Building schemes with certain characteristics in the arrangement of rooms and functions; new patterns of use today also require a further development of traditional school building typologies (e.g., the »classroom-corridor« school).

Urban densification

Densification results from the urban planning provision of inner development: future land requirements should be met primarily on already developed sites, while the designation of new greenfield sites should be largely avoided; this often results in a higher-density development of school sites.

Variability

Schools are constantly evolving in response to changing societal demands. Learning spaces should therefore be adaptable in the medium term and capable of being modified to meet new requirements. In order to create sustainable buildings, it should also be possible to change their use in the long term, if necessary.

Year-group team

A collaborative team within a school staff in which teachers of the same student year group work together and jointly support a group of students over several years; enables well-coordinated, joint planning in smaller, manageable structures; requires flexible spatial concepts that give each respective year group a »home.«

BIBLIOGRAPHY

AAGAARD, T. / LUND, A. (2020): *Digital Agency in Higher Education. Transforming Teaching and Learning*. London, New York.

ABS, H.J. / HAHN-LAUDENBERG, K. / DEIMEL, D. / ZIEMES, J.F. (EDS.) (2024): *ICCS 2022. Schulische Sozialisation und politische Bildung von 14-Jährigen im internationalen Vergleich*. Münster, New York. www.waxmann.com/buecher/ICCS-2022

AGBF BUND – ARBEITSGEMEINSCHAFT DER LEITER DER BERUFSFEUERWEHREN IN DER BUNDESREPUBLIK DEUTSCHLAND (2014/2015): *Moderne Schulbau- und Unterrichtskonzepte. Empfehlungen zur Sicherstellung der Rettungswege aus Lernbereichen*. www.agbf.de/downloads-fachausschuss-vorbeugender-brand-und-gefahrenschutz/category/28-fa-vbg-oeffentlich-empfehlungen

AINLEY, J. / CARSTENS, R. (2018): Teaching and Learning International Survey (TALIS) 2018 Conceptual Framework. *OECD Education Working Papers*, No. 187. OECD Publishing. Paris. doi.org/10.1787/799337c2-en

AINSCOW, M. / BOOTH, T. / DYSON, A. (2006): *Improving Schools, Developing Inclusion*. London.

AKTIONSRAT BILDUNG (2013): *Zwischenbilanz Ganztagsgrundschulen: Betreuung oder Rhythmisierung? Gutachten*. Published by vbw – Vereinigung der Bayerischen Wirtschaft e.V. Münster. www.aktionsrat-bildung.de/publikationen/gutachten/gutachten-zwischenbilanz ganztagsgrundschulen-betreuung-oder-rhythmisierung.html

ALLERT, H. / ASMUSSEN, M. (2017): Bildung als produktive Verwicklung. In Allert et al. *Digitalität und Selbst. Interdisziplinäre Perspektiven auf Subjektivierungs- und Bildungsprozesse*. Bielefeld, pp. 27–68. doi.org/10.14361/9783839439456-004

ALLERT, H. / ASMUSSEN, M. / RICHTER, C. (2017): *Digitalität und Selbst. Interdisziplinäre Perspektiven auf Subjektivierungs- und Bildungsprozesse*. Bielefeld. doi.org/10.14361/9783839439456

ALT, C. (ED.) (2005): *Kinderleben – Aufwachsen zwischen Familie, Freunden und Institutionen. DJI-Kinderpanel*, vol. 2. Wiesbaden.

ALT, C. / HÜSKEN, K. (2016): Betreuungsdefizite am Nachmittag. In *Viel Tempo, wenig Plan. DJI Impulse. Das Bulletin des Deutschen Jugendinstituts* 2/2016, pp. 18–21. www.dji.de/fileadmin/user_upload/bulletin/d_bull_d/bull113_d/DJI_2_16_Web.pdf

ANDRÄ, C. / MACEDONIA, M. (EDS.) (2020): *Bewegtes Lernen – Handbuch für Forschung und Praxis*. Berlin.

ANGER, C. (2024): *Auswirkungen der Corona-Pandemie auf die Schulbildung, Gutachten für die Initiative Neue Soziale Marktwirtschaft (INSM)*. Cologne. www.iwkoeln.de/fileadmin/user_upload/Studien/Gutachten/PDF/2024/Bildungsmonitor_Corona_und_Schulbildung_2024.pdf

ANGER, C. / BETZ, J. / PLÜNNECKE, A. (2024): *Bildungsmonitor 2024*. Studie im Auftrag der Initiative Neue Soziale Marktwirtschaft (INSM). Cologne.

ARNOLD, R. / ERPENBECK, J. (2014): *Wissen ist keine Kompetenz. Dialoge zur Kompetenzreifung.* Baltmannsweiler.

ARNOLD, R. / SCHÜSSLER, I. (1998): *Wandel der Lernkulturen*. Darmstadt.

ARONSON, E. ET AL. (2008): *Sozialpsychologie.* Munich.

AUTOR:INNENGRUPPE BILDUNGSBERICHTERSTATTUNG (2016): *Bildung in Deutschland 2016. Ein indikatorengestützter Bericht mit einer Analyse zu Bildung und Migration*. Bielefeld. www.bildungsbericht.de/de/bildungsberichte-seit-2006/bildungsbericht-2016
(2024): *Bildung in Deutschland 2024. Ein indikatorengestützter Bericht mit einer Analyse zu beruflicher Bildung*. Bielefeld. www.bildungsbericht.de/de

AUTOR*INNENGRUPPE KINDER- UND JUGENDHILFE-STATISTIK (2024): *Kinder- und Jugendhilfereport 2024. Eine kennzahlenbasierte Analyse mit einem Schwerpunkt zum Fachkräftemangel*. Opladen, Berlin, Toronto.

BAMFORD, A. (2006): *The Wow Factor. Global research compendium on the impact of the arts in education*. Münster / New York / Munich / Berlin.

BARTELS, K. / PAMPE, B. (2020): Nachhaltigkeit im Schulbau: Planungsprozesse und Raumkonzepte. In Hofmeister, S. (Ed.): *Schulbauten: Räume zum Lernen und für die Gemeinschaft*. München 2020, pp. 6–13.
doi.org/10.11129/9783955535094

BASS (2010): *Bereinigte Amtliche Sammlung der Schulvorschriften NRW 2010/2011*. Frechen.

BAUER, J. (2007): *Lob der Schule. Sieben Perspektiven für Schüler, Lehrer und Eltern*. Hamburg.

BBC (2018): *The BBC Loneliness Experiment – School of Environment, Education and Development*. The University of Manchester.

BELLENZIER, P. / WEYLAND, B. (2015): *Schulen bauen in Südtirol zwischen Architektur und Pädagogik. Costruire scuole in Alto Adige tra architettura e pedagogia*. Published by the Autonomous Province of Bolzano – South Tyrol, Department of Italian Schools, Vocational Training and Culture, Housing and Public Buildings. Bolzano. www.schulen-planen-und-bauen.de/schulen-bauen-in-suedtirol-ein-ausstellungskatalog

BERTELSMANN STIFTUNG (ED.) (2010): *Soziale Gerechtigkeit in der OECD – Wo steht Deutschland?* Gütersloh.
(2011A): *Jugend in der Zivilgesellschaft. Freiwilliges Engagement Jugendlicher von 1999 bis 2009*. By Sibylle Picot in cooperation with TNS Infratest. Gütersloh.
www.bertelsmann-stiftung.de/fileadmin/files/BSt/Presse/imported/downloads/xcms_bst_dms_34522_34523_2.pdf
(2011B): *Wie steht es um das Engagement von Jugendlichen in Deutschland? Kluft zwischen Bereitschaft und tatsächlichem Engagement.* Press release 26.04.2011.
www.bertelsmann-stiftung.de/de/presse/pressemitteilungen/pressemitteilung/pid/freiwilliges-engagement-von-jugendlichen/
(2014): *Bildung und Vielfalt. Lernen für morgen.* Change – Das Magazin der Bertelsmann Stiftung 3/2014.
www.bertelsmann-stiftung.de/de/publikationen/publikation/did/change-32014-bildung-und-vielfalt

BILZ, L. / SUDECK, G. / BUCKSCH, J. / KLOCKE, A. / KOLIP, P. / MELZER, W. / RAVENS-SIEBERER, U. / RICHTER, M. (EDS.) (2016): *Schule und Gesundheit. Ergebnisse des WHO-Jugendgesundheitssurveys »Health Behaviour in School-aged Children.«* Weinheim.

BLATCHFORD, P. / BAINES, E. / KUTNICK, P. / MARTIN, C. (2001): Classroom contexts: Connections between class size and within class grouping. In *British Journal of Educational Psychology* 71, pp. 283–302.

BMBF – BUNDESMINISTERIUM FÜR BILDUNG UND FORSCHUNG (2011/2015): *Nationale Strategie für Alphabetisierung und Grundbildung Erwachsener.* www.bmbf.de/de/nationale-strategie-fuer-alphabetisierung-und-grundbildung-erwachsener-1373.html
www.bibb.de/dokumente/pdf/a33_grundsatzpapier_nationale_dekade.pdf

BMEL – BUNDESMINISTERIUM FÜR ERNÄHRUNG UND LANDWIRTSCHAFT (ED.) (2014): *Verpflegungskonzepte in Schulen. Grundlagen und Planungseckdaten für die Küchenplanung. IN FORM 5.* Berlin.

BMFSFJ – BUNDESMINISTERIUM FÜR FAMILIE, SENIOREN, FRAUEN UND JUGEND (2015): *Qualitätsstandards für die Beteiligung von Kindern und Jugendlichen.*
www.bmfsfj.de/resource/blob/94118/c49d4097174e67464b56a5365bc8602f/kindergerechtes-deutschland-broschuere-qualitaetsstandards-data.pdf
(2021): *Das Ganztagsförderungsgesetz.* www.recht-auf-ganztag.de/gb/politik/ganztagsfoerderungsgesetz
(2024): *17. Kinder- und Jugendbericht. Bericht über die Lage junger Menschen und die Bestrebungen und Leistungen der Kinder und Jugendhilfe.*

BMG – BUNDESMINISTERIUM FÜR GESUNDHEIT (2022): *Bewegungsförderung bei Kindern und Jugendlichen in Deutschland. Bestandsaufnahme.* www.bundesgesundheitsministerium.de/service/publikationen.html

BMUV / UBA – BUNDESMINISTERIUM FÜR UMWELT, NATURSCHUTZ, NUKLEARE SICHERHEIT UND VERBRAUCHERSCHUTZ / UMWELTBUNDESAMT (2024): *Zukunft? Jugend fragen! – 2023. Umwelt und Klima in Zeiten vielfältiger Krisen: Wie junge Menschen den Herausforderungen begegnen.* Berlin, Dessau.
www.umweltbundesamt.de/sites/default/files/medien/479/publikationen/zukunft_jugend_fragen_2023_0.pdf

BMVBS / BBSR – BUNDESMINISTERIUM FÜR VERKEHR, BAU UND STADTENTWICKLUNG / BUNDESINSTITUT FÜR BAU-, STADT- UND RAUMFORSCHUNG (EDS.) (2009): *Stadtquartiere für Jung und Alt. Europäische Fallstudien.* Werkstatt: Praxis Heft 63. Bonn.
d-nb.info/1000128016/34

BMWSB – BUNDESMINISTERIUM FÜR WOHNEN, STADTENTWICKLUNG UND BAUWESEN (ED.) (2017): *Bewertungssystem Nachhaltiges Bauen für Unterrichtsgebäude.*
www.bnb-nachhaltigesbauen.de/bewertungssystem/unterrichtsgebaeude/
(2024): *Co-designing spaces for the common good. The German Federal Government's guidelines for Baukultur.*
https://www.bmwsb.bund.de/SharedDocs/downloads/Webs/BMWSB/DE/publikationen/bauen/Baukulturelle-Leitlinien-eng.pdf?__blob=publicationFile&v=5

BRÄGGER, G. / POSSE, N. (2007): *Instrumente für die Qualitätsentwicklung und Evaluation von Schulen (IQES). Wie Schulen durch eine integrierte Gesundheits- und Qualitätsförderung besser werden können.* Bern.

BRAUM, M. / HAMM, O.G. (EDS.) (2010): *Worauf baut die Bildung? Fakten, Positionen, Beispiele*. Basel.

BREUER, A. (2015): *Lehrer-Erzieher-Teams an ganztägigen Grundschulen. Kooperation als Differenzierung von Zuständigkeiten*. Wiesbaden (Schule und Gesellschaft, 59).

BROEKHUIZEN, D. (2015): *Scholenbouwatlas – Verbouwen als nieuwe opgave voor basisscholen en kindcentra*. Rotterdam.

BUHREN, C.G. (1997): *Community Education*. Münster / New York / Munich / Berlin.

BUNDESREGIERUNG – PRESSE- UND INFORMATIONSAMT (2021): *Rechtsanspruch auf Ganztagsbetreuung ab 2026. Fragen und Antworten*. 10.09.2021. www.bundesregierung.de/breg-de/service/archiv/ganztagsausbau-grundschulen-1766962

BUNDESSTIFTUNG BAUKULTUR (2024A): *Baukulturbericht 2024/25 »Infrastrukturen«*. Potsdam. www.bundesstiftung-baukultur.de/publikationen/pdf-zum-download/baukulturberichte
(2024B): *Schulbuch Baukultur. Gebaute Umwelt erkennen, verstehen, gestalten*. Potsdam.

BURKHALTER, G. (ED.) (2016): *The Playground Project*. Zurich.

CAPRESI, V. / PAMPE, B. (2013): *LearnMovePlayGround. How to improve Playgrounds through Participation*. Berlin.

CHILES, P. (ED.) (2015): *Schulen bauen: Leitlinien für Planung und Entwurf*. Basel.

CODE CONSORTIUM (2018): *Leading from the Middle: Spreading Learning, Well-being, and Identity Across Ontario. Council of Ontario Directors of Education Report*. Principal Investigators: Andy Hargreaves and Dennis Shirley with Shaneé Wangia, Chris Bacon, and Mark D'Angelo. www.ccsli.ca/downloads/2018-Leading_From_the_Middle_Final-EN.pdf

COELEN, T. (2014): *Kooperationen zwischen Ganztagsschulen und außerschulischen Organisationen*. In Coelen, T. / Stecher, L. (Eds.): *Die Ganztagsschule. Eine Einführung*. Weinheim, Basel, pp. 29–45.

COELEN, T. / HEINRICH, A.J. / LOTH, C. / MILLION, A. / SOMBORSKI, I. (2017): *Gebaute Bildungslandschaften – Verflechtungen zwischen Pädagogik und Stadtplanung*. Berlin.

DAHM, K. (2006): *Freier Lernort Schulbibliothek – Raum für ein zeitgemäßes Lernen. In Schulen ans Netz e. V.: Freie Lernorte – Raum für mehr*. Medien in der Ganztagsschule, Bonn, pp. 12–15.

DANNER, A. / BOCK, F. / ROHDE, D. / GRASSHOFF, G. / IDEL, T.S. / SAUERWEIN, M. (2023): Laien als Akteure im Ganztag. Explorative Analysen im multiperspektivischen Mixed-Methods-Design *(*LAKTAT*)*. In *Soziale Passagen* 15, pp. 281–287. doi.org/10.1007/s12592-023-00443-x

DEINET, U. / ICKING, M. (2020): Offene Kinder- und Jugendarbeit und Schule. In Bollweg, P. et al. (Eds.) (2020): *Handbuch Ganztagsbildung*. Wiesbaden, pp. 875–886. doi.org/10.1007/978-3-658-23230-6_65

DESTATIS – STATISTISCHES BUNDESAMT (2016): *Veränderung der Zahl der Lebendgeborenen zum jeweiligen Vorjahr*. Wiesbaden. www.destatis.de/DE/Themen/Gesellschaft-Umwelt/Bevoelkerung/Geburten/_inhalt.html
(2018): *Schulen auf einen Blick*. Wiesbaden. www.destatis.de/DE/Themen/Gesellschaft-Umwelt/Bildung-Forschung-Kultur/Schulen/Publikationen/_publikationen-innen-schulen-blick.html

(2023): *Bildungsfinanzbericht 2023*. On behalf of the Federal Ministry of Education and Research and the Standing Conference of the Ministers of Education and Cultural Affairs of the Länder in the Federal Republic of Germany. Wiesbaden. www.destatis.de/DE/Themen/Gesellschaft-Umwelt/Bildung-Forschung-Kultur/Bildungsfinanzen-Ausbildungsfoerderung/Publikationen/Downloads-Bildungsfinanzen/bildungsfinanzbericht-1023206237004.pdf

DEUTSCHE BUNDESSTIFTUNG UMWELT (ED.) / AUER, T. / NAGLER, F. (2017): *Zukunftsfähiger Schulbau. 12 Schulen im Vergleich*. Bauband 2. Edition DETAIL. München 2017.

DEUTSCHE UNESCO-KOMMISSION E.V. (2010): *Inklusion: Leitlinien für die Bildungspolitik*. Bonn.
(2016): *Jahresbericht 2015*. Bonn. www.unesco.de/dokumente-und-hintergruende/publikationen/detail/jahresbericht-der-deutschen-unesco-kommission-2015/
(2017): *Bildungsagenda 2030 – Aktionsrahmen für die Umsetzung von Sustainable Development Goal 4. Inklusive, chancengerechte und hochwertige Bildung sowie lebenslanges Lernen für alle*. Abstract by Deutsche UNESCO-Kommission. www.unesco.de/assets/dokumente/Deutsche_UNESCO-Kommission/02_Publikationen/Publikation_Bildungsagenda_2030_Aktionsrahmen.pdf
(2021): *Bildung für nachhaltige Entwicklung. Eine Roadmap*. Published by UNESCO, the United Nations Educational, Scientific and Cultural Organization and the Deutsche UNESCO-Kommission e.V. (DUK). Paris/Bonn. www.unesco.de/assets/dokumente/Deutsche_UNESCO-Kommission/02_Publikationen/Publikation_Bildung_für_nachhaltige_Entwicklung_Eine_Roadmap.pdf

DEWEY, J. (1916): *Democracy and Education*. New York.

DGNB – DEUTSCHE GESELLSCHAFT FÜR NACHHALTIGES BAUEN: *Bildungsbauten. Nachhaltige Bildungsbauten mit der DGNB zertifizieren*. www.dgnb.de/de/zertifizierung/das-wichtigste-zur-dgnb-zertifizierung/nutzungsprofile/bildungsbauten

DIFU – DEUTSCHES INSTITUT FÜR URBANISTIK (2008): *Investitionsrückstand und Investitionsbedarf der Kommunen – Ausmaß, Ursachen, Folgen und Strategien*. Berlin.

DJAHANSCHAH, S. (2011): *Qualität und Nachhaltigkeit. Ein Kommentar des Referats Architektur und Bauwesen der Deutschen Bundesstiftung Umwelt.*

DKJS – DEUTSCHE KINDER- UND JUGENDSTIFTUNG (2019): *Well-Being als Faktor für Bildungserfolg. Diskurs, Studien und Praxisbeispiele*. Berlin.

DORNES, M. (2012): *Die Modernisierung der Seele. Kind – Familie – Gesellschaft*. Frankfurt am Main.

DREIER, A. / KUCHARZ, D, / RAMSEGER, J. / SÖRENSEN, B. (1999): *Grundschulen planen, bauen, neu gestalten*. Grundschulverband – Arbeitskreis Grundschule e.V. Hemsbach.

DUDEK, M. (2015): *Entwurfsatlas Schulen und Kindergärten*. Basel.

EDITION HOCHPARTERRE (ED.) (2015): *Grundrissfibel Schulbauten*. 30 Wettbewerbe in der Schweiz 2001–2015. Zurich.

EGER, N. (2014): *Arts Education. Zur Qualität künstlerischer Angebote an Schulen. Ein internationaler Vergleich*. Bochum, Freiburg.

EL-MAFAALANI, A. / KURTENBACH, S. / STROHMEIER, K.P. (2025): *Kinder – Minderheit ohne Schutz: Aufwachsen in der alternden Gesellschaft*. Cologne.

EXPERTENKREIS AMOK (2009): *Gemeinsam Handeln, Risiken erkennen und minimieren. Prävention, Intervention, Opferhilfe, Medien. Konsequenzen aus dem Amoklauf in Winnenden und Wendlingen am 11. März 2009.* www.baden-wuerttemberg.de/fileadmin/redaktion/dateien/Altdaten/202/BERICHT_Expertenkreis_Amok_25-09-09.pdf

FACHHOCHSCHULE NORDWESTSCHWEIZ FHNW (ED.) (2015): *SpielRäume. Möglichkeiten der Raumnutzung im Quartierkindergarten aus der Perspektive von Architektur, Pädagogik und Psychologie.* Windisch.

FAUSER, P. / PRENZEL, M. / SCHRATZ, M. (EDS.) (2007): *Was für Schulen! Der Deutsche Schulpreis. Herausgegeben für die Robert Bosch Stiftung und die Heidehof Stiftung.* Seelze.

FISCHER, N. (2020): *Wirkungen außerunterrichtlicher Angebote an Ganztagsschulen.* In Bollweg, P. / Buchna, J. / Coelen, T. / Otto, H.U. (Eds.): *Handbuch Ganztagsbildung.* Wiesbaden. doi.org/10.1007/978-3-658-23230-6_113

FULLAN, M. / SCOTT, G. (2014): *Education PLUS. The world will be led by people you can count on, including you! New Pedagogies for Deep Learning Whitepaper.* Washington. www.michaelfullan.ca/wp-content/uploads/2014/09/Education-Plus-A-Whitepaper-July-2014-1.pdf

GARDNER, H. (1991): *The Unschooled Mind: How children think and how schools should teach.* New York.
(1993): *Frames of Mind: The theory of multiple intelligences.* New York.
(1997): *Extraordinary Minds: Portraits of Exceptional Individuals and an Examination of our Extraordinariness.* New York.

GERMAN TOILET ORGANIZATION E.V. (ED.) (2023): *Toiletten machen Schule – Studie zu Sanitäranlagen an Berliner Schulen.* Berlin. www.germantoilet.org/de/schulen/toiletten-machen-schule-studie/

HAMMERER, F. / ROSENBERGER, K. (EDS.) (2015): *Raum Bildung³.* Kirchliche Pädagogische Hochschule Vienna / Krems in cooperation with the Federal Ministry of Education and Women's Affairs. Vienna / Krems.

HASCHER, T. / MORINAJ, J. / WABER, J. (2018): Schulisches Wohlbefinden – Eine Einführung in Konzept und Forschungsstand. In Rathmann, K. / Hurrelmann, K. (Eds): *Leistung und Wohlbefinden in der Schule: Herausforderung Inklusion.* Weinheim, pp. 66–82.

HASCHER, T. / HAGENAUER, G. (2011): Schulisches Wohlbefinden im Jugendalter – Verläufe und Einflussfaktoren. In Ilttel, A. / Merkens, H. / Stecher, L. (Eds.): *Jahrbuch Jugendforschung.* Wiesbaden. doi.org/10.1007/978-3-531-93116-6_1

HATTIE, J. (2023): *Visible Learning: The Sequel. A Synthesis of Over 2,100 Meta-Analyses Relating to Achievement.* London, New York.

HAUSMANN, F. / PFAFF, F. (2004): *Das offene Klassenzimmer. Dokumentation zur Untersuchung der FH Aachen an der Montessori-Schule Aachen.*

HECKMAN, J. (2008): *Die Dynamik von Bildungsinvestitionen im Lebensverlauf. Warum Sparen in der Bildung teuer ist.* Presentation at the Bertelsmann Stiftung's congress »Kinder früher fördern – Wirksamere Bildungsinvestitionen« on March 13, 2008.

HERTZBERGER, H. (2008): *Space and Learning.* Rotterdam.

HOFMANN, S. (ED.) (2015): *Partizipation macht Architektur. Die Baupiloten – Methode und Projekte*. Berlin.

HÖHMANN, K. / HOLTAPPELS, H.G. (2006): *Ganztagsschule gestalten: Konzeption – Praxis – Impulse*. Seelze.

HUNGER, I. / ZIMMER, R. (2024): »Wie Bewegung die Entwicklung, das Lernen und die Bildung von Kindern beeinflusst.« In *Bundeszentrale für politische Bildung*, 11.03.2024. www.bpb.de/themen/bildung/dossier-bildung/545753/wie-bewegung-die-entwicklung-das-lernen-und-die-bildung-von-kindern-beeinflusst

HURRELMANN, K. / KLOCKE, A. / MELZER, W. / RAVENS-SIEBERER, U. (2003): WHO-Jugendgesundheitssurvey – Konzept und ausgewählte Ergebnisse für die Bundesrepublik Deutschland. In *Erziehungswissenschaft* 14, 27, pp. 79–108. www.pedocs.de/volltexte/2021/1725/pdf/ErzWiss_27_2003_Hurrelmann_et_al_WHO-Jugendgesundheitssurvey.pdf

HÜTHER, G. (2010): *Die Macht der inneren Bilder. Wie Visionen das Gehirn, den Menschen und die Welt verändern*. Göttingen.

IAE – THE INTERNATIONAL ASSOCIATION FOR THE EVALUATION OF EDUCATIONAL ACHIEVEMENT (2002): *Civic Knowledge and Engagement*. An *IEA Study of Upper Secondary Students in Sixteen Countries*. By Amadeo, J. A. / Torney-Purta, J. / Lehmann, R. / Husfeldt, V. / Nikolova, R. Amsterdam. www.iea.nl/sites/default/files/2019-04/CIVED_Phase2_Upper_Secondary.pdf

IMHÄUSER, K.H. (2016): Typologien für lokale Bildungslandschaften. In *Schulen planen und bauen – Blog der Montag Stiftung Jugend und Gesellschaft*, 25.07.2016. www.schulen-planen-und-bauen.de/2016/07/25/typologien-fuer-lokale-bildungslandschaften

IT.NRW (2010): *Regionalisierte Schülerprognosen in Nordrhein-Westfalen 2010*. Düsseldorf.

KAHLERT, J. / NITSCHE, K. / ZIERER, K. (EDS.) (2013): *Räume zum Lernen und Lehren. Perspektiven einer zeitgenössischen Schulraumgestaltung*. Bad Heilbrunn.

KALANTZIS, M. / COPE, B. (2008): *New Learning: Elements of a Science of Education*. Cambridge.

KFW BANKENGRUPPE (ED.) (2016): *KfW-Kommunalpanel 2016*. Content editing: Deutsches Institut für Urbanistik, Scheller, Dr. H. / Schneider, Dr. S. Frankfurt am Main. www.kfw.de/PDF/Download-Center/Konzernthemen/Research/PDF-Dokumente-KfW-Kommunalpanel/KfW-Kommunalpanel-2016.pdf
(2025): *KfW-Kommunalpanel 2025*. Content editing: Deutsches Institut für Urbanistik, Raffer, C. / Scheller, H. / von Zahn, F. Frankfurt am Main. www.kfw.de/PDF/Download-Center/Konzernthemen/Research/PDF-Dokumente-KfW-Kommunalpanel/KfW-Kommunalpanel-2025.pdf

KLEMM, K. (2013A): *Ganztagsschulen in Deutschland – eine bildungsstatistische Analyse*. On behalf of Bertelsmann Stiftung. Gütersloh. www.bertelsmann-stiftung.de/fileadmin/files/BSt/Publikationen/GrauePublikationen/GP_Ganztagsschulen_in_Deutschland.pdf
(2013B): *Inklusion in Deutschland – eine bildungsstatistische Analyse*. On behalf of Bertelsmann Stiftung. Gütersloh. www.bertelsmann-stiftung.de/fileadmin/files/BSt/Publikationen/GrauePublikationen/GP_Inklusion_in_Deutschland.pdf
(2014B): *Ganztagsschulen in Deutschland: Die Ausbaudynamik ist erlahmt*. On behalf of Bertelsmann Stiftung. Gütersloh. www.bertelsmann-stiftung.de/de/publikationen/publikation/did/ganztagsschulen-in-deutschland-die-ausbaudynamik-ist-erlahmt

(2015): *Inklusion in Deutschland – Daten und Fakten*. On behalf of Bertelsmann Stiftung. Gütersloh.
www.bertelsmann-stiftung.de/fileadmin/files/BSt/Publikationen/GrauePublikationen/Studie_IB_Klemm-Studie_Inklusion_2015.pdf

(2016A): *Demografische Rendite war gestern. Zum mittelfristigen Ausbaubedarf bei Grundschulen*. Essen.
www.grundschulverband.de/wp-content/uploads/2017/02/anlage_1_zur_pm_schueleranstieg_ausbaubedarf.pdf

(2016B): *Finanzierung und Ausstattung der deutschen Grundschulen. Expert opinion on behalf of Grundschulverband e. V.* Essen.
www.pedocs.de/volltexte/2019/17719/pdf
GSV_2017_Klemm_Gutachten_Finanzierung_und_Ausstattung_der_deutschen_Grundschulen.pdf

(2016C): Warum sinkt die Zahl der Schüler an den Förderschulen kaum? Wo Inklusion gelingt – und wie sie scheitert. In *DIE ZEIT* No. 16, April 7, 2016

(2017): Ganztagsschulen im Spannungsfeld von Nachfrage, Finanzierung und Qualität. In Maschke, S. /Schulz-Gade, G. / Stecher, L. (Eds.): *Jahrbuch Ganztagsschule 2017. Junge Geflüchtete in der Ganztagsschule*. Schwalbach / Taunus.

(2021): *Inklusion in Deutschlands Schulen. Entwicklungen – Erfahrungen – Erwartungen*. Weinheim, Basel.

(2022): *Inklusion in Deutschlands Schulen: Eine bildungsstatistische Momentaufnahme 2020/2021*. On behalf of Bertelsmann Stiftung. Gütersloh.
www.bertelsmann-stiftung.de/de/publikationen/publikation/did/inklusion-in-deutschlandsschulen-eine-bildungsstatistische-momentaufnahme-202021-all

KLEMM, K. / ZORN, D. (2016): Die landesseitige Ausstattung gebundener Ganztagsschulen mit personellen Ressourcen. Ein Bundesländervergleich. Gütersloh.

KLIEBISCH, U.W. / MELOEFSKI, R. (EDS.) (2009): *Lehrer-Gesundheit. Anregungen für die Praxis*. Hohengehren.

KMK – KULTUSMINISTERKONFERENZ (2006): *Erklärung der Kultusministerkonferenz vom 03.03.2006 zur Umsetzung des Übereinkommens der Vereinten Nationen über die Rechte des Kindes*. Resolution of March 3, 2006.
www.kmk.org/fileadmin/veroeffentlichungen_beschluesse/2006/2006_03_03-UN-Kinderrechte_.pdf

(2011): *Schüler, Klassen, Lehrer und Absolventen der Schulen 2000 bis 2009. Statistische Veröffentlichungen der Kultusministerkonferenz, Dokumentation Nr. 190*. Berlin.
www.kmk.org/fileadmin/pdf/Statistik/Dokumentationen/Dok_190_SKL.pdf

(2017): *Bildung in der digitalen Welt. Strategie der Kultusministerkonferenz*. Resolution of December 8, 2016, in the version of December 7, 2017.
www.kmk.org/fileadmin/Dateien/pdf/PresseUndAktuelles/2018/Digitalstrategie_2017_mit_Weiterbildung.pdf

(2019): *Erklärung der Kultusministerkonferenz vom 17.10.2019 zum nachhaltigen Entwicklungsziel 4 der Vereinten Nationen und zu globalen Agenda Bildung 2030*.
www.kmk.org/fileadmin/veroeffentlichungen_beschluesse/2019/2019_10_17-Entwicklungsziel4-Bildung2030.pdf

(2021A): Der Ertrag inklusiven Unterrichtens: Ergebnisse der Bildungsforschung. In Klemm, K.: *Inklusion in Deutschlands Schulen. Entwicklungen – Erfahrungen – Erwartungen*. Weinheim, Basel.

(2021B): *Lehren und Lernen in der digitalen Welt. Die ergänzende Empfehlung zur Strategie »Bildung in der digitalen Welt.«* Resolution of December 9, 2021.
www.kmk.org/fileadmin/veroeffentlichungen_beschluesse/2021/2021_12_09-Lehren-und-Lernen-Digi.pdf

(2023): *Empfehlungen zur Weiterentwicklung der pädagogischen Qualität der Ganztagsschule und weiterer ganztägiger Bildungs- und Betreuungsangebote für Kinder im Grundschulalter.* Resolution of October 12, 2023.
www.kmk.org/fileadmin/veroeffentlichungen_beschluesse/2023/2023_10_12-Ganztag-Empfehlung.pdf
(2024): *Vorausberechnung der Zahlen der Schüler/-innen und Absolvierenden 2023 bis 2035.* Resolution of November 8, 2024.
www.kmk.org/dokumentation-statistik/statistik/schulstatistik/vorausberechnung-der-schueler-und-absolventenzahlen.html
(2025): *Allgemeinbildende Schulen in Ganztagsform in den Ländern in der Bundesrepublik Deutschland. Statistik 2019 bis 2023.* Berlin.
www.kmk.org/fileadmin/Dateien/pdf/Statistik/Dokumentationen/GTS_2023_Bericht.pdf

KNAUF, H. (2024): (Schul-)Kultur der Digitalität? Eine Analyse der Organisation Schule im digitalen Wandel. In *Zeitschrift für Grundschulforschung* 17, pp. 55–68.
doi.org/10.1007/s42278-024-00195-4

KOCAJ, A. (2018): *Zusammenhänge zwischen der Beschulungsart und den schulischen Kompetenzen sowie der schulischen Motivation von Kindern mit sonderpädagogischem Förderbedarf.* Dissertation. Berlin.

KOCAJ, A. / KUHL, P. / KROTH, A.J. / PANT, H.A. / STANAT, P. (2014): Wo lernen Kinder mit sonderpädagogischem Förderbedarf besser? Ein Vergleich schulischer Kompetenzen zwischen Regel- und Förderschulen in der Primarstufe. In *Kölner Zeitschrift für Soziologie und Sozialpsychologie* (2014/66), pp. 165–191.

KOMPETENZNETZWERK GEGEN HASS IM NETZ (2024): *Lauter Hass – leiser Rückzug. Wie Hass im Netz den demokratischen Diskurs bedroht. Ergebnisse einer repräsentativen Befragung.* Authors: Bernhard, L. / Ickstadt, L. Berlin.
toneshift.org/wp-content/uploads/2024/02/Studie_Lauter-Hass-leiser-Rueckzug.pdf

KRICKE, M. (2016): Die Auswahl von Lehramtsstudierenden: Ein Beispiel aus Finnland. In Boeger, A. (Ed.): *Eignung für den Lehrerberuf – Eignung und Förderung.* Wiesbaden, pp. 305–332.
doi.org/10.1007/978-3-658-10041-4_14

KRICKE, M. / REICH, K. (2016): Teamteaching: *Eine neue Kultur des Lehrens und Lernens.* Weinheim, Basel.

KRICKE, M. / REICH, K. / SCHANZ, L. / SCHNEIDER, J. (2018): *Raum und Inklusion. Neue Konzepte im Schulbau.* Weinheim, Basel.

KROWORSCH, S. (2023): *Inklusive Schulbildung: Warum Bund und Länder gemeinsam Verantwortung übernehmen sollten.* Berlin: Deutsches Institut für Menschenrechte (DIMR).

KURTH, B.-M. / SCHAFFRATH ROSARIO, A. (2010): Übergewicht und Adipositas bei Kindern und Jugendlichen in Deutschland. In *Bundesgesundheitsblatt – Gesundheitsforschung – Gesundheitsschutz* 7, pp. 643–652.
doi.org/10.1007/s00103-010-1083-2

KURZ, D. / WAKEFIELD, A. (2004): *Schulhausbau. Der Stand der Dinge. School Buildings. The State of Affairs.* Basel.

LADENTHIN, V. / REKUS, J. (EDS.) (2005): *Die Ganztagsschule. Alltag, Reform, Geschichte, Theorie.* Weinheim, Munich.

LANDESHAUPTSTADT DRESDEN (ED.) (2016): *Dresdner Schulbauleitlinie.* November 2016.
www.dresden.de/media/pdf/schulen/20170116_SBLL.pdf

LANDESHAUPTSTADT MÜNCHEN, REFERAT FÜR BILDUNG UND SPORT (ED.) (2015): *Das Münchner LERNHAUS. Funktionsschemata und Auszüge der Standardraumprogramme für Grundschulen, Mittelschulen, Realschulen und Gymnasien.* Munich.
stadt.muenchen.de/dam/jcr:2163989c-893e-47a0-a0e4-d986d7ce8314/Lernhaus_Einleger_final_web.pdf
(2016): *Praxisbuch Münchner LERNHAUS.* Munich.
www.lernhausfilm.de/wp-content/uploads/2019/04/Praxisbuch_Muenchner_Lernhaus_2016.pdf

LANDESHAUPTSTADT STUTTGART: *Neuausstattung von bestehenden Fachräumen im naturwissenschaftlichen Bereich an Stuttgarter Schulen im Rahmen der Bildungsplanreform.* 10.09.2007.

LANDESINSTITUT FÜR SCHULENTWICKLUNG (2008): *Abschlussbericht Modellversuche zur Arbeitsorganisation und zu einer Neubewertung der Arbeit von Lehrerinnen und Lehrern.* Stuttgart.

LARGO, R. (2009): *Schülerjahre. Wie Kinder besser lernen.* Munich.

LAWRENZ, W. / PAMPE, B. (2024): Zukunftsfähige Stadtentwicklung durch Bildung – Bildungslandschaft Altstadt-Nord Köln (BAN). In *Beispielhafte Projekte der Quartiersentwicklung – Neue Materialien zur Planungskultur.* Band 42 Projekte. Ed. by Wékel, J. / Ohnsorge, D., Institut für Städtebau und Wohnungswesen (ISW). München, pp. 172–175.

LEDERER, A. / PAMPE, B. (2010): *Raumpilot Lernen.* Stuttgart.

LORENZ-SPREEN, P. / OSWALD, L. / LEWANDOWSKY, S. ET AL. (2023): A *systematic review of world-wide causal and correlational evidence on digital media and democracy.* In Nat Hum Behav 7, 2023, pp. 74–101.
doi.org/10.1038/s41562-022-01460-1

LUEG, A. (2024): *Mit dem Körper lernen – Wie Bewegung das Gehirn trainiert.* SWR Kultur: Das Wissen. 16.11.2024.
www.swr.de/swrkultur/wissen/mit-dem-koerperlernen-wie-bewegung-das-gehirn-trainiert-das-wissen-2024-11-16-104.pdf

LÜTJE-KLOSE, B. / MILLER, S. / SCHWAB, S. / STREESE, B. (EDS.) (2017): *Inklusion: Profile für die Schul- und Unterrichtsentwicklung in Deutschland, Österreich und der Schweiz. Theoretische Grundlagen – Empirische Befunde – Praxisbeispiele.* Münster.

MATTHEWES, S.H. (2020): *Längeres gemeinsames Lernen macht einen Unterschied.* WZBrief Bildung 40. Berlin.
bibliothek.wzb.eu/wzbrief-bildung/WZBriefBildung402020_matthewes.pdf

MONTAG STIFTUNG JUGEND UND GESELLSCHAFT (ED.) (2015A): *Fünfmal Phase Null. Dokumentation der Pilotprojekte »Schulen planen und bauen.«* Bonn.
www.issuu.com/montagstiftungen/docs/151105_5xphasenull_72ppi_einzelseit
(2015B): *Phase Null – Der Film. Pädagogik und Architektur im Dialog: Die Planung der Geschwister-Scholl-Stadtteilschule in Hamburg.* A film by Jan Marschner and Flash Filmproduktion Armin Maiwald GmbH. Phase 0: bueroschneidermeyer and Institut für Schulentwicklung. Published by Montag Stiftung Jugend und Gesellschaft. Berlin.
(2017): *Bildungsband Osdorfer Born. Die Bildungslandschaft Osdorf / Lurup finden und entwerfen.* Bonn.
www.issuu.com/montagstiftungen/docs/brosch__re_bildungsband_osdorfer-bo
(2023/2024): *Ganztag und Raum. Pilotprojekte. Five documentaries.* Bonn.
www.montag-stiftungen.de/gur
(2025A): *Phase Zehn Playbook.* Bonn.
www.phase-zehn.de

(2025B): *Schulbau Open Source – Planungswissen für Innovationen im Schulbau*. Bonn. www.schulbauopensource.de

MONTAG STIFTUNG JUGEND UND GESELLSCHAFT / BUND DEUTSCHER ARCHITEKTINNEN UND ARCHITEKTEN BDA / VERBAND BILDUNG UND ERZIEHUNG (VBE) (EDS.) (2022): *Leitlinien für leistungsfähige Schulbauten in Deutschland*. 4., revised edition. Bonn, Berlin. www.issuu.com/montagstiftungen/docs/mon_lls_brosch_komplett_46rz_3teauf
(2024): *Akustik im Schulbau. Neue Konzepte und Empfehlungen*. Bonn, Berlin. www.issuu.com/montagstiftungen/docs/akustikimschulbau_mjg_web
(2025): *Qualität im Schulbau – Sondervermögen für Qualitätsoffensive im Schulbau nutzen*. Berlin. www.issuu.com/montagstiftungen/docs/qualitaetsoffensive_2025

MONTAG STIFTUNG JUGEND UND GESELLSCHAFT / BUND DEUTSCHER ARCHITEKTINNEN UND ARCHITEKTEN BDA / DEUTSCHE BUNDESSTIFTUNG UMWELT / TECHNISCHE UNIVERSITÄT KAISERSLAUTERN / UNFALLKASSE NRW / VERBAND BILDUNG UND ERZIEHUNG VBE (EDS.) (2017): *Brandschutz im Schulbau. Neue Konzepte und Empfehlungen*. Berlin, Bonn, Düsseldorf, Kaiserslautern, Osnabrück. www.issuu.com/montagstiftungen/docs/brandschutz_im_schulbau_interaktiv

MONTAG STIFTUNG JUGEND UND GESELLSCHAFT/ STADT KÖLN (ED.) (2022): *Management von Bildungslandschaften. Eine Vergleichsstudie*. Bonn. issuu.com/montagstiftungen/docs/220112_mjg_campusmanagement_studie_web

MONTAG STIFTUNG URBANE RÄUME (ED.) (2024): *Gemeinwohl bauen. Band 1: BOB CAMPUS – Transformation einer stillgelegten Textilfabrik*. By Debik J.M. / Ambrée, R. Berlin, Boston 2024.

MILLON, A./ BENTLIN, F. / HEINRICH, A.J. (EDS.) (2016): *Wenn Stadt Bildung mitdenkt, dann ... Perspektiven von Lehre, Forschung und Praxis auf die Idee einer bildenden Stadt*. Published by TU Berlin, Department of Urban Planning and Housing, in cooperation with Vodafone Stiftung Deutschland. Berlin. www.static.tu.berlin/fileadmin/www/40000092/FNEZ_Downloadliste/2016_Die_bildende_Stadt.pdf

NATIONALE AKADEMIE DER WISSENSCHAFTEN LEOPOLDINA, UNION DER DEUTSCHEN AKADEMIEN DER WISSENSCHAFTTEN, ACATECH – DEUTSCHE AKADEMIE DER WISSENSCHAFTEN (2021): *Digitalisierung und Demokratie*. Halle (Saale). doi.org/10.26164/leopoldina_03_00348

NODDINGS, N. (2006): *Critical Lessons – What our Schools Should Teach*. Cambridge.

OECD (2010A): *PISA 2009 Results: What Students Know and Can Do: Student Performance in Reading, Mathematics and Science* (Volume I). PISA, OECD Publishing. Paris. doi.org/10.1787/9789264091450-en
(2010B): *PISA 2009 Results: Overcoming Social Background: Equity in Learning Opportunities and Outcomes* (Volume II). PISA, OECD Publishing. Paris. doi.org/10.1787/9789264091504-en
(2010C): *PISA 2009 Results: What Makes a School Successful?: Resources, Policies and Practices* (Volume IV), PISA, OECD Publishing. Paris. doi.org/10.1787/9789264091559-en
(2010D): *The High Cost of Low Educational Performance: The Long-run Economic Impact of Improving PISA Outcomes*. PISA, OECD Publishing. Paris. doi.org/10.1787/9789264077485-en
(2011A): *Designing for Education: Compendium of Exemplary Educational Facilities 2011*. OECD Publishing. Paris. doi.org/10.1787/9789264112308-en

(2011B): *Wenn Schüler Klassen wiederholen oder die Schule wechseln müssen: Was bedeutet das für die Bildungssysteme? PISA IM FOKUS* 2011/6 (July).
(2018): *Equity in Education. Breaking Down Barriers to Social Mobility.* OECD Publishing. Paris.
doi.org/10.1787/9789264073234-en
(2019): *OECD Future of Education and Skills 2030. OECD Learning Compass 2030. A Series of Concept Notes.* OECD Publishing. Paris.
www.oecd.org/content/dam/oecd/en/about/projects/edu/education-2040/1-1-learning-compass/OECD_Learning_Compass_2030_Concept_Note_Series.pdf
(2020): *Back to the Future of Education. Four OECD Scenarios for Schooling. Educational Research and Innovation.* Paris.
doi.org/10.1787/178ef527-en
(2024): *Education at a Glance 2024: OECD Indicators.* OECD Publishing. Paris.
doi.org/10.1787/c00cad36-en

OELKERS, J. (2017): Ganztagsschulen: Ein neues Gutachten. In Maschke, S. / Schulz-Gade, G. / Stecher, L. (Eds.): *Jahrbuch Ganztagsschule 2017. Junge Geflüchtete in der Ganztagsschule.* Schwalbach / Taunus.

ORMROD, J.E. (2004): *Human Learning.* Columbus, Ohio.
(2006): *Educational Psychology. Developing Learners.* Upper Saddle River, New Jersey.

OSTER, H. / BEHLAU, S. (2024): Schulbeginn um 9 Uhr? In *Pädagogik* (12) 2024, pp. 40–41.

PAMPE, B. (2024A): Die Phase Null. Voraussetzung und Ausgangspunkt für einen zukunftsweisenden Schulbau. In Kirch, M. / Ramseger, J. / Grundschulverband e.V. (Ed.): *Lernräume und Schularchitektur. Grundschule mit Kindern neu denken, neu planen, neu gestalten.* Frankfurt, pp. 178–181.
(2024B): Schulbau Open Source – Wissenstransfer als Innovationstreiber. In *Bauwende. Zukunft Bau Kongress 2023.* Ed. by Bundesinstitut für Bau-, Stadt- und Raumforschung (BBSR). Bonn, pp. 196–201.

PAMPE, B. / WALTER, U. (2024): Von der Mensa zu Wohnküchen und Schulrestaurants. In Kirch, M. / Ramseger, J. / Grundschulverband e.V. (Ed.): *Lernräume und Schularchitektur. Grundschule mit Kindern neu denken, neu planen, neu gestalten.* Frankfurt, pp. 78–81.

PIB – PÄDAGOGISCHES INSTITUT BOZEN (2009): *Ein Rückblick zum Pilotprojekt »Mobiles Forscherlabor in der Grundschule.«* Bolzano.
www.schule.suedtirol.it/pi/faecher/documents/Bericht_Mobiles_Forscherlabor.pdf

PROGNOS / ITES (2023): *Bericht zum Ausbaustand der ganztägigen Bildungs- und Betreuungsangebote für Grundschulkinder nach §24a SGB VIII.* Bundesministerium für Familie, Senioren, Frauen und Jugend.
www.bmfsfj.de/resource/blob/234238/542e764d0223806ba63d913e3cc65da1/gafoeg-bericht-2023-data.pdf
(2024): *Zweiter Bericht der Bundesregierung zum Ausbaustand der ganztägigen Bildungs- und Betreuungsangebote für Grundschulkinder nach § 24a SGB VIII.* 2. GaFöG-Bericht. Bundesministerium für Familie, Senioren, Frauen und Jugend.
www.bmfsfj.de/resource/blob/251606/4eb97254232538a2b405d3a49705883d/2-gafoeg-bericht-data.pdf

RABENSTEIN, K. (2020): Rhythmisierung. In Bollweg, P. / Buchna, J. / Coelen, T. / Otto, H.U. (Eds.), *Handbuch Ganztagsbildung,* Wiesbaden.
doi.org/10.1007/978-3-658-23230-6_76

RACKLES, M (2021): *Inklusive Bildung in Deutschland. Beharrungskräfte der Exklusion und notwendige Transformationsimpulse.* Berlin.

RAMSEGER, J. / KIRCH, M. (2024): *Lernräume und Schularchitektur. Grundschule mit Kindern neu denken, neu planen, neu gestalten*. Frankfurt a.M.

RATHMANN, K. / HURRELMANN, K. (EDS.) (2018): *Leistung und Wohlbefinden in der Schule: Herausforderung Inklusion*. Weinheim.

RABENS-SIEBERER, U. / KAMAN, A. / OTTO, C. / ADEDEJI, A. / NAPP, A.K. / BECKER, M. / BLANCK-STELLMACHER, U. / LÖFFLER, C. / SCHLACK, R. / HÖLLING, H. / DEVINE, J. / ERHART, M. / HURRELMANN, K. (2021): Seelische Gesundheit und psychische Belastungen von Kindern und Jugendlichen in der ersten Welle der COVID-19-Pandemie – Ergebnisse der COPSY-Studie. In *Bundesgesundheitsblatt Gesundheitsforschung Gesundheitsschutz*. 12 2021, pp. 1512–1521. doi.org/10.1007/s00103-021-03291-3

REH, S. / FRITZSCHE, B. / IDEL, T.S. / RABENSTEIN, K. (EDS.) (2015): *Lernkulturen. Rekonstruktion pädagogischer Praktiken an Ganztagsschulen*. Wiesbaden.

REICH, C. / REICH, K. (2025): *Digitale Didaktik. Modelle und Methoden für eine erfolgreiche Praxis*. Weinheim, Basel.

REICH, K. (2007): *Lehrerbildung konstruktivistisch gestalten*. Weinheim, Basel.
(2008A): *Demokratie im Kleinen*. www.methodenpool.uni-koeln.de/download/demokratie_im_kleinen.pdf
(2008B): *Konstruktivistische Didaktik*. Weinheim, Basel.
(2010): *Systemisch-konstruktivistische Pädagogik*. Weinheim, Basel.
(2012): *Inklusion und Bildungsgerechtigkeit*. Weinheim, Basel.
(2014): *Inklusive Didaktik. Bausteine für eine inklusive Schule*. Weinheim, Basel.
(2023): *Faire Bildung für alle. Wie sich Schule neu erfinden kann*. Weinheim, Basel.

REICH, K. / ASSELHOVEN, D. / KARGL, S. (EDS.) (2015): *Eine inklusive Schule für alle. Das Modell der inklusiven Universitätsschule Köln*. Weinheim, Basel.

ROBERT KOCH INSTITUT (ED.) (2003–2017): *KiGGS – Studie zur Gesundheit von Kindern und Jugendlichen in Deutschland*. 2003–2006; 2009–2012; 2014–2017. www.rki.de/DE/Themen/Nichtuebertragbare-Krankheiten/Studien-und-Surveillance/Studien/KiGGS/kiggs_start_inhalt.html

ROLFF, H.G. ET AL. (2000): *Manual Schulentwicklung: Handlungskonzept zur pädagogischen Schulentwicklungsberatung*. Weinheim.

SALLIN, A. (2022): *Minorities in schools – Three empirical essays in education economics. Minderheiten in Schulen. Integration und deren Auswirkungen – Peer-Effekt der Klassenzusammensetzung*. Dissertation. St. Gallen. www.alexandria.unisg.ch/server/api/core/bitstreams/71c464ce-cac7-414b-b003-d399e1c100ed/content

SAUERWEIN, M. / HEER, J. (2020): Warum gibt es keine leistungssteigernden Effekte durch den Besuch von Ganztagsangeboten? Oder: Über die Paradoxie individueller Förderung. In *Zeitschrift für Pädagogik* (1) 2020, pp. 78–101.

SCHAARSCHMIDT, U. (2003): Psychische Beanspruchung im Lehrerberuf. In *Wirtschaft und Erziehung 2* (2003), pp. 8–21.
(2006): *Die Potsdamer Lehrerstudie. Ergebnisüberblick, Schlussfolgerungen und Maßnahmen*. www.vbe.de/service/potsdamer-lehrerstudie

SCHAARSCHMIDT, U. / KIESCHKE, U. (EDS.) (2007): *Gerüstet für den Schulalltag. Psychologische Unterstützungsangebote für Lehrerinnen und Lehrer*. Weinheim, Basel.

SCHAFFITZEL, W. (2023): Schule gestern und morgen – ein Blick auf die Rolle der Schulmöbel. In Kohlert, C. (Ed.): *Die menschliche (Hoch)schule*. Wiesbaden, pp. 125–142.

SCHMIDT, M. / SCHUSTER, R. (EDS.) (2017): *Schulgesellschaft. Vom Dazwischen zum Lernraum. 30 Schulgebäude im Vergleich*. Braunschweig.

SCHNEIDER, J. (2014): Lernen vom Schulbau. In Meuser, N (ed.) *Schulbauten. Handbuch und Planungshilfe*. Berlin.
(2012): *Typologien und räumliche Organisationsmodelle im Schulbau. Brief expertise on behalf of the Montag Stiftungen*. Cologne, Bonn.

SCHNEIDER, J. / SEYDEL, O. (2013A): *Empfehlungen für einen zeitgemäßen Schulhausbau in Baden-Württemberg. Grundlagen für eine Überarbeitung der Schulbauförderrichtlinien*. On behalf of the Baden-Württemberg Ministry of Culture, Youth and Sport. Stuttgart / Überlingen. www.schulentwicklung-net.de/images/stories/Anlagen/510%20schulhausbau_BW_2013.pdf
(2013B): *Schulbauleitlinien Landkreis Darmstadt-Dieburg. SBLLdadi®. Anlass und Ziele – Qualitäten – Quantitäten*. On behalf of Da-Di Werk Gebäudemanagement. Stuttgart, Überlingen.
www.ladadi.de/da-di-werk/downloads-formulare.html
(2019): *Neue räumliche Konzepte für den MINT-Unterricht*. Symposium Frankfurt am Main, January 22, 2019.

SCHNEPF, S.V. (2002): *A Sorting Hat that Fails? The Transition from Primary to Secondary School in Germany*. Florence.

SCHÖNIG, W. / SCHMIDTLEIN-MAUDERER, C. (EDS.) (2015): *Inklusion sucht Raum. Porträtierte Schulentwicklung*. Bern.

SCHRATZ, M. ET AL. (2000): *Qualitätsentwicklung: Verfahren, Methoden, Instrumente*. Weinheim.

SCHUHMACHER, H. (ED.) (2010): *Gestaltungsfibel Nachhaltiger Schulhof*. FH Erfurt.

SCHWEINHART, L.J. (2005): *The High/Scope Perry Preschool Study Through Age 40. Summary, Conclusions and Frequently Asked Questions*. www.highscope.org/wp-content/uploads/2024/07/perry-preschool-summary-40.pdf

SCHWEINHART, L.J. ET AL. (2005): *Lifetime Effects: The High/Scope Perry Preschool Study Through Age 40*. HighScope.

SEIDEL, S. ET AL. (2009): *The Qualities of Quality – Understanding Excellence in Arts Education. Project Zero*. Harvard Graduate School of Education.

SEYDEL, O. (2015): Überlegungen zur Beziehung von Schule und Stadt. In Coelen, T. / Heinrich, A.J. / Million, A. (Eds.): *Stadtbaustein Bildung*. Wiesbaden, pp. 23–32.
(2019): Abschaffung der Schule? Pädagogische Konsequenzen der digitalen Revolution. In Burow, O.A. (Ed.): *Schule digital – wie geht das? Wie die digitale Revolution uns und die Schule verändert*. Weinheim, Basel, pp. 129–138.
(2023): *Anforderungen an ein Schulgebäude. Lernräume – Arbeitsräume – Lebensräume*. Hannover.
(2024): Raus aus der Flexibilitätsfalle! Ein elementares Problem der Schulbauplanung. In *Räume und ihre Nutzung. Lernende Schule*, no. 106/2024.

SHELL YOUTH STUDY – DEUTSCHE SHELL HOLDING GMBH (ED.) (2024): *Jugend 2024. 19. Shell Jugendstudie. Pragmatisch zwischen Verdrossenheit und gelebter Vielfalt. (Shell Youth Study 2024 – with an English summary)*. Weinheim. www.shell.de/ueber-uns/initiativen/shell-jugendstudie-2024.html

SINUS JUGENDSTUDIE (2024): *Wie ticken Jugendliche 2024? Lebenswelten von Jugendlichen im Alter von 14 bis 17 Jahren in Deutschland.* By Calmbach, M. / Flaig, B. / Gaber, R. / Gensheimer, T. / Möller-Slawinski, H. / Schleer, C. / Wisniewski, N. Bonn. www.sinus-institut.de/media-center/presse/sinus-jugendstudie-2024

SLAVIN, R.E. (2006): *Educational Psychology. Theory and Practice.* Boston.

SLIWKA, A. / FRANK, S. (EDS.) (2004): *Service Learning: Verantwortung lernen in Schule und Gemeinde.* Weinheim.

SPIEGEL ONLINE (2010): Späteres Aufstehen macht Schüler fitter. In *Spiegel Online* July 6, 2010. www.spiegel.de/lebenundlernen/schule/schlafmuetzen-studie-spaeteres-aufstehen-macht-schueler-fitter-a-704819.html
(2015): Warum die erste Stunde für Jugendliche Folter ist. In *Spiegel Online* July 6, 2015. www.spiegel.de/lebenundlernen/schule/unterrichtsbeginn-warum-die-erste-stunde-folter-ist-a-1042065.html

SPIEGEL, P. / PECHSTEIN, A. / TERNÈS VON HATTBURG, A. / GRÜNEBERG, A. (EDS.) (2021): *Future Skills. 30 zukunftsentscheidende Kompetenzen und wie wir sie lernen können.* By 69 co-creators. Munich.

STADT FRANKFURT AM MAIN (ED.) (2018): *Planungsrahmen Grundschulen.* Elaborated by bueroschneidermeyer, Schneider, J. in cooperation with Walter Heilmann. Frankfurt am Main. www.frankfurt-macht-schule.de/bibliothek.html
(2023A): *Planungsrahmen für FREIRAUM Kindertageseinrichtungen/Schulen und SCHULSPORT.* Elaborated by Voigt, A. Frankfurt am Main. www.frankfurt-macht-schule.de/bibliothek.html
(2023B): *Planungsrahmen Weiterführende Schulen.* Elaborated by bueroschneidermeyer, Schneider, J., in cooperation with Institut für Schulentwicklung, Seydel, O. Frankfurt am Main. www.frankfurt-macht-schule.de/bibliothek.html

STADT JENA (2021): *Schulnetz- und Schulentwicklungsplan 2021/22-2025/26.* Fachdienst Jugend und Bildung, Schulverwaltung, March 24, 2021. www.schulen.jena.de/system/files/2024-10/00%20SEP%20komplett%20im%20PDF-1.pdf

STADT KÖLN (2009): *Schulbauleitlinie. Integrierte Jugendhilfe- und Schulentwicklungsplanung.* Published by the Department of Education, Youth and Sport. Cologne.
(2016A): *Brandschutztechnische Anforderungen für den Bau und Betrieb von pädagogischen Raumkonzepten in Kölner Schulen.* Amt für Feuerschutz, Rettungsdienst und Bevölkerungsschutz. Notification dated March 21, 2016. Cologne.
(2016B): *Planungsrahmen für pädagogische Raumkonzepte an Kölner Schulen.* 2nd, revised edition. Published by City of Cologne. Office for School Development in cooperation with Montag Stiftung Jugend und Gesellschaft. Cologne. www.stadt-koeln.de/mediaasset/content/pdf40/planungsrahmen-fue-paedag-raumkonzepte.pdf
(2016C): *Stadt Köln legt aktualisierte Schulentwicklungsplanung vor.* Press release, June 14, 2016.

STALDER, F. (2016): *Kultur der Digitalität.* Frankfurt am Main.

STALDER, F. / KUTTNER, C. (2022): Schule in der Kultur der Digitalität – Schule als Reflexionsraum. Im Gespräch mit Felix Stalder. In Kuttner, C. / Münte-Goussar, S. (Eds.): *Praxistheoretische Perspektiven auf Schule in der Kultur der Digitalität.* Wiesbaden, pp. 3–19. doi.org/10.1007/978-3-658-35566-1_1

STATISTISCHE ÄMTER DES BUNDES UND DER LÄNDER (2009): *Demografischer Wandel in Deutschland. Heft 3: Auswirkungen auf Kindertagesbetreuung und Schülerzahlen im Bund und in den Ländern.* Wiesbaden.
www.destatis.de/DE/Themen/Querschnitt/Demografischer-Wandel/Publikationen/Downloads/kindertagesbetreuung-schuelerzahlen-5871103099004.pdf?__blob=publicationFile

STEG (STUDIE ZUR ENTWICKLUNG VON GANZTAGSSCHULEN) (2019): *Ganztagsschule 2017 / 2018. Deskriptive Befunde einer bundesweiten Befragung. Studie zur Entwicklung von Ganztagsschulen, StEG.* Frankfurt am Main, Dortmund, Gießen, Munich.
www.pedocs.de/volltexte/2019/17105/pdf/Ganztagsschule_2017_2018_StEG.pdf

STEG-KONSORTIUM (KONSORTIUM DER STUDIE ZUR ENTWICKLUNG VON GANZTAGSSCHULEN) (ED.) (2019): *Individuelle Förderung: Potenziale der Ganztagsschule.* Frankfurt am Main.
www.pedocs.de/volltexte/2020/19109/pdf/SteG_2019_Individuelle_Foerderung_Potenziale_der_Ganztagsschule.pdf

STEINMANN, I. / STRIETHOLT, R. (2019): Effekte nachmittäglicher Bildungsangebote auf sprachliche Kompetenzentwicklungen. In *Zeitschrift für Pädagogik* 65, 2019, pp. 285–306.

STÖBE-BLOSSEY, S. (2023): *Rechtsanspruch auf Ganztagsförderung für Grundschulkinder: Strukturen und Herausforderungen.* IAQ Report. Institut Arbeit und Qualifikation (IAQ), Universität Duisburg-Essen.

STRENGER, K. (2005): *Schule ist Partner – Ganztagsschule und Kooperation. Werkstatt Schule und außerschulische Kooperationspartner, Stadterneuerungs- und Stadtentwicklungsgesellschaft (STEG) Hamburg mbH.* Themenheft 4.

STRENGER, K. / FRITSCHE, N. (2006): *Partner in der Schule. Erfahrungen aus verschiedenen Kooperationsbereichen. Werkstatt Schule und außerschulische Kooperationspartner, Stadterneuerungs- und Stadtentwicklungsgesellschaft (STEG) Hamburg mbh.* Themenheft 5.
www.ganztaegig-lernen.de/materialien/themenheft-05-partner-der-schule/

TDSB – TORONTO DISTRICT SCHOOL BOARD: *About the TDSB.*
www.tdsb.on.ca/AboutUs.aspx
Accountability for Student Achievement Policy. Policy P.040 CUR. Toronto, August 26, 1998.
ppf.tdsb.on.ca/uploads/files/live/97/202.pdf

THIO, S.L. / GÖLL, E. (2011): *Einblick in die Jugendkultur – Das Thema Nachhaltigkeit bei der jungen Generation anschlussfähig machen.* Berlin.
www.umweltbundesamt.de/publikationen/einblick-in-jugendkultur

TU – TECHNISCHE UNIVERSITÄT DORTMUND (2011): *Leitfaden Gestaltung von Speiseräumen in Schulen (Raum, Organisation, Kultur). Arbeitsbericht Nr. 17,* Dortmund.
www.eldorado.tu-dortmund.de/server/api/core/bitstreams/6c3aba49-22ad-464a-88a8-66b8bbe99151/content

UMWELTBUNDESAMT (2008): Gesundheitliche Bewertung von Kohlendioxid in der Innenraumluft. Mitteilungen der Ad-hoc-Arbeitsgruppe Innenrichtwerte der Innenraumlufthygiene-Kommission des Umweltbundesamtes und der obersten Landesgesundheitsbehörden. In *Bundesgesundheitsblatt – Gesundheitsforschung – Gesundheitsschutz 51* (2008), pp. 1358–1369.
www.umweltbundesamt.de/sites/default/files/medien/pdfs/kohlendioxid_2008.pdf
(2023): *Umweltbewusstsein in Deutschland 2022. Ergebnisse einer repräsentativen Bevölkerungsumfrage*. Dessau.
www.umweltbundesamt.de/publikationen/umweltbewusstsein-in-deutschland-2022

UN UNITED NATIONS (2006): *Convention on the Rights of Persons with Disabilities and Optional Protocol*. New York.
www.un.org/disabilities/documents/convention/convoptprot-e.pdf
(2015A): Department of Economic and Social Affairs, Divison for Sustainable Development: *Sustainable Development Goals*. New York.
www.sdgs.un.org/goals
(2015B): *Transforming our World: The 2030 Agenda for Sustainable Development*. New York.
www.sdgs.un.org/sites/default/files/publications/21252030%20Agenda%20for%20Sustainable%20Development%20web.pdf
(2023): *Concluding Observations on the combined second and third periodic reports of Germany. Committee on the Rights of Persons with Disabilities*. October 3, 2023.
digitallibrary.un.org/record/4023219?v=pdf

UNESCO (2009): *Inklusion: Leitlinien für die Bildungspolitik*. Bonn. Policy Guidelines on Inclusion in Education. Paris.
www.unesdoc.unesco.org/ark:/48223/pf0000177849
(2016): *Education 2030: Incheon Declaration and Framework for Action for the implementation of Sustainable Development Goal 4: Ensure inclusive and equitable quality education and promote lifelong learning opportunities for all*
www.uis.unesco.org/sites/default/files/documents/education-2030-incheon-framework-for-action-implementation-of-sdg4-2016-en_2.pdf

UNIVERSITÄT HAMBURG (2018):
LEO 2018 – Leben mit geringer Literalität.
www.leo.blogs.uni-hamburg.de

VODAFONE STIFTUNG DEUTSCHLAND (ED.) (2011): *Schul- und Bildungspolitik in Deutschland 2011. Ein aktuelles Stimmungsbild der Bevölkerung und der Lehrer. A study by the Allensbach Institute for Public Opinion Research*.
www.vodafone-stiftung.de/schul-und bildungspolitik-in-deutschland-2011/

WILKINSON, R. / PICKETT, K. (2010): *The Spirit Level. Why Equality is Better for Everyone*. London.

WOOLFOLK, A.E. (2005): *Educational Psychology*. Boston et al.

WÖSSMANN, L. (2007): *Letzte Chance für gute Schulen: Die 12 großen Irrtümer und was wir wirklich ändern müssen*. Munich.
(2017): Das Wissenskapital der Nationen: gute Bildung als Wachstumsmotor. In *Wirtschaftsdienst, Zeitschrift für Wirtschaftspolitik*, 97th year, special issue 2017, no. 13, pp. 38–42.

WÖSSMANN, L. / PIOPIUNIK, M. (2009): *Was unzureichende Bildung kostet: Eine Berechnung der Folgekosten durch entgangenes Wirtschaftswachstum*. Gütersloh.

WORLD ECONOMIC FORUM (2018): *The Future of Education according to experts at Davos*. www.weforum.org/stories/2018/01/top-quotes-from-davos-on-the-future-of-education/

WÜSTENROT STIFTUNG (ED.) (2004): *Schulen in Deutschland: Neubau und Revitalisierung*. Stuttgart.
(2015): *Unterwegs in deutschen Bildungslandschaften*. Ludwigsburg.

ZENKE, C.T. (2019): Raumbezogene Schulentwicklung in einer inklusiven Schule: Zur Nutzungsgeschichte des Unterrichtsgroßraums der Laborschule Bielefeld. In *PFLB – PraxisForschung-Lehrer*innenBildung*, 2019, 1(1), pp. 20–41. doi.org/10.4119/pflb-3173

ZIMMER, J. / NIGGEMEYER, E. (1992): *Macht die Schule auf, laßt das Leben rein. Von der Schule zur Nachbarschaftsschule*. Weinheim.

ZÜCHNER, I. / MINK, N. (2016): Zu wenig Zeit für Hobbys? In *Viel Tempo, wenig Plan*. In DJI *Impulse. Das Bulletin des Deutschen Jugendinstituts* 2/2016, pp. 14–18.

INDEX

IMPRINT

Editor
Montag Stiftung Jugend und Gesellschaft

Idea and concept
Montag Stiftung Jugend und Gesellschaft,
Montag Stiftung Urbane Räume

Team of authors
Ernst Hubeli
Meike Kricke
Barbara Pampe
Ulrich Paßlick
Kersten Reich
Jochem Schneider
Otto Seydel

Project management
Caroline Eckmann

Support / collaboration (German issues)
Corinna Alpers, Stefan Bayer, Thomas Becker, Antonia Blaer-Nettekoven, Vittoria Capresi, Annalena Danner, Kristina Foidl, Kristin Gehm, Maria Gilbers, Dirk Haas, Nadine Koch, Barbara Köpfer, Katrin Oelsner, Marcus Paul, Lieselotte Rowley, Katrin Schüring, Carla Schwarz, Miriam Seifert-Waibel, Monika Söller, Franziska Spelleken, Thorsten Schulte, Maria Zach

Cover
Montag Stiftung Jugend und Gesellschaft
labor b designbüro

Project management Jovis
Franziska Schüffler, Regina Herr

Translation
Kersten Reich

Copy editing and Proofreading
Bianca Murphy

Production Jovis
Susanne Rösler

Design, setting and lithography
labor b designbüro, Dortmund

Illustration
Max von Bock Visuelle Kommunikation, Berlin (pp. 136–137)

Graphic
labor b designbüro,
based on a design by Jochem Schneider

Typography
National, Klim Type Foundry

Paper
Inhalt: Circle Offset white
Umschlag: Euroboard

Acknowledgements
In addition to the contributors mentioned here, many other committed people have contributed to this book: People in schools, city administrations, architectural offices, foundations, organizations, etc., who advised us in many ways and provided content or images. The editors would like to thank them all for their support.

Printed in the European Union.

For questions about the General Product Safety Regulation please contact
productsafety@degruyterbrill.com

Bibliographic information published by the Deutsche Nationalbibliothek
The Deutsche Nationalbibliothek lists this publication in the Deutsche Nationalbibliografie; detailed bibliographic data are available on the Internet at http://dnb.d-nb.de

Jovis Verlag
Genthiner Straße 13
10785 Berlin

www.jovis.de

Jovis books are available worldwide in select bookstores. Please contact your nearest bookseller or visit www.jovis.de for information concerning your local distribution.

Also available in German.

ISBN 978-3-98612-225-6 (Softcover)
ISBN 978-3-98612-226-3 (PDF)
DOI 10.1515/9783986122263